To End All Suffering

To End All Suffering

A Christian Analysis of the Buddha's Teaching

By Michael Collender

WIPF & STOCK · Eugene, Oregon

TO END ALL SUFFERING
A Christian Analysis of the Buddha's Teachings

Wipf & Stock
An Imprint of Wipf and Stock Publishers
199 W. 8th Ave., Suite 3
Eugene, OR 97401

www.wipfandstock.com

ISBN 13: 978-1-62032-250-5

Manufactured in the U.S.A.

Table of Contents

For Jennifer

Who possesses the five powers of a woman,
Especially virtue.

You made this possible.

Gratitude

Why is there an Acknowledgments page in books instead of a Gratitude page? People deserve honor for honest work, but "acknowledgments" removes the appreciation one human gives to another human as we live in community, helping and serving one another. It removes thankfulness. As St. Paul writes, "What do you have that you did not receive? And if you did receive it, why do you boast as if you had not received it?"[1] Every project one accomplishes should provoke gratitude.

To End All Suffering took many years to complete. It would not exist without the willingness of many people to enter into dialogue to challenge the philosophical arguments presented in this book.

I owe a debt of thanks to:

Stephen Hagberg, who first kindled my love for philosophy, especially for the dialogue between Eastern philosophy and the Christian faith.

Robert Zeuschner, a philosophy professor at Pasadena City College and a student of David Kalupahana at the University of Hawai'i, who initiated the particular journey this book represents. Dr. Zeuschner (he will always be Dr. Zeuschner to me) relentlessly assaulted my Christian faith for two and a half years, provoking me to write papers against his arguments. Yet he had the integrity to give me A's on those papers. He graciously invited me into his home to discuss Buddhist philosophy and have dinners with his family. Those years of debating Christian and Buddhist philosophy with him taught me how defensible Buddhism can be. Much of the material today that is supposed to prepare young Christians to defend their faith is nearly useless. Young Christians put their trust in what they have been taught, believing these materials supply good arguments. When a competent, unbelieving professor shreds them, it provokes deep soul searching. I had that experience, thanks to Dr. Zeuschner, and it is one of God's greatest gifts to me.

Win Corduan, professor emeritus at Taylor University, regularly encouraged me through the process of finding a publisher and provided counsel to me throughout the project.

1. 1 Cor. 4:7b

I am also grateful to Gary R. Habermas (especially for all the time at his house analyzing his video-taped debates as well as those of William Lane Craig), Roy Atwood, Doug Jones, David Beck, Steven Harms, Craig Hinkson, Douglas Wilson, Nick Gier, Peter J. Leithart, Myron B. Penner, Mitch Stokes, Quanhua Liu, Richard McClelland, David Calhoun, Eric Schmidt, Bruce Williams, Shann Ray Ferch, Chris Francovich, Travis M. Walker, Lt. Col. Matt Deller, the monks of Wat Tai Temple in North Hollywood, California (who were very kind to let me talk with them so much and who offered to let me become a Buddhist monk), Fr. Tim Clancy, Doug Kries, and my other colleagues and students at Gonzaga University who have interacted in group discussions to consider these ideas, as well as my doctoral level students who worked through some of this material in early stages.

I am thankful to Wisdom Publications and Mike Crawford for permission to quote from their beautiful translations of the Pali *Nikāyas*. I am also grateful to William Hamilton and University of Hawai'i Press for their kind permission to freely quote from three of David Kalupahana's books. I am especially grateful to David Kalupahana for his lifetime scholarship and his personal permission to quote from *Ethics in Early Buddhism*.

I am grateful to the folks at Wiph and Stock for their support, especially my editor, Christian Amondson. Michelle Walker and John Unger gave me invaluable support with proofing this manuscript and they are two of the sharpest and most detail-oriented people I have ever met. They saved me from a multitude mistakes. Of course, the many mistakes that remain are all my own.

There is no way I could have accomplished this project without the support of my family. My three children, Jackson, Benaiah, and Isabella, have each encouraged and supported me while their father spent more time in the office to finish this book. Most importantly, this book could never have been completed without the love and support of my wife, Jennifer, whose strength, wisdom, efficiency, intellectual competence, project management skills, thoughtfulness, and love make me strong enough, by God's grace, to do everything I do. She is a fortress for me, and I dedicate this book to her.

1

Introduction

. . . Saccaka the Nigaṇha's son [236] replied: "Master Gotama, we were bold and impudent in thinking we could attack Master Gotama in debate. A man might attack a mad elephant and find safety, yet he could not attack Master Gotama and find safety. A man might attack a blazing mass of fire and find safety, yet he could not attack Master Gotama and find safety. A man might attack a terrible poisonous snake and find safety, yet he could not attack Master Gotama and find safety. We were bold and impudent in thinking we could attack Master Gotama in debate.

"Let the Blessed One together with the Sangha of bhikkhus consent to accept tomorrow's meal from me."

The Blessed One consented in silence.

Majjhima-nikāya, 1.235–236

TWO GREAT DEBATERS

The Buddha was a fierce debater. At least that is how the earliest Buddhist texts present him, as an intellectually formidable opponent who confounds the arguments of any who oppose his teaching. During the age in which the Buddha taught, debate was something of an indoor sport. In the *Culasaccaka Sutta*, the source of the quotation above, Saccaka, a young hothead, tries to lock horns with the Buddha in debate. He begins with vaunting—praising himself, boasting of his prowess, and prophesying his future victory over the Buddha using various metaphors to explain just how great his victory over the Buddha will be.

> [J]ust as a strong man might seize a long-haired ram by the hair and drag him to and drag him fro and drag him round about, so in debate I will drag the recluse Gotama to and drag him fro and drag him round about. . . . Just as a strong brewer's mixer might take a strainer by the corners and shake it down and shake it up and thump it about, so in debate I will shake the recluse Gotama down and shake him up and thump him about.[1]

Finally, the young Saccaka gets his chance. He throws his best arguments, but Master Gotama, who is the Buddha, throws back at him a series of complex Socratic questions that are so powerful that after each Saccaka remains silent. Unlike Plato's Socratic dialogues, the *Culasaccaka Sutta* is a real debate. Saccaka is no sounding board for the Buddha. Needless to say, the Buddha makes some excellent points through these questions. All who are listening can see the implications of the questions that the Buddha asks. So much so that a spirit appears holding a burning iron thunderbolt and asks the Buddha whether he should split open Saccaka's head if he persists in not answering. The debate ends, as you read above, with Saccaka realizing he is completely out of his league. One ought to think long and carefully before debating the Buddha.

The Buddha is not the only religious founder known for his remarkable debating skill. Jesus of Nazareth was also a formidable debater. The Jesus of Nazareth portrayed in the canonical Gospels demonstrates remarkable skill in reasoning and debate. Many of his exchanges leave his enemies thunderstruck, unable to form a reply. Perhaps the most famous of these exchanges follows his great cleansing of the Temple. Each of the synoptic Gospels narrates his final public showdown with the scribes, Pharisees, Herodians, Sadducees, and the religious teachers of Judea. He bests each group repeatedly until none dare to ask him another question.

Given that both the Buddha and Jesus of Nazareth were brilliant debaters, we should find it startlingly odd that proponents of interreligious dialogue between Buddhism and Christianity en-

1. *Majjhima-nikāya*, 1.228–229.

courage both religions *not* to debate. While specific examples must wait until the following chapter, it should be no surprise that our age of tolerance is reticent to engage in meaningful discourse to adjudicate religious questions. Where would we even begin? We believe that answers to religious questions are matters of opinion. Who can say which opinion is best or more correct? Yet neither the Buddha nor Jesus Christ accept that religious questions can only be answered by opinions. On this point these two great teachers both agree.

Tolerance is the respect one offers to a person who disagrees with what one believes. Tolerance cannot exist in a vacuum. Rather, it must be based on some principle, some reason which animates and empowers it. There are at least two kinds of tolerance. One kind of tolerance is to believe and act as though *ideas* do not ultimately matter. The other is to believe that *people* do matter. The present age embraces the first kind of tolerance. If truth is relative, if meaning is suspect, then why should one pursue ideas and doctrines? It makes no sense. The other kind of tolerance is rooted in a belief in the intrinsic importance of human beings.

Contrary to contemporary Western culture, both Jesus and the Buddha believe the latter—that people are important—which is what motivated them to embrace tolerance, a specific kind of tolerance. The Buddha's patience and tolerance is evident in the way he talks with opponents like Saccaka. Likewise, Jesus taught tolerance in the Parable of the Field (Matt. 13:24–30, 36–43). Jesus tells the story of a field that Jesus says represents the world and the person who sowed the seed is Jesus. Good seed was sown in the field. But an enemy of the sower plants wheat-like weeds in it. The servants of the field owner ask their boss what if he wants them to cut down the weeds. The boss says, "No. Let them grow together till harvest time, lest any wheat is cut down by mistake." Jesus encourages us to have mercy and patience with all people because his aim is mercy. Both of these teachers embraced a tolerance that was informed by their worldview. Neither muddles their messages for the sake of tolerance as informed by their respective religious worldviews. For the Buddha, there is no way to end suffering outside of the Dharma. For Jesus Christ, there is no other way to end suffering and evil but through him. Therefore, the Dharma and the Gospel are wholly different in their content and their goals.

Tolerance opens a space for mercy and the getting of wisdom. However, both the Dharma and the Gospel teach that logic in itself is not enough to persuade someone of religious truth. Like Saccaka in the *Culasaccaka Sutta*, the religious leaders who confront Jesus will not let logic persuade them even though the listening crowd knows they lost. Sometimes even the best reasoning fails to move the heart. As Pascal observed, "The heart has reasons that reason cannot know."[2]

INTERRELIGIOUS DIALOGUE IN A FLAT WORLD

In the past twenty-five hundred years since the Buddha ministered at the base of the Himalayas, the world has most certainly changed. Today the world is flat, as Thomas Friedman has famously told us.[3] And on this flat earth the upheavals that tip its political corners push billions of inhabitants into collisions with one another. Since 9/11, religion has intruded itself all the more into matters of politics, and we have no reason to think this intrusion will end soon. The technology that flattened the earth has permitted an unprecedented interaction of worldviews. In the ancient world, the rich interaction of worldviews occurring today was only possible in locations such as Alexandria, Egypt, a nexus of Eastern and Western trade routes, where Latin, Greek, Aramaic, Parthian, and possibly Chinese could have been heard in the tumult of its markets. Today, the Internet and the global supply chain make Earth a global Alexandria.

Given this reality, Christians should prepare for thoughtful engagement with Eastern philosophy, and especially with Buddhism. Before the economic rise of the East, some may have thought Buddhism and the other movements in Eastern thought should be dismissed as curiosities suited to the academy, or as spiritual diversions in a postmodern world. However, the twenty-first century is shifting the cultural ground underneath our philosophical feet. In the "post-Christian" West, a new ideological continent appears to be forming underneath us with cultural weather currents of its

2. Pascal, *Pensées*, sect. 4, no. 277.

3. Friedman, *The World Is Flat* 3.0.

own. In this developing eco-system of ideas, Christians must think clearly and deliberately about the relationship between the cultural forms of the East and the Christian heritage. I do not call it the Western heritage. The Greeks and Romans saw Christianity as an Eastern religion. According to the New Testament, the Advent of Christ proves no nation holds more privilege to the grace of God than another. Christ commissions the international benefits of his ministry to be shared with everyone (Matt. 28:18–20).

I have written *To End All Suffering: A Christian Analysis of the Buddha's Teaching* to promote Buddhist/Christian dialogue that respects the reasoned doctrines taught by the Buddha and Jesus of Nazareth. This work attempts to model an honest approach to dialogue that recognizes real disagreement and enters into debate regarding critical points of difference, in order to determine which view is true, good, and beautiful. But let me be very clear. *To End All Suffering* is primarily written to Christians. I am preparing Christians to dialogue with Buddhists who are intellectually prepared to defend their tradition. This book should be useful to Christian scholars, pastors, and college students, primarily in religiously-oriented institutions of higher learning or in ministry. It is not written from some "neutral" point of view, which surreptitiously insinuates a third, arbitrating authority in this dialogue. I will examine Buddhism and Christianity, each from within its own specific criteria. Both Buddhism and Christianity have distinct epistemologies, and that reality requires interlocutors to be both careful and creative. Let me forthrightly state up front: *In this book I intend to bring early Buddhist thought and the Christian Gospel into philosophical dialogue with one another. In doing so, I will make the case that Buddhism undermines itself while the Christian faith does not.*

The only other book available today that comes close to what *To End All Suffering* aims to achieve is *Buddhism: A Christian Exploration and Appraisal* by Keith Yandell and Harold Netland. Yandell and Netland wrote their book to acquaint Christians with Buddhism. Most of the book offers general, clear introductions to aspects of Buddhist philosophy and Buddhist history, with footnotes that recommend more specific books for further study. *Buddhism* then goes on to explain how Buddhism came to the West, particularly through D. T. Suzuki. The next two chapters survey some key doctrines of Buddhism and some of the contradictions in those doctrines. As a general introduction to Buddhism, the book is helpful. Unfortunately, the introduction to Buddhism at the beginning is not precise enough to inform the critical sections at the end of the book. Also, the problems that Yandell and Netland raise near the end would most likely not phase a studied Buddhist who understands the difference between scholastic Buddhism, which does stumble into the sorts of problems they identify, and the outlook of the more pragmatic and defensible versions of Buddhist philosophy. Yandell and Netland present Christianity as a different religion, which the authors believe in, but little more. These problems are not defects *per se*. They are choices the authors made to find a direct road to making the book accessible, philosophical, and charitable. However, I will be taking the long road, working through the Buddha's teaching in great detail, organizing its history, goals, and good arguments in order to eventually make the case against Buddhism I outlined above. *To End All Suffering* engages with contemporary Buddhist scholarship; herein a Buddhist will find his faith thoughtfully and fairly treated. Anyone who disagrees with my conclusions is invited to respond.

I do hope this book will find its way into the warm hands of Buddhists interested in honest dialogue between these two great religious traditions. *Charitable, argumentative discourse should be the norm of interreligious dialogue if Buddhists and Christians are to follow the example of their traditions' founders.* Should Buddhists and Christians not honor their founders by following their example and entering into reasoned discourse together?

To End All Suffering also aims at an appreciation of Buddhism. This book has been a labor of love over many years. In my undergraduate years I had the privilege of studying with Robert Zeuschner, who obtained his doctorate under the world-renowned Buddhist scholar David Kalupahana at the University of Hawai'i, which has the premiere Eastern philosophy program in the United States. At the time I had a keen interest in apologetics and Dr. Zeuschner took the brunt of that interest. Truth be told, he encouraged this interest by regularly attacking the Christian faith in his courses and conversations with students. Over the years we became friends. We would meet at his house to bring Buddhism and

Christianity into rigorous debate. His influence led me to write a B.A. thesis on the relationship between Buddhist philosophy and Christian thought. I then pursued graduate study in Philosophy of Religion at Liberty University. Still interested in interreligious dialogue between Buddhist and Christian philosophy, I requested permission to build my M.A. thesis on my previous B.A. thesis and received permission to do so from Dr. Craig Hinkson, then Director of Graduate Studies for Liberty's School of Religion. The M.A. program in Philosophy of Religion gave me occasion to further test and refine my arguments. In addition, I have had opportunities to engage in dialogue with colleagues at Gonzaga University regarding the case I present here and have used portions of the manuscript to teach Buddhist philosophy to my doctoral students. The Buddha is asking significant questions that deserve real answers.

While this book does engage the different tributaries in Buddhist thought, it pays special attention to early Buddhist philosophy. Why? While some complex doctrines and emphases in Buddhism have evolved, the core of Buddhism is simple and has remained relatively stable over the two and a half millennia since the death of the Buddha. The Buddha's teaching demonstrates the insightfulness of one of the sharpest minds in history. Our inquiry will focus on the philosophy presented in the Pali Canon, the oldest record of the Buddha's teaching. Over time, the individualist spirit of the Buddha's teaching permitted the addition of teachings that embellished some aspects of the Buddha's message and Mahāyāna Buddhism reflects some of these developments. Hirakawa Akira, in his book *A History of Indian Buddhism*, summarizes the rise of Mahāyāna Buddhism as:

> an example of how Buddhism responded to the demands of a new time. Mahāyāna Buddhism included many elements not found in early Buddhism. Despite these innovations, the original spirit of the Buddha's teachings was not lost in early Mahāyāna. . . . However, these innovative elements brought hidden dangers with them. As time passed, many Buddhists became more interested in the new additions than in the original message of the Buddha.[4]

4. Hirakawa, *History of Indian Buddhism*, 3.

For clarity, we will stick close to the source, and by doing so we will get to see the formidable mind of the Buddha at work. There is much philosophers can learn from him, whether they work within the Buddhist or Christian traditions.

The present-day tradition that remains closest to these early writings is the Theravāda School of Hīnayāna Buddhism. The primary Buddhist scriptures, the *Tripiṭaka* (the three baskets), contain the teachings of the Buddha, and in particular the Pali *Nikāyas* or Chinese *Āgamas* seem to bring us as close as one can get to the teaching of the Buddha. The size of this vast collection of texts, not to mention the many other Buddhist scriptures. far exceeds the length of the Bible. To remove the objection that my reading of the *Tripiṭaka* is a piñata of my own making, I have pursued conversation partners that represent some of the finest luminaries in Pali Buddhist philosophical scholarship of the late twentieth century; namely, the late K. N. Jayatilleke, whom Nancy McCagney calls "the greatest Buddhist philosopher since Buddhaghosa," and David Kalupahana, one of today's foremost Pali Buddhist scholars. Kalupahana, Jayatilleke's greatest student, is professor emeritus and former senior Buddhist scholar at the University of Hawai'i.

However, completely identifying early Buddhism with the Theravāda School of Hīnayāna Buddhism would be a mistake. In *To End All Suffering*, I am attempting to discuss aspects of core Buddhist doctrine, a core that will also resonate with Mahāyāna Buddhist scholarship that has its own varicolored readings of the *Nikāyas*. For this reason, along with Kalupahana and Jayatilleke, I will also include Mahāyāna dialogue partners, drawing them into my presentation and critique of early Buddhist philosophy. In text and footnootes I will interact with the Routledge published *Buddhist Thought: A Complete Introduction to the Indian Tradition*, Second Edition by Paul Williams with Anthony Tribe and Alexander Wynne, and also Rupert Gethin's *The Foundation of Buddhism*, both excellent introductions to Buddhism which approach the *Nikāyas/Āgamas* from the perspective of Mahāyāna Buddhist scholarship.

To End All Suffering is written to be self-contained, with a charitable introduction to the Buddha's teaching that sets the stage for the latter critique chapters. Everything the reader needs to follow the argument of this book is here presented. However, one will better get the significance of the case I present if one concurently reads other competent Buddhist philosophers. To get the most fulfilling experience, consider reading Jayatilleke's *Early Buddhist Theory of Knowledge*, Kalupahana's *Buddhist Philosophy* and/or *A History of Buddhist Philosophy*, Williams' *Buddhist Thought*, or Gethin's *The Foundation's of Buddhism*. For my chapter on Nāgārjuna consider reading Jay Garfield's excellent commentary *The Fundamental Wisdom of the Middle Way: Nāgārjuna's Mulamadhyamicakārikā*. If one is interested in better following my arguments from the early Buddhist scriptures, one should consider examing the passages I interact with in their original context. Even better, work through all the *Nikāyas*. Wisdom Pulbications has produced beautiful and affordable translations of the first four Pali *Nikāyas*. University professors interested in building comparative religion courses using *To End All Suffering* may wish to start with the books listed above. Potential syllabi are avaliable on my academic webiste (collender.org). My hope is that this book will encourage interreligious dialogue between Christians and Buddhists, and in particular, more Christian study of early Buddhist philosophy and the early Buddhist scriptures.

OVERVIEW OF *TO END ALL SUFFERING*

To End All Suffering is divided into three parts. Part One introduces the way in which this book will conduct interreligious dialogue.

Part Two presents an overview of Buddhist philosophy and its historical context. It will interact with a number of modern and contemporary commentators on Buddhist thought. It will also follow Kalupahana's basic pedagogical outline for explaining Buddhism, drawing on a number of his works to bring Buddhist philosophy into conversation with modern philosophers like Wittgenstein, Quine, and William James. Finally, I will outline the historical development of Buddhist philosophy, showing how these themes grew and developed through doctrinal controversies throughout the history of Buddhism. This outline will show both that the philosophical core of Buddhism is more or less preserved and that distant aspects of the tradition, like Zen and Mahāyāna Buddhism, make sense when considered in view of the questions that gave rise to them.

Part Three offers a Christian critique of Buddhist philosophy comprised of eight chapters. The first four chapters critically examine Buddhist logic. The next two examine the Buddhist problem of other minds, and the Buddha's doctrine of interdependent co-origination. The last two chapters engage the problem of suffering from a biblical perspective, bringing the Buddhist notion of suffering (*dukkha*) to terms with the Cross within Christian theology and, finally, address Buddhist pragmatism and Buddhism's claim to be able to end suffering.

I have given the barest outlines of these sections. This is because the coming chapters that introduce the Buddha's teaching should be read sympathetically. Give the Buddha your faithful and open mind. There will be time to critically engage with the Buddha's teachings. C. S. Lewis warns against reading a book at first with a critical eye, looking for faults:

> We can find a book bad by only by reading it as if it might, after all, be very good. We must empty our minds and lay ourselves open. There is no work in which holes can't be picked; no work that can succeed without a preliminary act of good will on the part of the reader.[5]

Should we not first hear the voice of the Buddha with an honest and open ear? I believe that even badly mistaken traditions have something of value to share. If so, the Buddhist tradition, which arises out of one man's sincere desire to end suffering, most certainly deserves a fair and patient hearing.

Let us begin.

5. Lewis, *Experiment in Criticism*, 116.

Part I

A Methodology for Interreligious Dialogue Between Buddhism and Christianity

2

A Methodology for Interreligious Dialogue Between Buddhism and Christianity

Sensual pleasures have been compared to a dream by the Blessed One; they provide much suffering and much despair, while the danger in them is great. . . .

Potaliya Sutta, Majjhima-nikāya 1.365

And in this mountain shall the LORD of hosts make unto all people a feast of fat things, a feast of wines on the lees, of fat things full of marrow, of wines on the lees well refined. And he will destroy in this mountain the face of the covering cast over all people, and the veil that is spread over all nations.

Isaiah 25:6–7 (KJV)

BUDDHIST-CHRISTIAN DIALOGUE

HOW DOES ONE JUDGE between the rival claims of competing religions? Both Buddhism and Christianity are competing religions in that both are evangelistic, striving to bring deliverance or salvation to people. Yet both define "deliverance" or "salvation" in very different ways, representing answers to very different questions. They are actually talking about totally different things when they appear to agree.

The problem with finding the correct methodology for interreligious dialogue arises from one simple fact: each religion claims its own standards for self-adjudication. Buddhism claims experience ultimately tests truth. Christianity claims the God Yahweh is the ultimate judge of truth and the Bible is God's own revelation of himself, given as a textual heritage to his people. Islam has its own holy book, but it claims humans cannot know the character of the God Allah, only his revealed will to which all humans must submit. Mormonism claims that a "burning in the bosom" authenticates divine revelation. Other religions make their claims. However, one must ask Who gets to pick the rules that all religions have to follow to be proven true? To be reckoned useful? To be fully bona fide?

Perhaps logical consistency could be the test? The so-called laws of logic seem to be the lone universal, objective set of standards beyond any religion's claim to authority. However, careful study of the world's religions proves that simple logical consistency will not work as a test. Each religion has a worldview that tells its own story about the nature, use, and significance of human thought. The Christian Church has taught, throughout her history, that God is wise and consistent, that he does not lie, and that he desires humankind to think, reason, and judge wisely on the basis of God's public revelation (see Deut. 1:12–18 in the context of Deut. 30:11–14 and Romans 10:5–8). In Islamic theology, however, Allah can contradict himself because his nature is not revealed to us. He can say that Christians and Jews should be loved as People of the Book in the early Surahs (i.e. Qur'an 2:62 and 3:64), but he can order their deaths in holy war in later revelation (i.e. Qur'an 9:5) without contradiction because he can change his will over time.[1] The deep contradictions in Mormonism's early historical records do not move Mormons to reconsider the truthfulness of their religion because reason plays almost no part in authenticating their religion's

1. When anti-Muslim apologists indolently point out apparent contradictions in the Qur'an without first reading the Qur'an in light of Islamic theology's doctrine of revelation, they end up building very weak arguments against Islam. No one likes having one's holy texts read carelessly. We ought to do our best, imperfect as we all are, to carefully read and interpret the holy texts of another religion. Even if another religion is mistaken, it is imperative not to do shoddy exegesis so as to model the moral equity our own religious faith has cultivated within us, no matter our religious tradition (Exod. 20:16).

worldview; rather, an emotional sensation "in the bosom" fulfills this role. As we will discover in later chapters, even Buddhism redraws its own boundaries of logic, to fence its limits in terms of human sense experience and its usefulness toward human goals. And the religion of the *Upaniṣads*, as we will see in chapter 3, completely alters the place of logic as a test for truth. For the Upaniṣadic teachers, rational consistency is part of the folly of the illusion-lived experience that confuses humans as to the nature of what is actually reality. Any strategy that makes an unqualified appeal to logical consistency will meet disaster on all fronts.

One potential *Via Dolorosa* to test a religion's claims is the process of consensus building. Get together a group of believers from various religions and ask them to find some basic principles that they agree on, principles critically necessary to the integrity of their own belief systems. Then test all religions according to those principles. If a religion fails the test, it will be judged false or week. Simple enough. However, the authority of consensus begs one critical question: Why should the opinions held by believers in one religion have any authority to criticize the tenants of another religion? The consensus test for truth assumes human opinions are the highest standards of truth. If more humans believe or support a particular religious claim, that claim somehow becomes more "true." The consensus test for truth is, therefore, patently silly and useless in interreligious dialogue because it mistakenly equates rhetorical proof with logical proof. Sure, one can persuade or dissuade a group of people by building a case upon their shared values and assumptions. If the only type of proof in religious matters is rhetorical proof, then the "consensus" test for truth proves too much. If there are no truths beyond one's own faith commitments, then what is the point of establishing the pretentious trial of consensus building?

However, our task is simpler than having to come up with the one and only standard to measure absolutely all religions because this book is an interreligious dialogue only between Buddhism and Christianity. Thus, we should focus our resources on these two great religions. From discussing these religions and the way they interact with one another, we can, perhaps, draw more general conclusions at some later point about how interreligious dialogue should be handled.

The challenges with bringing Buddhism and Christianity into dialogue are illustrated in *Buddhist-Christian Dialogue: Mutual Renewal and Transformation*, which assembles scholars of comparative religion to face this challenge.[2] The editors and contributors want to play nice and keep these two religions on friendly terms (which is easy to do as both religions want to end suffering). These scholars pursue different strategies to accomplish this purpose. Some try to poke mutual holes in each religion as if to say, "It is okay. You do it, too." For example, Fritz Buri finds fault with the Buddha's silence about what happens after death rather than praising his silence as honorable consistency.[3] Is the Buddha not allowed to be consistent? Regarding Jesus' teachings, Buri carelessly argues, "By [Jesus'] own actions, he tried to reach a goal, which like his message proved to be illusionary in its eschatological expectations." Yet Jesus bet his reputation as a prophet on the prediction that Jerusalem would be destroyed by Rome within one generation and that this event would bring an end to Israel as previously constituted by the civic portions of the Mosaic law.[4] His prediction of the end of the age was spot on. His words are the historical explanation for why Jewish Christians fled Jerusalem on the eve of her destruction in A.D. 70. Is it necessary that each religion somehow have its legs broken before it can sit at the table of discourse? No. The philosophies presented by the Buddha and by Christ deserve to be presented in their full strength.

Paul O. Ingram makes a different proposal.[5] He recommends Christian theologians follow the dictates of Alfred North Whitehead's process philosophy in order to make Christian theology "submit

2. Ingram, *Buddhist-Christian Dialogue.*

3. Ibid., 18.

4. Jesus made this prediction many times throughout his ministry. In fact, each of the synoptic gospels presents a major discourse devoted to explaining that Jerusalem will be destroyed by the Romans within one generation (Matt. 24, Mark 13, and Luke 21). For a detailed study of this theme in Jesus' teaching throughout his ministry and in these passages, see Wright, *Jesus and the Victory of God*, 320–68. Jesus' warning to his disciples to flee Jerusalem when Rome would come to destroy it is one of the reasons Christianity survived the Roman purge against Judaism, which is recorded in Josephus's *Wars of the Jews.*

5. "Interfaith Dialogue as a Source of Buddhist-Chrisitan Creative Transformation."

itself to creative transformation by assimilating not only new aspects of Western culture, but to open itself to still more radical transformation through dialogue with the non-Christian Ways."[6] Yet why should Christianity, or Buddhism for that matter, be forced to undergo Ingram's radical transformation? Because Ingram says they should? Ingram advocates that Christianity and Buddhism meet in a way that transforms them both without either falsifying the other.[7] Yet his recommended methodology is antithetical to the methodologies adopted by both Jesus and the Buddha. Perhaps a better methodology would be for the more robust, debate-oriented methodologies of the Buddha and Jesus to "transform" Ingram's process philosophy, which he uses to dictate rules of engagement to Buddhism and Christianity.

Shohei Ichimura approaches the problem of religious dialogue by way of the second century Buddhist philosopher Nāgārjuna and his book the *Mulamadyamikakārikā*.[8] Instead of faulting Buddhism or Christianity for some doctrinal problem to make them equal, or requiring each to transform one other into things they are not, Ichimura criticizes the process of doctrine making. In a later chapter, I will address Nāgārjuna in detail, but some cursory remarks are appropriate here. Nāgārjuna taught that human language is a way that humans organize their own understanding of the world, but doctrine will always be logically incomplete and contradictory. So Nāgārjuna recommends people pass over doctrinal debates in order to find enlightenment, and his arguments are the historical source of the non-conceptual formulations of Zen Buddhism. Ichimura takes Nāgārjuna's point and applies it to interreligious dialogue, arguing that discussions about different religious positions are merely conflicts between various ways that humans linguistically and conceptually organize their views of the world. In his view, religious experience is ultimately paradoxical.[9] Why should we expect one religion to encompass all of it?

6. Ibid., 85.

7. Ingram, Buddhist-Christian Dialogue, 93.

8. Ichmura, "Sunyata and Religious Pluralism," in Ingram, *Buddhist-Christian Dialogue*.

9. Ibid, 112.

Thus, we see Ichimura takes a similar approach to Fritz Bury, except Ichimura does not fault either the Buddha or Jesus; rather, he blames the limitations of language and human conceptualization. Furthermore, he follows a similar approach to Ingram in that he finds one overall philosophical structure—in Ichimura's case, that of Nāgārjuna, who was himself a Buddhist—and this is a much wiser move on Ichimura's part. But the use of Nāgārjuna's philosophy here proves too much. If Nāgārjuna's method is to be used as an overall framework for religious dialogue, and Nāgārjuna proves (so Nāgārjuna thinks) that that all linguistic conceptual constructs are necessarily problematic and incomplete, then substantive interreligious dialogue is impossible. This approach is like the kid at the ball game who turns to his friends and says, "This game is stupid. We are going home." Depending on his standing in the group, so much for that game.

Buddhist-Christian Dialogue is a helpful read, and it could be worthwhile to continue my critique of each contributor. However, the limits of space here require me to move to a general point, which a careful read of this book in its entirety will support. *Buddhist-Christian Dialogue* is representative of many other books that attempt similar strategies. I chose this one because its contributors are well-reputed scholars in the field of comparative religion. The book represents the common, well-accepted methodologies of pluralism, or relativism, or mutual humbling, or finding some other standard outside of both religions to which each must submit. Are these the only ways? Is there not a more creative, more interesting, more daring way of doing comparative religious dialogue than these four methodologies?[10]

Could we not build a rapport between these two religions? After all, these two religions are both rooted in honest debate regarding doctrines and both make heartfelt attempts to outdo one another in acts of kindness for each other and the world. Is this not better than inventing procedures to force Buddhism and Christianity to meet some definition of "getting along" or redefining them into things they are not? Both Jesus and the Buddha encouraged debate—

10. There may be fewer than four methodologies because one can collapse some of these methods into others.

evaluating evidence, "mixing it up," as it were—in order to help people and bring them to wisdom. Their vibrant debates were not the stuff of unreadable journal articles or awkward academic conference presentations given in order to build promotion and tenure scores. These two religions deserve to run together without first being hamstrung at the gate. Let them flourish in full strength in a fellowship fit for worthy rivals.

WHY WE CAN KNOW THE WORLDVIEWS OF ANCIENT PEOPLES

Given that we are attempting to bring the teaching of Jesus and the early church into discourse with early Buddhist philosophy, it is important to address the question of whether it is even possible to know what early Buddhists and Christians thought and taught. After all, they taught and wrote in the ancient past, in a different socioeconomic, cultural, linguistic setting. The Buddha likely spoke Magahdi, a linguistic cousin to Pali, the language of the Pali Canon.[11] Likewise, all evidence points to Jesus of Nazareth being a native speaker of Aramaic, a cognate language of Hebrew. He most certainly read Hebrew.[12] Likely he spoke Latin,[13] and potentially Greek, given the Greek language was the trade language in the region of Galilee.

Since the scope of this book is interreligious dialogue between early Buddhist philosophy and early Christianity, we should address the possibility of even doing such a study given the vast ages and cultural differences that span between the modern reader and the authors of these two religious traditions. The basis for the possibility of such study is rooted in the semiotic structure of language itself. Aristotle wisely observes that the single word is not the smallest unit of meaning. The sentence (*logos* in Greek) is. A sentence must have both a subject and a predicate.[14] Now in Greek there are verbs that can be both, due to the grammar and syntax of Greek, which uses verb endings to communicate the number of persons acting as well as the time and duration of that action. This same structure

11. Mizuno, *Buddhist Sutras*, 26.

12. Luke 4:17–20.

13. John 18:33–38.

14. Aristotle, *Categories; On Interpretation*; Prior Analytics, 16b 26–17a 24.

also shows itself in Hebrew, Aramaic, Latin, German, Japanese, and Arabic. One can confidently say that anywhere language is used, something ends up doing the work of these parts of speech. The critical observation from Aristotle, though, is that the subject and predicate work together to make the fundamental unit of meaning, namely, the sentence.[15]

The late Paul Ricoeur has traced the significance of Aristotle's observation in great detail, especially for the study of history and literature.[16] Discourse is something that occurs at a specific time and place, wherein a speaker discourses to another person. This discourse is spoken in time, to someone. And text is the written form of discourse, with one caveat: it is inscribed and is readable beyond the immediate context of the one discoursing. If one has ever written a hasty, angry email and hit "send" only to regret the words, he or she has experienced this phenomenon firsthand. The technical term for this is "distanciation, the transport of the signification from one discourse context to another through the vehicle of symbolic representation."[17] The most readily accessible example of distanciation is the inscription of discourse in text.[18] Text carries an act of discourse beyond the immediate context of that speech, beyond that immediate narrative, which gives context to that utterance.[19] Nevertheless, it is possible to preserve the narrative in which a speaker or writer gives his or her discourse.

These qualities of discourse and text are what make possible the study of ancient worldviews and ancient cultures. It was the postmodern turn in the last century that made much of the problems of identifying the meaning of a text. While aspects of postmodernism and various philosophers within the movement are commendable, the popular criticism of the possibility of meaning in language comes from a mistaken conflation of the meaning of individual words and the meaning of discourse. Paul Ricoeur specifically addresses the postmodernism of Jacques Derrida on this particular

15. Ibid., 16b 26–28.

16. *The Rule of Metaphor*.

17. Ricoeur, *From Text to Action*, 75–101.

18. Ibid.

19. Ricoeur, *Interpretation Theory*, 43–44.

point in *The Rule of Metaphor.* Ricoeur makes a careful study of metaphor to show that Aristotle's distinction between the meaning of individual worlds and individual sentences is necessary to grasp what metaphors mean and how they are used.[20] Put very briefly, words do not have meaning.[21] We should not expect them to. Words have uses but not meanings unless they are in sentences. A sentence has a meaning because it is discourse articulated by a human being at a particular time and place and the words spoken have a specific reference or context.[22] A full recapitulation of Ricoeur's case in *The Rule of Metaphor* is beyond the space available here. It is because discourse has an intended meaning and a corresponding natural way of being understood within a given context that discourse reveals "a world," as Ricoeur puts it.[23] There is a "world of the text" that inscribed discourse permits. The face of the sentence, the *logos*, permits the act of discourse, the moment of speech or writing, to be preserved so that the logos can speak to us in the current moment.[24]

Jesus seems to have had something of this in mind in Luke 16. Jesus tells the story of a rich man who has mistreated a poor man named Lazarus. Both men die. Both men wake up in an afterlife of some sort. The rich man awakes in Hades while Lazarus awakes in a peaceful place called "Abraham's Bosom." The rich man calls across a great chasm to Abraham and to Lazarus, who is now safe. He begs Abraham to send someone to his brothers to warn them of the torments of Hades. Abraham then replies, "They have Moses and the Prophets; let them hear them." In Jesus' story, Abraham rejects sending messengers to the rich man's family because they already have Moses and the Prophets. But, in reality, they do not. They only have the prophets' writings. However, notice that the prophets' writings, per Ricoeur's observations, have distanciated their message. Abraham treats having the text of Scripture as having Moses and the prophets physically present. This is the principle of distanciation at work in texts. *It is not* as though the intent of Moses

20. *The Rule of Metaphor*, 9–43.

21. Ricoeur, *The Conflict of Interpretations*, 79–96.

22. Ibid.

23. *From Text to Action*, 96.

24. Collender and Deller, "Scoping Complex Systems," 70.

and the prophets is somehow in the texts. To Jesus of Nazareth, the texts *are* the discourses of Moses and the prophets. Those discourses can be read such that the engagement with the text is like engaging with and listening to Moses and the Prophets as though they were present and speaking.

Now the property of distanciation in discourse does not warrant that one should lazily and naively understand a text. After all, to understand in this way is to misunderstand. Rather, distanciation enables historical research and the study of historical contexts. Jesus rebukes many of his hearers for not understanding his own action within the context of his own time (John 5:38–40). Jesus says, "You do not have His word (*logos*) abiding in you, for you do not believe Him whom He sent. You search the Scriptures because you think that in them you have eternal life; it is these that testify about Me; and you are unwilling to come to Me so that you may have life." Jesus castigates the religious leaders of his own time for not believing in him and his message. He also identifies the cause of their unbelief— reading the text blindly, letting the words pass through the mind, without letting them become the discourse they really are—which would make the religious leaders responsible for drawing conclusions they want to deny. To draw the correct conclusions, they would have had to understand Jesus according to his own literary context. In one sense, Jesus is saying they are making themselves poor historians in order to fail to skillfully interpret Jesus discourse. Discourse events provide anchors, or data points in time, which allow for the development of an historical narrative. The best narrative is one that makes sense of the relevant data points.[25]

This framework, called Critical Realism, allows us to reconstruct ancient worldviews and historical events that occurred in the ancient past. The eminent Christian historian and theologian N. T. Wright explains the methodology of Critical Realism in much greater detail in the opening of his work *The New Testament and the People of God*. The teachings of Jesus and the Apostles are not presented in the Bible as mere collections of sayings per some hypothetical source documents that some higher-critical scholars

25. Wright, *New Testament People of God*, 38–46.

may claim as the source for portions of the four Gospels. The books of the New Testament reveal a narrative, or, rather, a collection of narratives, which, as Ricoeur observes, cannot be compressed into a univocal super-plot. From a Christian perspective, the Gospels and the Book of Acts tell the story of the culmination of the tributaries of Israel's history, and these books teach, among other things, a new way of being Israel. Obviously, the Gospels presume the multifaceted worldview of the Hebrew Scriptures, and Jesus specifically interacts with the multifaceted expectations, we might even call them "Judaisms," which Jews of the first century embraced. We know about these worldviews through the writings of the various sects of Judaism at the time, the multitude of intertestamental texts, the first century texts, the Mishnah, Talmudic material, and the Anti-Nicene writings.

Likewise, the earliest Buddhist texts reflect the original teachings of Buddha. These are the Five *Nikāyas* in the Pali Canon and the Chinese equivalent to the *Nikāyas*, the Four *Āgamas* (which were once Five *Āgamas* corresponding to each of the Pali *Nikāyas*; unfortunately, one *Āgama* was lost). These texts (the *Nikāyas* and the *Āgamas* together) are called the *Sūtra*-(Pali *Sutta*) *piṭaka* or the Sūtra Basket. The *Sūtra-piṭaka* is a critical part of the *Tripiṭaka* (which means "The Three Baskets"), the collection of scriptures embraced by the Theravāda School of Hīnayāna Buddhism, the oldest sect of Buddhism. However, we are going to focus on the *Sūtra-piṭaka*, particularly the Pali Canon, rather than the rest of the *Tripiṭaka*, and there is a good reason for this. The other two baskets of the *Tripiṭaka* are either ordinances for the monks (the *Vinaya-piṭaka*) or philosophical commentaries on the Buddha's sermons (the *Abhidhamma-piṭaka*).[26] However, these other two baskets further confirm the existence of an extensive community of monks that had formed around the Buddha's teaching and lend historical credibility to the claim that the Buddha was a real, historical figure akin to one presented in the *Nikāyas*. These other two baskets play something of the role that the Anti-Nicene writings play in Christian theology.

Some have suggested that the *Nikāyas* are unreliable because, as far as we know, they were orally transmitted by the monks and

26. Mizuno, *Buddhist Sutras*, 13–23.

not written down until centuries later; however, this seems to be an unfair dismissal of the historical record and of Buddhist tradition. The Buddha taught for about over forty years. His disciple Ānanda, so legend has it, possessed a copious memory and remembered all of the Buddha's sermons. Anyone who has been around an itinerant teacher who has a "shtick" that he repeats again and again to different audiences in different settings, learns the sermons very well. Since Ānanda was known to have a very sticky memory, and since the Buddha had a large community of followers, it seems only reasonable to accept that if Ānanda had started changing the sermons the community would have known. Also, the circumstances under which the monk Mahākāsyapa, the Buddha's chief disciple, allegedly convened the Buddhist council that compiled the first collection of sūtras seems to be a further reason to trust the general authenticity of the *Nikāyas.*[27] Mahākāsyapa had overheard an old monk express his exuberance at the death of the Buddha since now they could all be free to do what they wanted. So he convened a council of the five hundred monks who were still at Kushinagara, the place where the Buddha had just died. The monk Ānanda being among their number, Ānanda recited the Buddha's sermons. If the sūtras were compiled this way, or approximately in this way, there is good reason to accept their reliability.

Richard H. Robinson and Willard L. Johnson dismiss the legend of the composition of sūtras as "an anachronistic and idealized story."[28] Nevertheless, even if the idealized story is embellished, the possibility of an oral tradition retained by memory for a few centuries has its own good mechanism for accurately retaining the Buddha's teaching. For those more familiar with the Bible than the Buddhist sūtras, it is certainly true the sūtras are not the heart-pounding action narratives of the books of 1 and 2 Samuel, Mark, or Acts. If it was not so offensive, I would say most of the Buddhist sūtras are . . . boring. *Very tedious reads.* Yet their repetitive structures and sundry qualities suggest they were meant to be memorized and repeated. Only someone who *truly* wanted to preserve this content would exert the kind of mental energy necessary to organize and retain

27. Mizuno, *Buddhist Sutras,* 19.

28. *The Buddhist Religion,* 64.

the sūtras in one's memory. This is the view held by Rupert Gethin, namely that the Buddha's teachings were accurlately remembered by the community of the Buddha's followers and written down later.[29] It is true that Buddhist teaching has its own philosophy of history, which in some way compromises the very project of vindicating the reliability of sūtras, as we shall see in chapter 4. However, by having good will and common sense regarding human care for deeply held convictions, we should respect the diligence of the ancient monks who devoted themselves strenuously to the teaching and practice of the *Dharma*.

We may draw a lesson regarding the legends surrounding the composition of the Greek translation of the Hebrew Scriptures, the Septuagint, which can be applied to the composition of the Buddhist sūtras. Legend has it that seventy or seventy-two rabbinical scholars met for seventy days and over that time translated the Hebrew Scriptures into Greek. This legend hypes the Septuagint as more powerful and miraculous, but the point of the story is that the Hebrew God is working to preserve his word as it translates to a new target language. The Septuagint is not an attempt to change the meaning of the Bible as much as it is an effort to relocate the content of the Hebrew in a new language. The Septuagint takes pains to distinguish the Hebrew worldview from Greek philosophy contrary to the claims of Roger Corless, who blames the Septuagint for imposing Greek philosophy on the Hebrew worldview of Torah.[30] One anecdotal piece of evidence for this lack of syncretism which Corless claims is the "mis-translation" in chapter 7 of Septuagint Proverbs, which turns the seductress wife of Hebrew Proverbs, who

29. Gethin, *Foundations of Buddhism*, 35-38.

30. Corless perpetuates the myth that early Christians did not study Torah and did not maintain the antithesis between Hebraic and Greek thought. He writes, "It is time to say that this is nonsense, and that Christians have themselves been responsible for the nonsense, because they wrote in Greek and Latin and did not study Torah" in "The Mutual Fulfilment of Buddhism and Christianity in Co-Inherent Superconsciousness," *Buddhist-Christian Dialogue*, 116. As someone who reads Hebrew, Greek, and Latin, and who has carefully studied Torah, its legal code, and the way the New Testament writers use Torah, I do not know how any person competent in Torah and in these three languages could write this sentence or the folly that follows it. I am embarrassed for Mr. Corless.

preys on young men, into a personification of Greek philosophy.[31] The Septuagint intended to present the content of the Hebrew text to the faithful Jews of the Diaspora who perhaps had lost facility with the mother tongue of their faith. The Buddhist sūtras serve something of this role. They preserve the teaching of the Buddha for the service of a community that seeks to follow and spread his teaching.

So whether written early or remembered and written later, we have good reason to trust the sūtras, especially the *Nikāyas/Āgamas*. If the texts appear to be memorized and then written down, why would these features not arise according to a scenario similar to that presented in the Kushinagara council narrative? If that story is not persuasive, it seems quite reasonable to conclude that a community of Buddhist monks invested a great deal of energy in preserving these texts in their own memories. If they strenuously worked to memorize this teaching, caring for it so diligently, then it also would be realistic to assume they wrote it down as an aid to memory.

The New Testament and the *Sūtra-piṭaka*, as well as their voluminous surrounding literature, make it possible to use Critical Realism in order to reconstruct their respective worldviews. Therefore, it remains with us to ask the question How can we bring the worldview of the early Church, articulated in the New Testament, and that of early Buddhism, articulated in the *Sūtra-piṭaka*, into reasoned discourse with one another?

HOW TO PRACTICE INTERRELIGIOUS DIALOGUE

We have established that both Jesus and the Buddha were excellent debaters. A debater uses evidence and reason to persuade by making a cogent case. Jesus and the Buddha used debate not only to persuade but also to serve others by moving them to life-changing insights. With more skill than a scholar, and more wit than a public intellectual, they both spoke to human emotions, human dispositions, and human goals.

Since they debated in the hearing of real and normal people, it may be worthwhile to examine what the rhetorical tradition teaches

31. Johann Cook is the world's leading scholar in Septuagint Proverbs. See his discussion of this matter in Cook, *The Septuagint of Proverbs*.

regarding effective debate. In *Rhetorica ad Herennium,* one of the great works of the rhetorical tradition written in the first century B.C., its anonymous author explains how to argue a decisive case. He gives the following advice while explaining legal argumentation for the Roman courtroom: He advises that the speakers discern the *Point to Adjudicate.* This Point to Adjudicate is where the case of prosecution and the case of defense meet over their central question of contention. The Point to Adjudicate:

> . . . will be established from the meeting of the prosecutors Central Point and the defendant's Justifying Motive, as follows: When Orestes says that he killed his mother to avenge his father, was it right for Clytemnestra to be slain by her son without a trial? This then is the proper method for finding the Point to Adjudicate. Once the Point to Adjudicate is found, the complete economy of the entire speech ought to be directed to it.[32]

Although *Rhetorica ad Herennium* is discussing legal pleading, the author's point applies to debate in general. Well-reasoned debate helps judge and jury most when the interlocutors argue toward the Point to Adjudicate. In legal pleading, this is the point at issue between the prosecution and defense.

The problem with finding the Point to Adjudicate between two religions is that this point "moves" depending on what claims are made by the two religions in dialogue. Given that Buddhism and Christianity are in discourse here, we can find the Point to Adjudicate more quickly. Unfortunately, the identity of the Point to Adjudicate must wait to be revealed till later in *To End All Suffering.* To attempt to explain it now would only confuse since we have yet to examine Buddhist philosophy on its own terms. Were I to suggest a Point to Adjudicate now, it would just seem like a guess.

However, some light on the road might help us better see where we are going. Allow me to highlight some terrain and say, "Keep an eye on this." Both religions aim to actually accomplish a goal, to do something that impacts all suffering. Perhaps we could even call this suffering 'evil'. Since each religion aims in some way to address suffering, it will be important to understand why the proposed "cure" for suffering will work. Why, if one follows a certain doctrine,

32. [Cicero], *Rhetorica Ad Herennium*, 53.

will one's suffering end? Is it a real cure? What measures the success of the cure? How would one know if one has encountered success? It follows that the questions of where one's standards come from and why those standards are reliable become very important.

Since standards will turn out to be important, we now turn our attention to the question of how to find standards which can apply to dialogue between Buddhism and Christianity.

Four Options for the Source of Standards

As I mentioned earlier, the question of standards in interreligious dialogue presents many challenges. How do we know the truthfulness of a religion, especially when different religions define truth differently? How do we discern the usefulness of a religion, especially when religions have different goals? In the four options I present below, I am assuming that there are only two potential locations for standards:

- *in a religion* (a designation which has polysemy; in this case, an ambiguity including both the beliefs of adherents, confessions of faith communities, holy texts, ritual praxis, and the culture these produce, etc., so one must grant me something of the same latitude Aristotle deserves when he defines a term with multiple overlapping definitions, e.g. happiness or virtue),
- *or in the world,* which includes the natural world of physical processes and the human world of humanly experienced cultural awareness and social processes phenomenologically bracketed from religion.[33]

To step beyond these two locations requires us to consider the kind of worldview doctrines we are attempting to adjudicate, so this antinomy between religion and the world seems fair to me. Based on this antinomy, the following four options arise:

1. There is an objective standard outside a religion to which a religion must submit. (A)

33. Ricoeur wisely observes, though, that the "world as nature" and the "world as the human real" are not so easy to for us to wholly separate because both require humans to reflect about time, which is both a subjective and an objective phenomenon. See Ricoeur, *Time and Narrative: Volume I*, 3–30.

2. There is no objective standard outside a religion, only inside a religion; therefore, we cannot adjudicate between religions. (B)
3. The standard is both in a religion and outside of a religion in the world. (Both)
4. The standard is neither in a religion nor in the world. (Neither)

This seems to me a complete enumeration of the options.

Option 1: There is an objective standard outside a religion to which a religion must submit. (A): This corner means that a religion's doctrine may not define the categories of reality. Put another way, the Buddha cannot make claims without first getting permission from Greek philosophy and logic, or Darwinian natural science, or Russell and Whitehead's *Principia*, etc. If a religion's claims are justified according to a standard or another narrative that is culturally acceptable and authoritative, then and only then can the religion claim to be true.

The obvious problem with this view is that it is a subtle way to require a religion to actually deny itself before it can come to the table and enter into discourse. To have potency, it must first castrate itself. Both Buddhism and Christianity make world-defining claims. Furthermore, this requirement is hypocritical since, at least in my illustration, Greek philosophy and logic, or Darwinian natural science, or the *Principia* of Russell and Whitehead get to claim to be the "true" standard by which a view must be measured when in fact they are each a view, like early Buddhism taught in the *Sūtra-piṭaka* and the Christian Gospel taught in the New Testament. This is not to say that these three views actually do make this kind of claim. Perhaps they do. But if they did, it would be a sly attempt to win on the cheap.

Option 2: There is no objective standard outside a religion, only inside a religion; therefore, we cannot adjudicate between religions. (B): This position claims there is no standard, or reference point by which one can judge between competing religious claims. However, this position is absurd. By drawing a conclusion about the limits of what a religion can claim as true or useful, a person is adjudicating between views. If one claims to make this claim by reasoning, he or she is insane. Nietzsche saw right through this argument, even though he was sympathetic to its premises. He understood that the lack of objective grounds meant that a stronger view could impose itself on weaker ones. All is rhetoric. Socrates suffered from "terrifying ugliness."[34] Nietzsche's clear head on this matter is one of the reasons I like him.

Option 3: The standard is both in a religion and outside of a religion in the world. (Both): It may be a blind spot in contemporary Western culture to force the antinomy between the doctrine a religion teaches and one's knowledge of the physical world and the human social world. A religion need not be wrong about the operation of the world; in fact, it may actually illumine and explain the world. If a religion is true and/or useful, if it describes our human world and the natural world, and if it helps us to make wiser choices within it, Option 3 seems perfectly reasonable.

This position must be distinguished from Natural Law Theory, which is actually an example of Option 1. Natural Law Theory, which developed in the Western philosophical tradition, treats the regularities in the natural world and in the human world of moral experience as though these regularities are part of the world independent of God. At the beginning of the 1700s, Natural Law Theory began to decisively replace biblical casuistry, the study of the Bible for wisdom regarding social counseling and public policy. If the principles of morality and wisdom are as clearly presented in nature and society as they are in the Bible, and more universally, Natural Law becomes the standard to measure the Bible's teaching. Natural Law Theory supplanted the authority of Biblical moral teaching leading to the view, common throughout the later 1700s and early 1800s, that Natural Law operates in the world as a surrogate for God's direct oversight, or in such a way that a methodological naturalism is possible. The universe runs in such a way, by such predictable laws, that it takes on its own God-like properties. Natural processes unfold so predictably that the burden of proof rests on the believer in God to show his God is necessary. When explained like this, it is clear that Natural Law Theory is an example of Option 1. However, it also explains why Darwinian evolution completely dismantled Natural Law Theory. Darwinian evolution claims the universe is a

34. Nietzsche, *Twilight of the Idols*, 14.

place where accidents compound to make order. This means that there is *no* natural law or moral law. Everything changes. Humans must evolve to survive in an evolving world. Old ways of doing things may not work in the new world that natural selection has selected for us. This is why current adherents of Natural Law Theory can only problematically defend it. This philosophical relic from the heady days of a pervasive cultural Christianity fails to find legitimacy in today's post-Christian West. Today, defenders of Natural Law Theory tend to preach to their choir, but society has moved on.[35]

Option 3 is not a kind of Natural Law Theory. Rather, it recognizes that if either Christianity or Buddhism is true and useful, then the natural world and the human world together are either the Buddhist world, or they are the Christian world. If this is the case, facts are not bald facts that can be interpreted apart from Buddhism or Christianity. As we shall see in the next chapter, the Buddha vigorously criticized his Vedic opponents for distorting what direct experience in meditation told them about the universe by reading their own Vedic religious teaching into their experience. The Buddha believed that the natural world and the human world both operate according to the same process, dependent co-origination (Pali: *paṭiccasamuppāda*, Skt: *pratītiasamupāda*), which I will discuss in detail later. Put briefly, the Buddha taught that everything arises out of causal interactions. Nothing is outside the realm of causation. There are no self existent gods like the Christian God. No one ordains all things. Even the gods arise out of dependent co-origination. This doctrine and reality is what makes introspection possible. The reason why a Buddhist should accept this is because experience seems to confirm it, and because understanding it and using experience is the best way to end suffering. We see the Buddha claims his teaching, his Dharma, is both in his mouth and in the world.

35. For an example of this, see the "Preface to the First Edition" in Budziszewski, *What We Can't Not Know*. In the second edition, Budziszewski describes his position in different terms suggesting that Natural Law Theory is leaving Option 1 and moving in the direction of Option 3. What is important about this rebranding of Natural Law Theory is the admission that what lives under the name "Natural Law Theory" has been Option 1. It seems apparent that if "Natural Law Theory" does eventually becomes the name for Option 3, that will lead to confusion since some will attack Option 3 as though it has the critical weaknesses of Option 1.

Likewise, the Christian Gospel makes the same sort of claim within its own worldview. Since God created the world and sustains it, all knowledge relates to him. No fact of experience, no object, no moral sentiment, can be accurately understood apart from the Creator. If the Bible is correct, then the entire universe is God's private property. He knows everything about it. He has the final say regarding the future of everything. The natural world and the human world point to the attributes and character of God, as St. Paul explains in the first chapter of his letter to the Romans. Paul explains that people look at the created world that testifies to its Creator and then they suppress that knowledge (Rom. 1:18–23). Though St. Paul is arguing from a different worldview, his observation that people suppress the testimony of nature about God's character is markedly similar to the Buddha's observation that Vedic religion distorted a person's observations of the world.

However, St. Paul and the Buddha differ on what our world experience teaches. St. Paul believes that it reveals the nature and attributes of its Creator. The Buddha, on the other hand, believes it reveals a universal causal law (see chapter 5). At first, St. Paul's natural theology in Romans 1 may sound like Natural Law Theory, a version of Option 1. However, the Bible also teaches that in order to know God and his revelation, humans must exercise faith. The author of the letter to the Hebrews writes, "without faith it is impossible to please *Him*, for he who comes to God must believe that He is and *that* He is a rewarder of those who seek Him" (Heb. 11:6; emphasis in translation). So which view of experience is true?

Both. Throughout the Bible, God asks people to believe what he tells them. Faith is belief based on testimony.[36] It is a particular process of belief, one that places trust in the one testifying.[37] When a person has faith in the sense that we are referring to here, the person believes based on the fact that this is *God's* testimony.

Our use of trust based on testimony pervades human experience more than one would think. Consider what a person does when navigating a large room filled with things. It could be a warehouse, a supermarket, even a vast office floor holding a

36. Packer, *Concise Theology*, 159.

37. Ibid.

cubicle maze. When one walks across such a room, one must retain a memory of one's journey, which one then recalls in the process of the journey through the room. If one forgets the memory "map" mid-journey, if one forgets where one has been, then one will be quite disoriented. Imagine if this were to happen to you, how frightening and disorienting it would be to find yourself in such a room suddenly without the benefit of your memory. In the film *Memento*, written and directed by Christopher Nolan, a man faces life with no long-term memory. He can only remember three minutes into the past, and he uses written notes to himself to remind him of his past. However, he uses his memory crutch for evil purposes and turns it into a weapon by writing a lying note to himself to deceive himself into committing a murder. But texts can also serve the memory for good. Cognitive scientist Andy Clark has written about how some Alzheimer's patients will use a system of organization and notes to inform themselves about what they cannot remember and, thus, lead relatively normal lives.[38] In contrast to *Memento*, they and their caregivers put trustworthy information into their notes and into the organization of their environment, and they prosper as a result.

Returning to the example of navigating a large room, when we navigate such a room we need to trust not only our eyes but also trust the testimony of our memories. Trust then gives access to information we use in the present moment, which is confirmed by sense experience. This trust allows us to use information as a context to make sense experience intelligible. If one cannot trust one's memory, one is paralyzed. Military strategist John Boyd described this mental process through his strategic model of the OODA Loop.[39] According to Boyd, individuals maneuver in military operational environments through four stages in time. First they observe, then orient, then decide, then act. Then they observe again, and then orient again, etc. The most important part of the OODA Loop is the second "O": Orienting. The success of one's ability to maneuver and make good decisions in reaction to the outside world depends on one's orientation. At any given moment one must be able to trust one's orientation. Human life orientations are built through trust,

38. Clark, *Being There*, 66.

39. Osinga., *Science, Strategy and War*, 1–6.

through teachers and mentors, through formative experiences, but most importantly, through parents. In an all-things-being-equal world, we are born trusting. We look to our parents. This trust makes us sponges that soak up what our parents and other adults teach us in our youth. We must believe in order to understand.

In a way somewhat analogous to how people can trust their eyes to help them observe and their memories to help them orient them through a large room, the nation of Israel could trust God to help them observe the creation and trust his revelation to orient them on their sojourn through the ancient world. The Hebrew word for a chronicler (or historian) means a "rememberer." Texts are the public memories of a people. In the case of Israel's progressive revelation, the people had the opportunity to observe, orient, decide, and act. The Bible thus became Israel's written history of how God interacted with them in the past, but it also oriented then to understand God, their world, and how to make effective decisions.

Among other things, what separates the Bible from all other textual traditions is this extended period of repeated passes through a massive civic, cultural OODA Loop, wherein a people have the repeated opportunity to interact with their God, to understand him. There is so much that could be studied regarding the relationship between the OODA Loop and how God's revelation oriented his people over time.[40] Like a man making his way through a room looking to his memory to guide him to help him make educated guesses about what to do next, the Bible acts as a cultural memory, a history of a people and their interaction with their God.

If one doubts that faith in one's memory is important, one need only spend a little time with people who have come to seriously doubt their memory. Sometimes, there are things they can still remember, but they fear they cannot. They fear that they do not remember. Assuming the biblical account is true, God interacted with his people, repeatedly orienting them to understand him and the world. In doing so, also made sure to provide them with a public memory, *a public text*, a shared communal memory. Where a person's memory might fail them, the intertextuality of the various texts composed at different times and different regions ("of the room," so

40. This is one of those projects I hope to get to one day.

to speak) provide multiple witnesses to memory and sanity, and a repeated confirmation that the orientation, which has been taught and trained into a people through each successive generation over two thousand years, is not only true but also wise and competent.

This naturally raises an important question: How does the one who believes God know he is hearing from God? The Christian tradition provides many consistent answers to this question, but the thrust of those answers is summarized well by the examples of Romans 1 and Hebrews 11. According to Romans 1, the evidence in the world is so strong that men are without a "reasoned excuse" (Greek: *apologia*, as in Socrates' reasoned defense before the court of Athens). However, as stated in Hebrews 11, without faith no one can see God. Yet the rest of Hebrews 11 describes the historical evidence of God's faithfulness, generation after generation for two millennia, showing that God protects and vindicates his people in history. According to Hebrews 11, this vindication has culminated in the advent and victory of Messiah, an historical event in the recent memory of the readers of both Romans and Hebrews. In Romans, Paul faults humans for not believing in the face of overwhelming evidence. Hebrews identifies the evidence of God's faithfulness in history, generation after generation. Why would the author of Hebrews offer evidence when he has already stated that without faith no one can even please God? (Heb. 11:6). Because, according the biblical worldview, God gives ample evidence that he makes good on all his promises. He keeps his word to his people—real promises, revealed in history and fulfilled in this world. For the readers of Romans and Hebrews, the question of how God's people know that God is real and that he keeps his promises is not an academic debate, since the Christian community suffered in many ways during the turbulent first century. Romans and Hebrews affirm both faith and evidence, albeit in different but very practical ways.

In the Bible, faith and evidence work together. Some Christian theologians have tried to separate these or prioritize one over the other. Yet, there is a long tradition, reaching back through Augustine, through the New Testament, deep into the Old Testament, showing that we need not prioritize these in such a way that faith must believe without evidence or that evidence must be perfectly evaluated before faith is justified. John Calvin explains this relationship in the first two chapters of Book 1 of his *Institutes of the Christian Religion*.[41] According to Calvin, without knowing ourselves, we cannot know God. Nevertheless, without knowing God, we cannot know ourselves. Thus, a hermeneutical circle demands that man know both God and himself in order to know anything at all.

The late French philosopher Paul Ricoeur approaches Calvin's Augustinian hermeneutical circle through the gate of textual hermeneutics by way of the human process of interpreting symbols and narratives. This process *is* human reflective thought. Human thought is not computational, as such. Rather, " 'the symbol gives rise to thought.' And this conjunction is a circular relation between a believing and an understanding."[42] Ricoeur goes further to show that the circular relation between believing and understanding does not destroy thinking or reason. Ricoeur clarifies, "The circle is not vicious; still less is it deadly. It is quite alive and stimulating. You must believe in order to understand. No interpreter in fact will ever come close to if he does not live in the aura of meaning that is sought. And yet it is only by understanding that we believe."[43] Given the finitude of humans, no one will ever be able to exhaustively prove all one's beliefs without reference to beliefs that are accepted based on faith in testimony. *The question is not whether we should accept some things based on faith but rather* What *things will we accept by faith?*

The biblical approach to faith and evidence as well as the Buddha's theory of knowledge both fit squarely under Option 3. Both need to be developed in more detail. It should be clear, though, that the simple, direct appeal to logic or evidence or citing holy texts is not quite so easy when engaging in religious discourse. Both religions have their own standards and goals. They each have a worldview that defines what counts as "winning" the debate. Nevertheless, if either one of these religions is correct in what it claims about what is true and useful, then the world is either a Buddhist world or a Christian world. This means, assuming that one or the other is *the* truthful or *the* useful religion, that the natural world and the human

41. Calvin, *Institutes*, 35–38.

42. Ricoeur, *The Symbolism of Evil*, 352.

43. *Conflict of Interpretations*, 298.

world must follow an attraction—a natural gravity, if you will—as both are pulled into the orbit of one view or the other.

Option 4: The standard is neither in one view nor in the world. (Neither): If Option 4 is true, both Buddhism and Christianity are mistaken, and there is no such thing as interreligious dialogue. If Option 4 holds, then a ratio to measure either religion is nowhere to be found. And if one tries to salvage Option 4 by suggesting that the means of measurement could be in heaven, with God or the bodhisattvas, notice that his particular interpretation of Option 4 actually collapses into Option 2. If someone was going to seriously present Option 4 as a rival position for either New Testament Christianity or early Buddhist philosophy, notice that the debate ends.

However, Option 4 creates a very silly situation. Option 4 is actually making a claim about which norms or standards apply to interreligious discourse; thus, when it engages either Christianity or Buddhism, it creates a new Point(s) to Adjudicate, though different issues would be joined between New Testament Christianity than between early Buddhism. It actually resets the debate. We now end up with a new debate between either Buddhism or Christianity and Option 4.

Someone familiar with the history of the development of Buddhist doctrine may spot the shallow analogies between Option 4 and Mādhyamika Buddhism or Zen Buddhism, and their emphasis on the non-conceptual nature of Buddhism. Later on, I devote an entire chapter to the philosophy of Nāgārjuna, the founder of Mādhyamika Buddhism, and it will be clear at the end of that chapter that Nāgārjuna does not represent Option 4. Furthermore, Zen Buddhism is actually a historical tributary flowing from Nāgārjuna's philosophy, and Zen's apparent hostility to conceptual formulation is based on the conceptual formulations, which are discussed in the chapter on Nāgārjuna. Zen is not Option 4.

By looking over these four options, one can see both Buddhism and Christianity seem best situated under Option 3. This chapter on methodology will conclude by addressing one thorny problem raised by Option 3: the perilous danger of reasoning in a circle, otherwise known as *begging the question.*

Begging the Question

Aristotle and the logicians that followed him throughout the centuries have reckoned it a logical fallacy to have an argument's conclusion also be one of the premises. Circular proof "is proof by means of the conclusion."[44] In short, this is what it means to argue in a circle, to prove by means of the conclusion.

Consider the following two sentences: "The Constitution of the United States is a wise document because it was written by the Founding Fathers. And we know that the Founding Fathers were wise men because they were wise enough to write the Constitution!" These two sentences clearly offer a circular argument since the second sentence assumes the conclusion. The argument is meant to prove that the Constitution is a wise document, but the supporting premise assumes that the Constitution already is a wise document. This argument is clearly bogus.

Consider this argument: "We know that the human eye is reliable because we can test it. When we look at the way the human eye works and match that with the world we see, we can tell that the human eye sees the world." This argument is clearly also begging the question. The human eye is being used to test the human eye. This is arguing in a circle. This argument is clearly fallacious if begging the question is never allowed. However, a lot hangs on this argument. If we cannot use the human eye to test the human eye, what do we use? Our ears? Our noses? There is a kind of information that comes through the human eye that does not come through any other sense. If one is not permitted to use the eye because it is begging the question to do so, then the use of human sight is suspect.

Consider this example: "If a sequence of three sentences is organized in the structure of modus ponens, then the third sentence will be a valid conclusion. These three sentences are organized in the structure of modus ponens. Therefore, this conclusion is valid." Notice that this argument also begs the question since it is using modus ponens to prove the conclusion of a modus ponens syllogism valid. While my first example of begging the question pointed out that trusting in our eyes is actually built on begging the question, this argument demonstrates something equally insidious. When one

44. Aristotle, "Prior Analytics," 57b 17.

attempts to prove the validity and reliability of logic, one must use logic to do so. Logic is one of those things that one must assume to prove anything at all. Scientific experimentation does not prove a universal law of thought. Rather, what we might call "the laws of thought" are first necessary for humans to even begin planning the process of scientific experimentation. Therefore, at least two things require humans to beg the question: human sight and the human use of logic. Are these two things important? How much can we know without sight or reason?

If using sight and reason require humans to beg the question and question begging is fallacious, then all human thinking is perpetual insanity. Or Aristotle missed something.

Let us consider the hypothesis that Aristotle did miss something. What could it have been? Aristotle explains why he believes begging the question is a fallacy in his masterwork on logic, the *Organon*, which contains two sub-works called *Prior Analytics* and *Posterior Analytics*. These two sub-works discuss deductive logic (primarily in *Prior Analytics*) and inductive logic (primarily in *Posterior Analytics*), but a careful reading of both texts will show that they cannot be so neatly compartmentalized. *Prior Analytics* provides an extended framework for what Aristotle discusses in *Posterior Analytics*, the latter being more of a guide to doing scientific research rather than anything that we would consider as an inductive logic textbook today.

Aristotle offers three arguments for why begging the question cannot count for proof, or "logical demonstration" as he calls it. He offers arguments from (1) immediate knowledge, (2) certainty, (3) and self-evidence. I will explain each argument and then demonstrate the deep problem with each one in turn.[45]

First, in *Posterior Analytics*, Aristotle argues against circular reasoning in the context of talking about necessity in scientific

45. The eminent Aristotelian scholar Jonathan Barnes identifies these problems in his commentary *Posterior Analytics*. However, he does not assemble the faults in Aristotle's case against begging the question into a refutation of Aristotle's position on the question of begging the question, which I am doing here. The fact that Barnes did not do this is no failure on his part. His commentary covers many helpful areas, and his exegesis of the passages I discuss here is very helpful. However, he does not choose to address the same issues that I am addressing here.

knowledge.[46] Aristotle wants to make it possible to argue from premises to a conclusion, and he believes that circular reasoning will injure that project. To make his case, he argues against two particular schools of thought. The first thinks that all premises have to be demonstrated, which of course leads to an infinite regress since there must be a proof for every proof, and the string of proofs can never stop by definition. The second uses the mistake of the first to say, "See! We can get around those other guys by having a circular proof. You just let each premise prove itself by itself. There. No problem!"

Aristotle rejects both schools of thought by claiming that a person knows the premises "immediately." However, he does not explain what this means. "Immediately" when? And in relation to what? He does not say.[47]

Aristotle then goes on to argue against circular reasoning because what is less known must be proved by what is more known "and the same things cannot be simultaneously prior and posterior to one another, so circular demonstration is clearly not possible in the unqualified sense of 'demonstration' "[48] While Aristotle is correct that in a single syllogism it may be the case that the same things cannot be prior and posterior to one another, we have already seen (above) that in the case of both sight and reason, the eyes and modus ponens are simultaneously prior and posterior and they are central to all human knowledge. Clearly, Aristotle's observation must have limited scope. The question that remains for us to discern is in what way is it limited?

Second, Aristotle argues against circular reasoning by fencing his case through maintaining that one cannot establish certainty by that which is uncertain. Using A, B, and C as term variables, he traces hypothetical relationships between a variable A and its relationships to B and C.

> If then it is uncertain whether A belongs to C, and also whether A belongs to B, and if one should assume that A does belong to B, it is not yet clear whether he begs the original question,

46. Aristotle, "Posterior Analytics," 72 b.

47. See the extended discussion of this passage in Barnes, *Posterior Analytics.*

48. Aristotle, "Posterior Analytics," 72b 26–28.

> but it is evident that he is not demonstrating: for what is as uncertain as the question to be answered cannot be a principle of a demonstration.[49]

Subsequently, one cannot argue from what is less certain to what is more certain. If one is trying to prove a conclusion to be true, by definition the conclusion is not yet proven so it is uncertain. To then take what is uncertain and make it a premise in the argument to prove that conclusion, well, it is madness, all things being equal.

However, all things are not equal. Notice this argument depends upon the question of certainty. Yet certainty is a mental state, not a property of the world.[50] A person must reflect and assemble a conviction that something is the case based on deduction based on first principles and observation, in which one is driven from the particulars of experience to the forming of more abstract conceptions, which Aristotle believes reflects universal first principles and natural forms. Nevertheless, certainty is not certain. It is a product of reflection, and is, thus, somewhat transient and subjective. It can change. It follows that the measure of how certainly a person believes a premise in his heart is an ill-suited basis for a case against begging the question.

Finally, Aristotle argues against circular reasoning based on self-evidence. Anything that is not self-evident and which must be proved must be proved by means of something else. According to Aristotle:

> Whenever a man tries to prove what is not self-evident by means of itself, then he begs the original question. This may be done by assuming what is in question at once; it may also be proved through the thesis proposed, and demonstrate it through them. . . . So it turns out that those who reason thus merely say that a particular thing is, if it is, in this way everything will be self evident. But that is impossible.[51]

Thus, according to Aristotle, if one wishes to prove something, he must do so by means of something else. If he assumes what he in-

49. Aristotle, "Prior Analytics," 65a 11–14.

50. For an extended discussion of the concept of certainty in Aristotle, see "Aristotelian Certainty," in Grene, *The Knower and the Known*, 36–63.

51. "Prior Analytics," 64b 36–65a 9.

tends to prove in the process of proof, one of two things must be the case: Either he is actually appealing to something that is self-evident or he is begging the question. For Aristotle there is no *teritam quid.*

However, there is a serious problem with this dichotomy. There is no universal agreement regaring what (if any) things are in fact "self-evident," or which principles or truths are self-evident. Now, to be fair, I am not suggesting here that there has to be universal agreement on anything for it to be confirmed. Though one ought not flippantly reject a crowd's wisdom, still, the assent of the majority is not proof. Yet the question of what counts for self-evident truths is intimately connected to the question of worldview. While the question of what counts for self-evident truths and the question of worldview are different questions that should not be confused with each other, they are still intimately related to one another.

While we cannot hope to number every possible self-evident truth, at least we can find three typical areas in which people have claimed that there are self-evident truths: logical truths, natural science, and human rights. Logical truths have long been considered necessary, self-evident truths. The apparent regularity of the behavior of the universe has, at least at times, persuaded men that the regularity of the natural world is self-evident as a component of experience. The Buddha certainly holds this view, as we shall see. And regarding human rights, one need look no further than the American Declaration of Independence for an example of a claim that human rights are self evident: "We hold these truths to be self-evident, that all men are created equal, that they are endowed by their Creator with certain unalienable Rights, that among these are Life, Liberty and the pursuit of Happiness." However, the claim to self-evidence in each of these domains is shaky at best.

In logic, the question of logical truth has become even more problematic at the hands of many twentieth century philosophers, most notably the Harvard logician Willard Van Orman Quine, who argued convincingly against the analytic and synthetic distinction between propositions because he found "synonymy" a problematic concept both to define and to use. He believed there is no necessary relationship between a sentence's subject and predicate beyond that which a behavioral criteria will account for in their relationship. In other words, Quine denies one of the cornerstones of Aristotelian logic, the proposition or the meaning of a sentence, which can be understood apart from a sentence. To make his point, Quine suggests that, at best, subject and predicate are not related by their participation in a proposition but rather their relation to one another is more akin to what David Hume called "constant conjunction." For Quine, the very notion of "logical truths" is a difficult one since he believes that logic is just a way of handling sentences. His book *Philosophy of Logic* promises to explain logical truths, which he defines in this way: *"A logical truth . . . is definable as a sentence from which we get only truths when we substitute sentences for its simple sentences*"[52] The simple sentences he is referring to are the kind that are found in logical truth trees. Notice for Quine, logic is not the application of a set of laws or principles; rather, it is a set of behaviors. It is a correct way for humans to handle sentences. This makes for a very interesting, albeit frustrating, ending to his little book. In his last chapter, "The Ground of Logical Truth," he finally tells us what the ground of logical truth is: "The reason is just that logic is obvious, potentially obvious."[53] So logical truths are "just . . . obvious." His book builds up to this revelation, and he takes pages to explain what he means by obvious.[54] He really does mean that it is just *obvious.* As we read Quine, we can hear Aristotle's word for *obvious*: "self-evident." Yet notice that Quine has denied the existence of propositions, so what he is calling self-evident is not the same thing Aristotle describes by the term. The principles and the nature of logic itself are not quite so obvious.

Furthermore, the uniformity of causal relationships so hallowed by enlightenment science also fails to offer self-evidence, or at least philosophers have found enough reasons to doubt the existence of necessary causal relationships in nature. The most famous skeptic of causality is David Hume, who famously argued against the "self-evidentness" of causal relations by making the case that we have no proof that a causal event has taken place. We only have the constant conjunction of phenomena. Billiard ball A moves in the direction of billiard ball B. Billiard ball A stops when it meets B. Then B takes

52. *Philosophy of Logic*, 50.

53. Ibid., 96.

54. Ibid., 82–83.

off in the adjacent direction. A and B are conjoined in the event, but that is not the same as saying A caused B to move. Hume showed that one could not actually prove that one event caused another event without making an assumption that one event caused another. In his view, we do not actually see the causation, only the signs.

Hume's skepticism strikes at the very heart of Aristotle's claims regarding self-evidence, especially given the importance of Aristotle's theory of causality to his account of proof. Consider the following passage from *Posterior Analytics* in which Aristotle explains when one has uncovered the complete reason for something:

> Our search for the reason ceases, and we think that we know, when the coming to be or existence of the fact before us is not due to the coming to be or existence of some other fact, for the last step of a search thus conducted is *eo ipso* the end and limit of the problem. Thus: 'Why did he come?' 'To get the money—where with to pay the debt—*that he might thereby do what is right*.' When in this regress we can no longer find an efficient or final cause, we regard our selves as then only having full knowledge of the reason why he came.[55]

Aristotle defines the limits of the search for an explanation as that point "[w]hen in this regress we can no longer find an efficient or final cause . . ." While Aristotle doesn't specifically use the term "self-evident" here, notice that he is talking about what constitutes the limits of reason, or proof. On what is he basing this theory of the limits of proof? On his metaphysical account of the four causes, a theory that explains Aristotle's notion of substance, a theory that modern science has largely rejected. The only one of Aristotle's causes that modern science accepts is efficient cause, and even efficient cause is held in doubt. Causality is not self-evident, or at least it seems that one needs to make a case for it.

Finally, the reality that humans have innate human rights seems to be a self-evident, incontrovertible truth that only a wicked man would deny. Every human deserves his or her human rights. I believe this. I hope you believe this. However, our desire for it to be so does not make it a self-evident truth. Just because one *really* believes something does not mean that it becomes self-evident. However, throughout history, many people have denied the

55. 85b 28–34; Aristotle's emphasis.

human rights of humans. Recall the beginning of the Declaration of Independence. "We" may "hold these truths to be self-evident," but many do not. Not all people believe that all men are "created," let alone "created equal" Though we all want "Life, Liberty and the pursuit of Happiness" many who teach in Western universities and message in the mainstream media deny that the endowment of humans "by their Creator with certain unalienable Rights" is a self-evident truth.

Self-evidence is a deeply problematic concept, but one that does have limited utility. Whenever one hears the term "self-evident," one should immediately ask what is the worldview in which the claim to self-evidence is presented. The statement regarding the "self-evidentness" of human rights in the Declaration of Independence contains worldview metadata necessary to make sense of the claim of human rights. If there is a Creator God who made human beings, then we are his property, his workmanship. No one can argue with God if he decided to give us rights (assuming we know where to find his arguments!). No one can argue against causality if every argument against causal relationships assumes a universe in which causal relationships govern physical relationships. No one can argue against logical truths if all attempts assume a worldview in which logical truths apply in all places, and all times, to all things. But what is that worldview? Aristotle failed to see that what one accepts as self-evidence could not be separated from aspects of one's overarching metaphysical stance regarding the world. Put in Aristotle's terms, there are elements to a person's worldview that are prior and posterior to inquiry at the same time, but in different ways. Logical truths, trust in the human eye, faith in causal relationship, as well as human rights and the ethical responsibilities into and out of which they arise are each both prior and posterior to any attempt to demonstrate themselves. Scholarship becomes nothing more than lies if done unethically. Medical research devolves into torture if human rights are not assumed. Observation is impossible without reliable eyes. Science is impossible without causal relationships or logic (including quantum mechanics—I know what you're thinking). Epistemic demonstration of each of these is both prior and posterior. Is all consistent human knowledge built on the foundation of circular reasoning? Must we think in vicious circles?

The great German philosopher Immanuel Kant explored the answers to these questions in his short book titled *The One Possible Basis for a Demonstration of the Existence of God.* Kant published this book in 1763, almost twenty years before he published the first version of *The Critique of Pure Reason.* In *The One Possible Basis,* Kant criticizes the common strategy of some Christian philosophers of his own day to offer evidence for the existence of God based on particular examples. In his subsection titled "The advantages and also the errors of ordinary physico-theology," he points out that when scientists want to use elements of the natural world or certain physical behaviors or features as proof of God, they actually end up not quite proving what they intended.[56] The God they are trying to prove is the God who not only made the physical features but also the preconditions that make the laws, principles, physical features, etc., which make the object of scientific study even possible. To put this point in Aristotle's terms, this means that God cannot be treated as though he is posterior to whatever feature of evidence is being used to support his existence. He must be 'prior' to that bit of evidence or, in reality, the very existence of the thing being used as evidence, and the natural principles that govern the natural world have to depend on God necessarily. I am using 'prior' in the sense that Aristotle is using it, being logically prior, not chronologically prior. For this reason, Kant disparages this sort of piecemeal attempt at proof for the existence of God. Kant is not disparaging any evidence offered for the existence of God; rather, he is arguing that the evidence be presented through a different methodology. For Kant, God must be treated as the single unifying ground of any possibility. To be fair, Kant sees this line of reasoning as the only argument for the existence of God rather than what I am calling it, which is a methodology for offering worldview related arguments and engaging in worldview discussion. Kant transfers this methodology from theology to metaphysics in his *Critique of Pure Reason* in which he calls arguments presented within this methodology "transcendental arguments"—arguments that argue to the preconditions of an intelligible world.[57]

56. *One Possible Basis,* 147–59.

57. Though I am recommending transcendental arguments, this should not be taken as blanket support for the case that Kant presents in *Critique of Pure Reason.*

If we take Kant's methodology and apply it to Aristotle's case against circular reasoning, we can see that Kant's methodology can be applied not only to God but also to logical truth, faith in the human eye, causal relationships, and human rights. These self-evident claims are each a precondition to intelligible experience. Nevertheless, they are not "self-evident" if re-narrated and explained in a worldview that cannot make sense of them, as we shall see in the following chapter, in the context of certain Indian philosophies. By critiquing Aristotle and using Kant to identify what was missing in Aristotle's arguments against begging the question, we see that Aristotle was right, except in matters that need to be addressed with transcendental arguments and, thus, a transcendental methodology. We must argue to the preconditions that make inquiry possible. Both Jesus and the Buddha argued in this way, aiming to understand the fundamental nature of the world. In doing so we may return to truths that were used previously in other parts of an argument, but in new ways. Instead of a vicious circle, we may find ourselves reasoning *recursively* in a life-giving spiral that actually goes somewhere.

In bringing these two great religious traditions into discourse with each other, it will be necessary to treat them in accord with Option 3, which we discussed above. This means that we will have to consider whether each can be a standard for the other and hold each other to account. This is difficult work since both views have differing standards. Thus, it will be necessary that each view not only examine the other view but also examine itself. If a religion cannot account for its own tests for truth and usefulness, then that religion compromises itself. Does either Buddhism or Christianity compromise itself? That is a question we will have to answer.

CONCLUSION

When scholars bring Buddhism and Christianity into dialogue with each other, some have tried to hamstring one or both of these great religions either by preventing one or both from offering

---

While Kant's *Critique* contains many helpful insights regarding transcendental arguments, at the same time it betrays a number of metaphysical commitments which I am not making and do not support. *The One Possible Basis* contains a powerful initial insight which this chapter develops, but that should not be construed as support for the *Critique*.

good arguments or by glossing over differences to bring about the appearance of common ground. However, the better place to find common ground between these two religions is modeled in their respective founders who were both rigorous, winsome debaters. Christians and Buddhists should follow the practice of their traditions' respective founders while modeling the charity and winsomeness of both the Buddha and Jesus Christ.

Buddhism and Christianity both teach their own standards for evaluating truth claims, and these standards flow out of the doctrines taught by each religion. The worldviews of these two religions can be comprehended in the present through the use of the exegetical methodology of Critical Realism, which defends both the historical reliability of the texts of Buddhism and Christianity as well as our ability to interpret them today. These religions have their own worldviews, which also offer their own respective standards for what is true and useful. It follows that a third perspective should not be brought in to adjudicate between them. To bring in a third perspective is to deny either religion. Thus, a different methodology, something other than the third perspective, is necessary.

I suggested that of the four options I presented, Option 3 is the best; namely, that the standards for the evaluation of views must be both in the world and in the religion. This option, though, gives rise to the supposed problem of begging the question since it would appear that each religion is using its own standards to prove itself and critically examine the rival religion. By examining Aristotle's three arguments against reasoning in a circle, his arguments from (1) immediate knowledge, (2) certainty, (3) and self evidence, I demonstrated that each of these arguments against begging the question are ill-founded. I demonstrated the final argument from self-evidence actually depends on the worldview in which the claim for self-evidence is offered. In some contexts, a thing that is believed by a community to be self-evident is not accepted by another community based on the worldview of that community. Worldview interprets what is reckoned as self-evidence.

Immanuel Kant's approach to transcendental arguments, which is introduced in his book *The One Possible Basis*, provided a way of approaching the problems in Aristotle's arguments against circular reasoning while also distinguishing what separates a vicious circle from productive recursive reasoning; namely, that productive recursive reasoning looks to the preconditions of intelligible experience. We found that this approach helped us rescue four things that are integral to human life, but which must first be assumed before they can be proved: specifically, logical truth, trust in the human eye, causal relations, and human rights.

I do not wish to provide a new framework for comparative religions by critiquing Aristotle's criticisms against circular reasoning or defending recursive reasoning. Instead, I have made a defense for allowing the worldviews and standards of Buddhism and Christianity to engage one another as full worldviews that make their own claims to what is true and useful. To that engagement we now turn.

Part II

An Overview of Buddhist Philosophy and Its Historical Context

3

Historical Background to Buddhist Philosophy

In the beginning this world was Self in the form of a person.

Bṛhadāraṇyaka Upaniṣad 4.1

In the beginning God created the heavens and the earth.

Genesis 1:1

INTRODUCTION

HUMAN BEINGS IN ONE region of the world are not by birth privileged to greater insight over those in another. So it follows that the Western history of philosophy might provide some philosophical context for those who want to study Eastern philosophy. However, when studying ancient thought there is always a danger of distorting ancient ideas by filtering them through a contemporary, more comfortable web of ideas.[1] When one hastily races to the conclusion that an Eastern idea is equivalent to a Western idea, one prepares a tragic, philosophical accident. Philosophy is the most dangerous discipline in the world because it establishes the value frameworks by which people make decisions. Consider the many Western children who have grown up lonely and ignored in a society that values individual pleasure and success more than loving and investing in

1. For an excellent discussion of this, see Tuck, *Comparative Philosophy.*

the lives of one's children. Or the many, many millions of people who were murdered in the last century as a consequence of whole societies embracing or submitting to totalitarian ideologies. It is a cliché deserving full acceptance that ideas have consequences. The teachings of Buddhism have consequences, too, albeit different and more peaceful ones. However, we risk misunderstanding both the Buddha's teaching and the consequences of that teaching if we do not take care to understand Buddhism within its own historical context. One cannot clearly see the shape and detail of the Buddha's teaching without the illuminating light of his religious and philosophical context.

Siddhārtha Gautama, who would become the Buddha, was born into a world of religious controversy. Indian religion arose more than a millennia before the Buddha, before the Aryans first conquered the well-developed civilization of the Indus Valley. Archaeological excavations of this civilization have revealed artifacts that suggest meditation was a part of the religious culture of the indigenous Indus people. For instance, statues have been found of figures seated in a lotus meditative position. According to David Kalupahana, these conquering Aryans were more mundane in their outlook. He cites as evidence their lack of an ascetic tradition.[2] Though the Aryan culture dominated this new civilization, the older ascetic tradition could not be dispatched. "The history of Indian philosophy may be described as the story of the struggle for supremacy between these two traditions (ascetic and Aryan)."[3]

A single-chapter summary of Indian philosophy must necessarily be overly simplistic. This is because there is no one single "Indian philosophy." Polytheism, monotheism, pantheism, atheistic naturalism, animism, and just about any other ism have an Indian counterpart. For four millennia, Indian religious culture has been mostly *bhakti*, devotional. Devout men and women pray regularly to their chosen deities. Every point made in this introduction has an opponent somewhere in the Indian tradition, and probably in present day India. Hence the goal of this chapter must remain limited and

2. *Buddhist Philosophy*, 3.

3. Ibid., 4.

focused. Here, I present a history of the movements within Indian thought relative to the Buddha's development of his own doctrine.[4]

THE CREATOR/CREATURE DISTINCTION IN ANCIENT INDIA

We can observe the evolution of Indian philosophy in the historical development of the Indian holy texts. The Indian scriptures called the *Vedas* are comprised of several compilations. First, the *Saṃhitās* (meaning "collections") include the *Ṛgveda*, a collection of hymns, likely composed about the middle of the second millennium before Christ[5], and finally transcribed around 800 *B.C.*, which praise the gods; the *Sāmaveda*, which are melodies relating to these hymns;

4. One may object that philosophical discussions are not relevant to daily religious culture, both in thinking and practice. As one critic put it, "This is like thinking that to be a Catholic, one must also be an Aristotelian just because Aquinas was." My critic does not understand either Aquinas or Aristotle's impact on Catholic theology through the influence of Aquinas. It is true most Catholics have little understanding of Aristotle, but the relationship between the Catholic and Aristotle is a helpful analogy for understanding the relationship between pious Hindus and the philosophical underpinnings of their beliefs. Catholic theology has taught that Catholics receive the grace of God through sacraments. Grace passes metaphysically from God to the believer through various means which God has set in place. In Catholicism, the Church has been given the responsibility to dispense this grace through God's means. Allegedly, this must be the case; otherwise, justification is a *legal fiction*, as Catholic apologists characterize it. Whether one agrees with Catholic apologists or not, the force of their point rests upon something of a connection between Catholic doctrine and Aristotelian metaphysics. The *legal fiction* objection holds in the Catholic mind because they hold that righteousness must be metaphysically implanted *in them* for it to be "real" and efficacious.

When Hellenistic philosophy was overturned within the church near the end of the Middle Ages in the later medieval movement toward nominalism, discussions of justification shifted from emphasis on *quod in se est* (that which is in him) to *ex pacta divinia* (out of the divine pact). With the rise of medieval nominalism came the emphasis on covenants and renewed interest in the Pauline discussion of the mechanisms of God's imputation of righteousness through Christ. (For an extended discussion, see McGrath, *The Intellectual Origins of the European Reformation.*

Again, without discussing the merit of Aristotle, the Catholic who takes the host so that righteousness can be infused into him is plainly thinking in Aristotelian terms. He may know nothing of the great philosopher, but that does not protect him from the man's influence. Unpacking a religious or philosophical perspective often requires asking *Where did this come from?* The Buddha's insights are no exception. The history of philosophy is very important in such matters, especially in the case of Eastern philosophy.

5. Hiriyanna, *Outlines of Indian Philosophy*, 13.

the *Yajurveda*, the sacrificial formulae; and the *Atharvaveda*, the magical formulae. The *Brāhamaṇas* are texts that deal with ritual and sacrifice, discussing their purpose and value. In a sense they are a commentary on the *Saṃhitās*. The *Upaniṣads* are commentaries on these earlier scriptures. For brevity's sake, we will focus on the *Ṛgveda* and the *Upaniṣads*.[6]

These holy books trace a fascinating change. The hymns of the *Ṛgveda* bear a strong resemblance to other *devotional* literature of the period. They deal with many of the same themes of praise and blessing found in Middle Eastern, Cananite, or even Hebrew religious poetry. Like the gods of the Sumerians, Egyptians, and Greeks, the *Ṛgveda* refers to a gathering of gods that stand behind the various phenomena of the world. These gods are praised and placated for certain ends. But some of the later hymns show a change. The people of India started to inquire about the nature of reality, as Greeks in Miletus would centuries later. With the increased skepticism toward their own gods came a degeneration in the later hymns when compared to their earlier, more noble counterparts.

The Indian people began to ask some insightful questions: "Who has seen that the Boneless One bears the Bony? When he is first born? Where is the breath, the blood and the soul of the earth? Who would approach the wise man to ask this?"[7] Or, stated in modern terms, How is it that an immaterial God could create a material world? The answer in the Indian mind was simple: He could not. Material, or what ever makes up the stuff of this world (one form of being) could not come from something that was not material (a completely different type of being).

The urgency of this philosophical problem in this period of Indian philosophical development points to a difference between the evolution of Indian thought during this period and both Christian theology and Greek philosophy, namely, the eradication of a Creator/creature distinction. Christian theology assumes the Creator/creature distinction. God as Creator is different from creation. At the same time, God provides purpose and structure for it. Greek philosophy, however, does not maintain a Creator/creature

6. Paul Williams has a helpful discussion of the consensus view that the early *Upaniṣads* predate the Buddha in *Buddhist Thought*, 8f.

7. *Ṛgveda*. 1.164.4 quoted in Jayatilleke, *Early Buddhist Theory*, 24.

distinction like Christian theology; yet it does retain an analogous distinction within kinds of being, which is at least reminiscent of a Creator/creature distinction. In the Greek philosophical systems of Plato and Aristotle, the universe itself is not assumed to be the same grade of being throughout. Instead, the *forms* structure reality, either through participation in a far-off realm (Plato) or from direct presence within the object receiving structure (Aristotle).[8] So Greek forms take the place God holds in Christian theology. While the form/matter distinction is not the same as a Creator/creature distinction, the clumsy, less-than-perfect similarities between these two distinctions make it possible for Augustine to incorporate a theory of forms within his own theology, which did teach a clear Creator/creature distinction.

The Upaniṣads

So, in the centuries before the Buddha, some Indian philosophers had become skeptical of the Creator/creature distinction. A group of religious teachers inspired by this skepticism began an aggressive, ambitious deconstruction of the Creator/creature distinction. Some of these teachers were the authors of the *Upaniṣads*. The *Upaniṣads*, were written from approximately 800 to 200 B.C. (though many were written after this period) as commentaries on earlier scriptures. The *Upaniṣads* themselves represent the thought of groups that pulled away from mainstream Hindu thought. As Gnostic Christianity was a heterodox movement challenging apostolic Christian teaching, so the *Upaniṣads* represent a secret tradition challenging Vedic orthodoxy. The *Upaniṣads* contain some of the first explorations of the concept of *ātman*, or the Self.

The Indian religious teachers who wrote the *Upaniṣads* did not want to accept distinction within being, so they began a forceful movement toward an ultimate radical monism, a view that all things are, in reality, ultimately one. They affirmed substance could not come from something (or someone) that does not possess the qualities of that substance. The boneless being could not have offspring with

8. Aristotelian forms here are described in language that suggests a more platonic interpretation of Aristotle. I do not favor the platonic interpretation of Aristotle, namely, that forms are imbedded within matter. My language here is merely identifying the location of forms.

bones. They affirmed that skepticism from those later hymns in the *Ṛgveda* which challenge the Creator/creature distinction: "[T] he gods are posterior to this creation: if so, who knows whence it evolved?"[9] If the gods are part of the creation and do not exist before the creation, this would make them poor sources of knowledge as to the origin of the universe. Thankfully, the developments in *Upaniṣads* emerge at a time when categories of contention were simpler, at a time when philosophical discourse was being conducted in more poetic language. To the reader more familiar with the history of Western philosophy, recall the debates in Miletus that kick-start Greek philosophy. Thales looks for a unifying principle to explain the universe and comes up with *water*. Anaximander, the next to try, posits one unidentifiable substance, "the boundless." Though none of the early developments on the Greek Islands quite parallel the movements of thought in far-off India, one can see that the steps taken at this stage, though revolutionary and foundational, are, by our standards, a bit more simplistic and, therefore, more easily grasped.

For a moment, let me ask *you*, the reader, to climb inside the point of view expressed in the *Upaniṣads*. (In academic writing, you are not supposed to write in the second person, but bear with me.) This will allow you to see how the ultimate unity of phenomena in the world would follow naturally in the developing Indian mind. If there can be no separation in the ultimate kinds of being, then how does that impact your current moment of consciousness right now—as you hold this book or ebook reader—and read these words?

As a first step, consider: The page or reader cannot be fundamentally different from the hand that touches it. Nor can the air around you be different from you, the one breathing. If it were, how could you, the breather, enjoy it?

The second step, ask: Can the self—you, the one who right now experiences this page—be different from the page being read? If we assume no divide between different types of being, then material and consciousness must somehow ultimately be the same being, if they are to interact. Consciousness and the object of consciousness are the same being.

9. *Ṛgveda*. 10.129.6 quoted in Jayatilleke, *Early Buddhist Theory*, 24.

The final step, notice: When you hand off this book to a friend who reads it, the book cannot be that distinct in being from his or her own consciousness. Otherwise, how could he or she understand it? The material (the book) and the immaterial (the self) must be the same being, though they do not appear to be. If this conclusion follows, it must also follow that two people who have the same knowledge can only have that same knowledge because they are both part of the same being. Therefore, *this oneness of being accounts not only for the cohesion of experience but also the objectivity of knowledge.* (Here ends my use of the second person.)

Ātman is Brahman

Our journey will now take some sharp conceptual turns. Hang on.

The mindset I have described in my illustrative thought-experiment above is developed at length in the *Upaniṣads,* where the importance of the critical concept of *ātman,* or the 'Self', is thrust into a greater position of importance. In the *Upaniṣads, ātman,* the 'Self', looks out and sees himself (*ātman*). Therefore, "the Upaniṣadic thinker is interested in utilizing this conception of self not only to account for the certainty of human knowledge or a rational justification of knowledge, but also to explain the origin and continuity of the world."[10] *Ātman* is not only the subject but also the object of consciousness. As we discussed above, since different people having the same knowledge must be aspects of the same being to have knowledge, then the concept of the individual self must expand into a public-self of which each person is an aspect, just as each side of a diamond is an irremovable facet. This one universal self, of whom all individual selves take part, is called *ātman.*

Let us summarize, then, this movement of thought from the latter hymns of the *Ṛgveda* to the *Upaniṣads* that we have discussed so far. Beginning with the *Ṛgveda,* we have seen how the abandoning of a Creator/creature distinction first started the Indian philosophical mind toward the notion of an undivided being. Oneness of being encompasses not only rocks and trees but also consciousness. Notice that questions regarding what is real are being answered by theories regarding how we know what we know. Or worded differently, the

10. Kalupahana, *History of Buddhist Philosophy,* 11.

expansion of *ātman* as a metaphysical concept is actually warranted by epistemic concerns. The knower and the object of knowledge were believed to be the same 'self'. Some Indian thinkers believed that this philosophical view explained the objectivity of knowledge. Since knowledge is not a mere personal thing, the Indian thinkers also accounted for the reality of mutual knowledge by the 'Self' (*ātman*). It follows then that no item can proceed from what it is not. Everything that proceeds must have proceeded from something that was the same as itself. Quickly, this thinking will reduce to the notion that behind all things must be the same thing. As the teaching of the *Upaniṣads* has been summarized many times, this is an "A one without a second."

The 'Self' (*ātman*) even takes responsibility for regulating the order of the universe. Before this time, *Ṛta* was the thing that provided the ever-pervasive order of the universe. *Ṛta* is roughly analogous to the stoic conception of the *Logos*, an order, logic, or formula that establishes the patterns, events, and operations of the universe. With the lack of a Creator/creature distinction, the order of the universe was conceived as objective phenomena with no place for the human perspective. As the period of the *Upaniṣads* dawned in India, *ṛta* was replaced by *ātman*.[11] This occurred even though *ātman* is not stuff: not water, not a person, not a group of people, not an object of knowledge. Yet, it expresses all of these things. Curiously, the term chosen to denote the grand unification of all these things is the 'Self' (*ātman*). Even the possibility of one type of being predicated out of another type of being was not allowed. The new philosophy moved toward assuming no difference in being. The 'Self' (*ātman*) became the ultimate unifying feature of reality.

'Self' is not just the personal sense of one's own identity, but instead an expansion on the concept of 'I', not a condition of experience, but instead a transcendental proposition, a precondition

11. Ibid., 7. I recognize there may be a disagreement here. Some rather see that *karma* replaced *ṛta*. In a sense, I agree. But *karma* describes the mechanism by which our choices cause our future circumstances and not the basis for knowledge. For my purposes here, *ātman* accounts for the basic ontological unity within consciousness between the mind and its objects since both are 'Self'. It seems to guide phenomena. In that sense, Kalupahana makes his connection between *ṛta* and *ātman*.

to all other rational thought.[12] The 'self' not only accounted for certainty in human knowledge but also the continuity of the world. It is more than just a self—*Ātman* is *the Self.*

The *Bṛhadāraṇyaka Upaniṣad* (1.4.1–16) gives an excellent summation of this driving influence in Upaniṣadic thought. In the beginning this world was soul or 'self' (*ātman*) in the form of a man who looked around the universe. Noticing nothing else, the being said, "I am." This 'self' felt lonely being without another, so this being separated into male and female forms. The man and the woman copulated and made the human race. Then this original male and female changed into a cow and bull and copulated, making cattle. They continued all the way to the smallest insect.

Nowhere in this creation account is there any suggestion that *Brahman* (the "-an" makes it a more abstract noun, like *divinity* rather than *Brahma*, a name for God) is distinct from *ātman*. The 'self' (*ātman*) is the substance of the universe and absolute. But *ātman* cannot be described in words. Words require the speaker and hearer to make distinctions. Even the simplest duality is not possible. Any term we use to describe the 'self' is merely a convention held between men, and how can a convention that cuts up the world describe the thing that envelops and supports all knowledge?

The *Bṛhadāraṇyaka Upaniṣad* tells us that *Brahman* tried to develop, but repeatedly the text uses the phrase, "he had no power to develop further." At different stages, Brahman develops princes, commoners, slaves, etc. With no more power to develop further, playing the part of Plato's Form of the Good, he develops law and morality. So it follows that 'self' should be worshiped alone, for out of *ātman, ātman* creates whatsoever we desire.[13]

Three themes curdle to the top in both this *Upaniṣad* and the *Bhagavadgītā*, which was likely written after the Buddha flourished, between the fifth and first centuries B.C. First, the ontology of the 'self' and the world combine in this one concept of *ātman*. Second, we are reminded of the four-tiered caste system (which shows up in chapter 10 of the *Ṛgveda*). Finally, we are introduced to the moral

12. Ibid., 11.

13. *Bṛhadāraṇyaka Upaniṣad* I.4.15 quoted from Goodall, *Hindu Scriptures*, 51.

system based on that caste system, termed *Brahma*.[14] When men follow the moral system (*dharma*), they show honor and reverence for *Brahma*. "'The ultimate truth' (*ātman*) and 'the ultimate value' (*brahma*) are thus combined in a salvific realization which is considered to be the highest blissful attainment a human being can achieve."[15]

The Evolution of Karma

Another important development during this period crucial to understanding Buddhism is the notion of karma. With the conception of 'Self' starting to function as the unifier of reality, death cannot be the end of a person. If death is not the end, it would seem that one's 'Self' lives on. If one does not live on in this life because, by definition, one is dead, then another life must follow. But what is the quality of this next life? Is it better or worse? But no two lives are the same, of course. Qualitatively, some are vastly better than others. Since this *ātman/brahman* oneness unifies *all* reality, then the 'Self' (*ātman*) also unifies the reality of the gods. Some souls may be incarnated as gods. In many other religions of the time, the gods maintained some sense of justice, or at least some type of final court of appeal for human disputes. When the relationship between the divine and the created collapsed by abandoning the Creator/creature divide, some other system of moral equity had to take up the slack. Karma naturally fills this role of the key regulator of moral consequences. In the period of the *Upaniṣads*, karma came to refer to the moral weight or value of actions that regulates the quality of future reincarnated states. The notion of karma as a regulator of the quality of reincarnated life developed as a response to the philosophical expansion of the concept of *ātman*.

Some may dispute my claim that *karma-as-reincarnation-regulator was a late bloomer*. One might do so on the basis that the use of the word 'karma' in ancient moral discourse predates this development of *ātman*. I grant this is true. The use of the term karma predates the developments of *ātman* found in the *Bṛhadāraṇyaka Upanishad*. However, the pre-*Upaniṣad* use actually strengthens my

14. Kalupahana, *History of Buddhist Philosophy*, 11–12.

15. Ibid., 12.

case. In earlier use, karma only describes actions and their effects. It took the addition of the concept of reincarnation to recontextualize the term karma, to transform it into *actions affecting future rebirths.* But the doctrine of rebirth does not show up till the time that the speculations regarding *ātman* also develop. About this, even K. N. Jayatilleke writes:

> There is no trace of a belief in rebirth in the Ṛgveda, where we only find sporadic references to a belief in life after death. The Arthavaveda, too, makes no reference to the doctrine. The Brāhmaṇas show a greater interest in the after-life and we meet with a variety of views on this subject but no conclusive reference to rebirth is found. The conception of a "second death" (punar mṛtyu) is pregnant with the possibility of developing the idea of rebirth and all that can be said is [and here Jayatilleke sights Radhakrishnan] "the Brāhamaṇas contain all the suggestions necessary for the development of the doctrine of rebirth."[16]

In other words, the early Vedic texts have no mention of rebirth. Thus, the concept of karma cannot be connected to rebirth in these early works since there was no doctrine of rebirth with which to connect. Rebirth does show up in the earliest *Upaniṣads* (850 B.C.) but only as one of a number of theories of the afterlife.[17] In fact, the first clear references to rebirth from one terrestrial life form to another are from *Bṛhadāraṇyaka Upaniṣad* 6.2.15–16, *Chāndogya Upaniṣad* 5.10.1–8, and *Kauśitakī Upaniṣad* 1.2[18] (all from 850 to 750 B.C.). Finally, in the *Kaha Upaniṣad*, we see that the theory has general acceptance.[19] Curiously, the development of the doctrine of rebirth not only parallels the speculation of *Upaniṣads* but also, at times, shows up in the same Upaniṣad. Clearly, this new use of karma as a regulator of rebirths was a new development, which coincides with the invention of reincarnation and the rise of *ātman* of as the preeminent, metaphysical, unifying concept.

So what does this "new" notion of karma as a regulator of rebirth have to do with the causes of suffering? This question

16. Jayatilleke, *Early Buddhist Theory*, 372.

17. Ibid.

18. Ibid., 373.

19. Jayatilleke, *Early Buddhist Theory*, 373–4.

was very important to the Buddha. The answer to the question is somewhat counterintuitive: karma is basically the cause of all our problems. To understand how, we will have to grasp karma's relationship to *saṃsāra*, the endless cycle of reincarnation. When they hear "karma," many Westerners think of phrases like "What goes around comes around." This slogan almost has it right, but there is more. With the rise of the Indian caste system also came the implication of a hierarchy of incarnations. The only social mobility came after death, based on what karma a person gained in that life. But could one step off the ladder altogether? If *ātman* is all there is, then the answer is *No, a person could never leave ātman*. This logically leads to the idea of *saṃsāra*, the continual miserable cycle of reincarnations, based on the obvious empirical truth that some of us just have it better than others. *Saṃsāra* is the amusement park ride that no one can ever get off, no matter how frightening.

Let us expand upon the popular conception of karma. Rather than equating karma with good works, or righteousness, or guilt, we should think of it as money. If one has a hoard of money, one can "put on the Ritz" for a long time, but eventually the money runs out. Then it is back to a flat, a friend's couch, or a cardboard box. When one has a lot of karma, one can live as a god, one can be a god, but thc karma will run out. When it does, one descends on the wheel of *saṃsāra*. The first time being a god is fun; maybe the tenth time is still a thrill. But like the Bill Murray character in the movie *Groundhog Day*[20] who kept living the same day over and over again, eventually one just wants it all to end. Gandhi understood this truth when he called *saṃsāra* "the wheel of suffering." According to Indian thought, we have all been on this wheel billions, maybe trillions of times. But no one can leave because *saṃsāra* is a necessary part of perceiving one's 'self' as a distinct being. If there is a 'you', then 'you' must reincarnate. As one reincarnates, one uses karma—the "money" of action (to continue the metaphor)—which one stores up, but which one must spend to live. Every ethical action one commits leads to a further accumulation of karma. More karma leads to more incarnations. It never ends.

20. Rubin, *Groundhog Day*.

Karma, as such, may seem far-fetched to westerners; however, it serves a very important role in bending Upaniṣadic philosophy into a cohesive worldview. The need for it logically follows from the philosophical developments in the Indian history of thought up through the period of the *Upaniṣads*. Some in the West may disdain Indian philosophy for its mystical speculations. However, when one considers the desire of these maverick philosophers,[21] and the lengths to which they went to maintain a notion of deity while denying a Creator/creature distinction, one can respect the remarkable, creative philosophical product they were driven to fashion in order to retain a complete worldview after abandoning that Creator/creature distinction. If one reasons through the starting presuppositions of the Upaniṣadic philosophers regarding oneness and the priority of *ātman* as the underlying unifier of reality, their philosophy does not seem as strange. Secondary concepts such as karma and *saṃsāra* naturally follow in the attempt to make the Upaniṣadic system livable. To a man inside the system, it will seem quite rational.

If karma is the money of action, then the trick is to learn *how not to spend* (the goal for many Indian higher-consciousness views), or better yet *how not to earn* (the goal of Buddhism and also the *Bhagavadgītā*)! It is no wonder that many Indian men, after providing financially for their families, would each renounce his old life and go into the forest to seek a deeper understanding of *ātman*. If a family member were to find him on the road begging, he was to treat him no differently than any other stranger. These men had renounced life, and with a bowl, a robe, or sometimes nothing at all, would study under a teacher, practicing meditative techniques in the hopes that *Ishvara* would be gracious and show them mystical insight, a final vision, or revelation.[22] This view involving *ātman*, *brahman*, *saṃsāra*, and karma we will call Brahmanism. Buddha would challenge this view with the greatest vigor.

21. As I mentioned earlier, this does not refer to every Indian philosophy, only to some very influential thinkers about the time of the Buddha.

22. Jayatilleke, *Early Buddhist Theory*, 169.

THE CREATOR/CREATURE DISTINCTION IN THE HEBREW SCRIPTURES

It goes without saying that the ancient Hebrews believed in a Creator/creature distinction. It would be helpful here to identify how this distinction enables a different mechanism to regulate the consequences of moral choices. This task is complicated by the development of the documentary hypothesis, which claims that the Hebrew Scriptures are an edited patchwork of older texts assembled during the postexilic period. Since our topic is not the validity of the documentary hypothesis but rather a comparison of worldviews, it is not appropriate to devote an extended discourse here to refuting the strongly critical form of the documentary hypothesis that dismisses the reliability of the Hebrew scriptures. That book has already been written.[23] As Paul Ricoeur laments regarding the current situation in higher critical studies, "the historico-critical method has more or less exhausted its resources.[24]

Instead, I will use the historical research methodology of critical realism articulated by N. T. Wright.[25] Wright's methodology embraces Paul Ricoeur's tensive hermeneutic of trust and suspicion. Wright advocates trusting the documents that history presents to us, but to do so critically, in a way that appreciates the postmodern turn. Historical documents do not present bald-fact statements of observations that can be accepted individually with mathematical certainty. Instead, they are units of discourse written by people that reflect a certain cultural context and worldview. For this reason, it is necessary to craft a narrative that explains all the data points without adding to them philosophical biases. This requires great discipline on the part of the historian. If the historian merely trusts the documents, without reading them in the cultural context of their period, like some biblical fundamentalists read the Bible, then text is more likely to be read in terms of the cultural context of the reader. Consider American fundamentalist support of American prohibition in the early part of the last century. I once heard a lecture by an old fundamentalist seminary professor defending the view that the

23. See Cassuto, *The Documentary Hypothesis.*

24. Reagan, *Paul Ricoeur,* 121.

25. Wright, *New Testament and People,* 33–144.

passages that support drinking wine are actually referring to grape juice because the Greek world for wine (*oinos*) is actually referring to grape juice. The problem with this view is that no one in Palestine owned refrigerators. There is no way that *oinos* could be drunk year around without having first turned to wine. To avoid problems like this, Wright advocates that cultural historians and textual interpreters do the hard work of gathering all the data points, as best as one can, in order to make a case.

Exilic and postexilic Judaism had a clear narrative of their national history. Robert Alter has famously pointed out that the narrative style of the Pentateuch and the historical books of the early monarchy have a very different style of historical narrative composition from the historical written narratives of the divided kingdom, exilic and postexilic periods, reflecting different literary periods in the development of Israel's narrative artistry.[26] Even during the centuries that gave the world the *Upaniṣads*, the Book of Isaiah affirms the culturally authoritative history, which we read in the Pentateuch.[27] Israel's God, YHWH, created the world out of

26. Robert Alter returns to this point, again and again, throughout Alter, *The Art of Biblical Narrative*.

27. Isaiah 40–48 is part of Deutero-Isaiah. Some scholars argue that Duetero-Isaiah was composed later because it refers to Cyrus, who became king of Persia; thus, this portion of the book must be late-dated in the period of the Persian Empire. However, the entire book of Isaiah is an argument that YHWH is the true God because he can predict the future. This is the case made to Ahaz, who had moved the altar of God in order to placate powerful Assyrians. In the narrative of the Book of Isaiah, Isaiah comes to Ahaz in God's name, and says, in short, "Ahaz you have made a bad political choice because I, the real King of Israel, know the future exhaustively, and I can prove it." After interaction with Ahaz (Isa. 7–8) God predicts the future fall of all the political powers surrounding Judah over the next few hundred years. (Isa. 9–35). The Book of Isaiah then narrates the reign of Hezekiah (Isa. 36–39), demonstrating that Hezekiah learned from his father's mistakes and believed God's promises and power, albeit imperfectly (39). It is in this context that chapters 40–48 of Isaiah make the argument that there is no other God. YHWH is making an argument based on his ability to predict the future. When higher critics claim that this book must be late-dated because of Cyrus, this claim needs to be called out for what it is. The higher critics' notion that Isaiah must be late-dated because of Cyrus needs to be called out for what it is: an accusation of forgery on the part of Isaiah and his God. If it was penned by a man after Cyrus lived, it is a forgery, for it claims to be prophecy but is not. My point here is not to prove Duetero-Isaiah was not written by another author as a separate unit. Rather, the warrant for even separating the two is not textual but philosophical. Methodological

nothing. He is the one and only creator God who made all things (Isa. 40–48).

YHWH as Creator is also lawgiver. When he created humankind, he made a unilateral covenant with them through Adam. The Book of Hosea, written to both northern Israel and Judah, shows that this narrative is still in the cultural consciousness of both. "But like Adam they have transgressed the covenant. There they have dealt treacherously with Me" (Hosea 6:7). Because YHWH is the Creator and lawmaker, he also takes responsibility as judge. Abraham recognizes this when he pleads for mercy for the city of Sodom, "Shall not the judge of all the earth deal justly?" (Gen. 18:25). YHWH creates the nation of Israel and establishes his law with the Israelites. Leviticus 26 and Deuteronomy 28 reveal how God rewards obedience and disobedience to his revealed law with positive and negative sanctions in history. These passages are the legal basis for the prophets' legal lawsuits against Israel and Judah in the prophetic books of the Hebrew scriptures.

This revealed law is not only for Israel but for all people. Deuteronomy 4:5–8 explains the relationship between the Mosaic Law and the surrounding nations.

> "See, I have taught you statutes and judgments just as the Lord my God commanded me, that you should do thus in the land where you are entering to possess it. So keep and do *them*, for that is your wisdom and your understanding in the sight of the peoples who will hear all these statutes and say, 'Surely this great nation is a wise and understanding people.' For what great nation is there that has a god so near to it as is the Lord our God whenever we call on Him? Or what great nation is there that has statutes and judgments as righteous as this whole law which I am setting before you today?"

While some of the specific regulations in the Mosaic Law are meant only for the nation of Israel, it is obvious that the Mosaic Law, when practiced, was intended to create a socially just, model society. Paul Ricoeur points out that the biblical law is not meant only to contain

naturalism, the view that the only acceptable scholarly and scientific research is that which presupposed there is no supernatural, is what turns the last half of the book of Isaiah into Duetero-Isaiah. However, Isaiah, in its present form, purports itself to be a 66-chapter-long argument against methodological naturalism.

just statements, but, when lived out, it should create just institutions.[28] Therefore, this passage explains the warrant for God's moral rebukes and judgments against other nations. The principles of his law are universal and reflect his own moral character. Whether one agrees with this view or not, the Creator/creature distinction is the warrant for YHWH's moral pronouncements in the Hebrew Scriptures.

While the Creator/creature distinction answers the question of where morality comes from and who enforces its sanctions in history, it also begs another problem which contemporary philosophers have called the existential problem of evil. Why is there suffering in the world? And why so much of it? During the first millennium *B.C.*, many philosophers around the world were wrestling with the place and purpose for suffering in the cosmos. Several biblical books address the question. Ecclesiastes, the most philosophical book in the Bible, wrestles with this question. In Ecclesiastes the narrator, whose title in Hebrew is *Qoheleth* (the teacher or preacher), affirms Leviticus 26 and Deuteronomy 28 (Eccles. 12:13–14), but he does so amidst the real appearance that oppressors seem to get away with evil. *Qoheleth* concludes that all of life's pursuits are "vanity," yet they are not to be abandoned. He examines the goals of pleasure, wealth, wisdom, power, and the like, showing that each, when taken out of its proper context, becomes "vanity" or "chasing after the wind." He considers the ebb and flow of time and chance, with the presupposition that God has absolute sovereignty over all things (Eccles. 3:1–11a). *Qoheleth* reasons that every event, even the atrocities of wicked men, are under the control of God. *Qoheleth* freely admits that the world is filled with injustice.

> There is a futility which is done on the earth, that is, there are righteous men to whom it happens according to the deeds of the wicked. On the other hand, there are evil men to whom it happens according to the deeds of the righteous. I say this too is futility. (Eccles. 8:14)

To answer the problem of injustice, *Qoheleth* turns to the same answer given by Job.

28. See Riceour, *The Just.*

The biblical Job comes under suffering for which God himself takes direct responsibility. Job believes that he had a final advocate with God, the Kinsman Redeemer or Avenger.

> And as for me, I know that my Redeemer lives. And at the last He will take his stand on the earth. Even after my skin is destroyed, yet from my flesh I shall see God; whom I myself shall behold, and whom my eyes shall see and not another. (Job 19:25–27b)

Many Christian theologians have interpreted this passage as retroactively referring to Jesus of Nazareth. While it may be messianic, it is clear that Job believes that God is sovereign and moral. Job affirms that YHWH is the kind of moral sanction-bringer described in Leviticus 26 and Deuteronomy 28. Both Job and his three rude friends all agree on this view of God. However, Job's friends believe that God is a kind of Skinner box. If a person does good deeds, then God mechanically rewards them. If they disobey, they get punished. Job disagrees with this view of divine behaviorism. Job knows that he is a righteous man. Even God affirms this at the beginning of the Book of Job. Job's issue with God is that he is apparently not fulfilling the kind of moral promises reflected in Leviticus 26 and Deuteronomy 28.

While the humans in the Book of Job debate whether God, who has sovereign free will and moral authority, has treated Job with justice, the characters in Heaven debate whether human moral choices are authentic and genuine. At the beginning of the Book of Job, God testifies to Satan regarding Job's moral actions. He declares Job righteous before Satan. Satan responds by denying that righteous humans choose good because of a righteous desire for good. Satan believes that humans are basically Skinner mice. They only choose good because they think God will reward them. They have ulterior motives: "Does Job fear God for nothing? Have You not made a hedge about him and his house and all that he has, on every side? You have blessed the work of his hands, and his possessions have increased in the land. But put forth Your hand now and touch all that he has; he will surely curse You to Your face." (Job 1:9–11) Satan is saying that Job is doing good only because he expects God to follow the plan reflected in Leviticus 26 and Deuteronomy 28.

God then makes a decision that begins the plot of the book of Job. God lets Satan hurt Job in order to vindicate Job's righteousness. This point is often misunderstood in commentaries and sermons on the book. God lets Job suffer in order to prove to the watching world what God already knows, that Job is a righteous man, not to prove that God is right. Satan already disrespects God. God is proving to Satan that he should not disrespect Job.

Satan and Job's rude friends do not believe in authentic moral sovereignty. Satan disbelieves that Job has it. Job's three friends disbelieve that God has it. However, both God and Job both believe in authentic free will. God believes that Job freely chooses good because it is good, not simply to earn favor with God. Job believes God is exhaustively sovereign over all things and events and can do whatever he chooses. So we see here that men choose freely, but God directs all history and is exhaustively sovereign over all things at the same time. The Augustinian and Calvinist traditions of Christian theology are littered with mountains of tomes, flooded with seas of ink that soak the dead flesh of forests to try to solve the paradoxical relationship between human free will and God's sovereignty. However, these matters are better grasped and explained through the compressed thickness of narrative. Theologians would do well to remember that the Book of Job is one of the best books to address this problem and is itself a combination of both narrative and logical reasoning.

Job affirms that God is sovereign, free, and just in the lives of all people, even those who suffer. Herein lies the deep psychological turmoil of the book. Job is not willing to say that God is in the wrong, yet he also knows he is experiencing unwarranted suffering. The dramatic question of the Book of Job is this: How will Job face undeserved suffering while also believing God is just and in control?

Job's response is not perfect, and God rebukes him at the end of the book for demanding that God answer him on Job's terms. The Bible affirms that God does not need to offer sons and daughters of Adam a reason for what he is doing under the sun. The Bible presents God's own character as the standard that measures all things. God is measured by nothing outside himself (Isa. 40–49, Job 38–41). He is the source of all redemption. He is the bringer of justice. It is in this context that the Redeemer passage discussed above (Job 19:25–27), makes sense. Not only does Job have a Kinsman Redeemer of the type described in the Pentateuch but a Redeemer who is himself also God. Job will see this Redeemer even if Job's flesh is destroyed. Job's affirmation is similar to the father who asked Jesus to deliver his son: "I do believe; help my unbelief." (Mark 9:24)[29]

In the end, Job is blessed with wealth and more children, positive sanctions in history consistent with Leviticus 26 and Deuteronomy 28. However, if one reads Job and thinks, "Ah, I see. God is a heavenly Skinner box. Job got the blessings!" then the narrative leaves unanswered questions, even for Job. God never explains to Job what the reader knows from the beginning chapters of the book, that the God of the universe deeply respects Job as a man and wants to vindicate Job to that watching universe. God never tells Job why. All but three of Job's servants are killed. All of Job's children are killed, even though he was offering sacrifices for their sins. Let us put the best construction on this and say God did not let his children die because of their sins, but rather because their deaths were part of a greater plan. Their covenantal relationship with their father is what led to their deaths. If they had been someone else's children they would not have died. God does not apologize, nor does he have to. Even Job defends God's right to take them (Job 1:21). The outlook of the Bible is clear in this regard; for those who know and love God, he wills them good according to his purposes (Rom. 8:28). God cares (Isa. 40:9-11; Jer. 23:5-6; 29:11; 30:18-22), even for those who may not understand how to relate to him (Ps. 107; Acts 14: 15-17). Nevertheless, sometimes this means hardship, suffering, and even death (Heb. 11:35–40, 2 Macc. 7). He gives good things but not mechanically and not on the terms one might wish them. So it is in the Book of Job, a book that is clear but not tidy.

This same moral teaching punctuates the finale of Ecclesiastes, but in a more universal form.[30] "The conclusion, when all has been

29. Much of this discussion of the theology of Job is based on North, *Predictability and Dominion: An Economic Commentary on Job.* Only about sixty pages long, his study is the most profound examination of the Book of Job I have read. An economist by vocation, North's commentaries examine the Bible from the perspective of the discipline of economics. Because of this focus, his observations regarding law, sanctions, and chance are quite helpful.

30. See North, *Autonomy and Stagnation.*

heard, *is*: fear God and keep His commandments, because this *applies to* every person. For God will bring every act to judgment, everything which is hidden, whether it is good or evil" (Eccles. 12:13–14; emphasis mine). After the wrestling back and forth between opposing arguments throughout the book of Ecclesiastes, *Qoheleth* draws a similar conclusion to the Book of Job, but the conclusion is applied universally. God will faithfully judge every person with integrity. Not even death, described in the middle of Ecclesiastes 12, can offer a person escape. The literature of Judaism during the exilic and postexilic periods traces out the implications of these insights toward the implications of God's covenantal faithfulness in this life and in eternity.[31]

The Judeo-Christian worldview's solution of faithful, precise divine judgment is not available to the Upaniṣadic thinkers. In the Bible, God has both the moral high ground and the raw power necessary to judge the cosmos since he is personally the standard of ethical norms and the foundation for all metaphysics. With the universe of *ātman*, such a grand story is not desirable. The doctrine of karma creates a system where the malefactor himself causally produces his judgment as the result of his own sins. If compared with the categories presented in the book of Job, not only do humans choose to create their own suffering by affecting the mechanism of the world, which then imposes consequences upon us, but there is no God to argue with because each man is the God who caused his own suffering. The "Job" of the *Upaniṣads* has no one to argue with but himself. If he tries, he learns that he is ultimately *ātman* and that making any argument for justice or non-justice is nonsensical. Evil and good are the same; all is *ātman*. This sort of problem is the central subject discussion in the *Bhagavadgītā*. Indian thinkers had no need for a higher creator or judge beyond the being of the one, or the 'Self' (*ātman*).

The Materialists

We now move on to a new group of Indian philosophers who provide a context for the Buddha's teaching. The first to react to Brahmanism's speculations were the Materialists who believed that

31. See Wright, *The Resurrection*, 102.

all should be explained in terms of the four elements—earth, water, fire, and air—and since they rejected the orthodox Brahmanical system they were of course considered heterodox. The Materialists were not the only naturalistic tradition. Another school of thought called the *Ājīvikas* fits that category and will be discussed later.

The Materialists can be placed in two main groups, the Reductionists and the Wholists.[32] The Reductionists reduced all things to the categories of matter and further reduced humanity to the matter composing the human body. They thought matter was permanent, operating in regular patterns, roughly analogous to today's Materialists. This matter acts according to determinism in a causal process. Since matter was the only permanent thing, all other things, including minds and personalities, are only derivative and impermanent based on matter. The personality and will are only the effect of a string of causes.

The second school of materialistic thought, the Wholists, Kalupahana labels the "more enlightened form of Materialism."[33] This nonreductionist school instead seems to have given more attention to human personality, considering people as wholes rather than parts. They believed that killing a man was a crime against nature. Both schools faithfully opposed any permanence regarding human personality.

The information available today regarding the ethical theories of these Materialists comes from their critics. We have no records from members of the schools. Either the records have not been preserved or the Materialists did not find ethics an important topic for compositions. The opponents of the Materialists may have grouped the ethical theories of all Materialists together and criticized them as nonethical.

We do find examples of terrible practices linked directly to materialist dogma and early Indian scientism. We see this in the horror story of the process used by which Pāyāsi, an ancient Indian Materialist, attempted to prove that the soul did not exist.[34]

32. Kalupahana does not use these terms to describe the two groups of Materialists. I have assigned these names for the purpose of making the discussion easier to follow.

33. Kalupahana, *History of Buddhist Philosophy*, 14.

34. Jayatilleke, *Early Buddhist Theory*, 105.

Pāyāsi flayed a man alive by "cutting off his integument, flesh, nerves, bones, and marrow to see if at any stage he could observe a soul."[35] He did this more than once. Why should Pāyāsi do anything different? In his own mind, the materialism he sought to prove had also justified his actions.

On the brighter side, we find Ajita Kasakambali, the most prominent Materialist of ancient India.[36] He agreed that:

> This human person consists of the four great elements. When he dies, the solidity returns the body to the earth, fluidity of the body of water, caloric to the body of heat, and viscosity to the body of air.[37]

Regarding moral concepts he writes:

> Ideas like generosity are simply the conceptualizations of a stupid person. He who speaks of their existence, his words are empty, confused and a cry of desperation.[38]

Kasakambali may sound like a wicked hedonist until we consider his second name, which means "one who wears human hair[.]"[39] This indicates he was an ascetic, not a pleasure-seeking Materialist. Instead, he was opposing the foundation of the Brahmanical moral theory, which he viewed as metaphysical speculation.

Pūraṇa Kassapa, another ancient Indian Materialist who held ideas resembling those of Kasakambali, thought that any kind of moral demerit was impossible. Conceivably, one could walk along the southern bank of the Ganges killing people and receive no demerit, while if one distributed charity along the northern bank, one would receive no merit.

These three approaches give us a flavor for ancient Indian materialism. Certainly not all Materialists committed acts like Pāyāsi.

35. Ibid.

36. Kalupahana, *Ethics in Early Buddhism*, 16–18.

37. From *Dīgha-nikāya*. 1.55 quoted from Ibid., 17.

38. Ibid.

39. Ibid.

THE ĀJĪVIKAS

The second school of Naturalistic thinking was the Ājīvikas. They held a similar conception of matter with the Materialists. Unlike the Materialist, though, they thought that the human personality survives after death.[40] They also held a notion of biological evolution with no known beginning or goal. Their philosophy involves three main concepts: fate (*niyati*), species (*saṅgati*), and inherent nature (*bhāva, svabhāva*).

Fate accounts for how beings are incarnated as a human or animal. No explanation is given as to how this event happens. Kalupahana argues that causal explanation by fate is no explanation at all.

An animal or human will always choose in accordance with their species and nature. This means that human will must not be free. Since all events in the universe are predetermined, then, by necessity, within this naturalistic framework no human exertion may change one's course. Kalupahana comments, "Like some modern philosophers, they seem to have possessed the courage to openly accept determinism, and reject free will."[41] A person is still free even though they have no free will. They simply choose in accordance to their nature. The Ājīvkas liken it holding onto the end of a ball of string while tossing the ball off of a mountain. No condition could possibly change the length of that string.

The Ājīvikas, unlike the Buddha, completely rejected extra-sensory perception as a reliable means for gaining understanding about the ultimate nature of reality. Apparently the Ājīvikas were trying to circumvent the need for metaphysical speculations. Instead, they sought to observe the world and draw conclusions; yet they saw the world as something that they could not change. The course of things will continue, as it must, according to the predetermined path.[42]

40. Warder, *Outline of Indian Philosophy*, 40.

41. Kalupahana, *History of Buddhist Philosophy*, 15.

42. *Dīgha-nikāya*. I. 54, quoted in Kalupahana, *Buddhist Philosophy*, 12. Analyzed in Kalupahana, *History of Buddhist Philosophy*, 15. See also discussion in Warder, *Outline of Indian Philosophy*, 42.

JAINISM

The Jainas are the final group we will consider. They emerged around 600 *B.C.* and continue to the present day. Today it is believed that the Jainas held a nonabsolutist view of knowledge. In other words, knowledge cannot be sure and fixed because the world described by one's knowledge is always changing, always becoming. 'Being' (*sat*), the Jainas claimed, is multiform because it shows many different characteristics of shaping or arising (*utpāda*), cessation or destruction (*vyaya*), and durability or permanence (*dhrauvya*). Since human knowledge of the world cannot have a quality of permanence due to the referent of our knowledge being an ever-changing, contingent world, one can see that everyday conclusions cannot be absolute. Every judgment must be from a certain point of view. However, the Jainas still claimed that one *could* have omniscience (*kevalajñāna*). Impermanence (*anicca*) is a part of existence yet the Jainas believed in the existence of the soul (*jīva*), analogous to the 'individual selves' (*ātman*) of the *Upaniṣads.*

Another point of analogy between Jainism and Upaniṣadic thought is the notion of karma. Yet the Jainas' theory of moral behavior (karma) is more deterministic since the choosing agent is responsible for his own choices. But once he chooses to act, the act becomes external to him and the effects of it are inescapable for him. The Buddhist texts lead us to think that the radical and severe asceticism of the Jainas may have been connected to their deterministic notion of karma; they may have engaged in such practices so that by non-action they could end the future production of karma. So there are certainly similarities between aspects of the Buddha's teaching and the doctrine of the Jainas, as we shall see in the chapters that follow. Nevertheless, the Buddha's middle way would fight against their asceticism.

CONCLUSION

This brief tour of pre-Buddhist thought is essential to understanding the counterpoint represented by Buddhist philosophy. The Brahmanism of the *Upaniṣads,* the Materialists, the Ājīvikas, and Jainism (with omniscience) suggest different types of absolutism. The Upaniṣadic thinkers held the absolute 'Self' as real and that change and impermanence were illusions. The Materialists and the Ājīvikas considered matter as the irreducible, ultimately real thing. The Jainas accepted both permanence and impermanence as characteristics of Ultimate Reality.

In attitudes of religious practice, the *Upaniṣads* suggest that the ultimate spiritual goal involves apprehending the unity between the 'Universal Self' and the 'Individual Self'. The Jainas strove after extreme mortification of the body to keep *karmic* particles from attaching to the soul, however the Materialists rejected any spirituality. The Buddha accepted aspects of these ideas while simultaneously cast aside the Upaniṣadic absolutist framework that was still developing in order to create a new doctrine.

4

The Life and Times of the Buddha

Between Gayā and the Place of Enlightenment The Ājīvaka Upaka saw me on the road and said: 'Friend, your faculties are clear, the color of your skin is pure and bright. Under whom have you gone forth, friend? Who is your teacher? Whose Dhamma do you profess?' I replied to him in stanzas:

'I am one who has transcended all, a knower of all,
Unsullied among all things, renouncing all,
By craving's ceasing freed. Having known this all
For myself, to whom should I point as teacher?

I have no teacher, and one like me
Exists nowhere in all the world
With all its gods, because I have
No person for my counterpart.

I am the Accomplished One in the world,
I am the Teacher Supreme.
I alone am a Fully Enlightened One
Whose fires are quenched and extinguished.'

Ariyapariyesanā-sutta, Majjhima-nikāya ???

Jesus therefore answered and was saying unto them, "Truly, truly, I say to you, the Son can do nothing of Himself, unless it is something He sees the Father doing; for what ever the Father does, these things the Son also does in like manner. For the

Father loves the Son, and shows Him all things that He Himself is doing; and greater works than these will He show Him, that you may marvel. For just as the Father raises the dead and gives them life, even so the Son also gives life to whom He wishes. For not even the Father judges anyone, but He has given all judgment to the Son.

John 5:19–22

INTRODUCTION TO THE BUDDHIST PROBLEM OF HISTORY

BEFORE EXAMINING THE BUDDHA'S teachings, we should examine his life and times. This task presents us with great challenges. In Buddhism, events in the universe have no particular goal or meaning, so preserving records of the past holds a lower priority than internal spiritual goals. Roger J. Corless, in the introduction to his book *The Vision of Buddhism*, makes this point regarding Buddhism and history:

> History is an academic discipline that has developed in the western hemisphere. The western hemisphere has been strongly influenced by the Abrahamic traditions (Judaism, Christianity, and Islam) and their conception of time as something created by God in and through which God manifests himself. On this view, time is meaningful. It has a beginning and the end is a goal, so that there is a development, a progressive achievement of the goal. . . . A Christian hymn says "God is working his purpose out as year succeeds to year." As soon as we substitute the word Buddha for God in this sentence, however, there is a problem.
>
> History as a secular discipline has many of the features of the Abrahamic tradition's view of time. God has been gradually eased out, and the notion of goal or purpose has become suspect. But the assumption that time is meaningful and that development is real does not seem to have been given up even by the most radical critics of the philosophy of history.
>
> Buddhism, on the other hand, sees things in constant change over time, but it does not see things as becoming more or less meaningful as they change. Change, for Buddhism, is a primary characteristic of cyclical existence (samsara), and his-

> tory is just a lot of change. All that one can say about history, Buddhistically, is that as time goes on we get more of it.[1]

Corless believes strongly that history is necessarily Abrahamic. The work of history "is non-Buddhist, even anti-Buddhist."[2] He even structures his book in a nonhistorical outline intentionally. The lack of interest in preserving the factual historical account of the Buddha seems to stem from the natural outworking of Buddhist doctrine itself.[3]

For this reason, the history of the Buddha's life is somewhat sketchy. Different traditions have conflicting versions of the Buddha's life. Many of the things attributed to the Buddha, such as the "The Flower Sermon," are additions that attach themselves to the tradition hundreds of years after the Buddha lived. This makes recovering the historical Buddha more difficult than recovering the historical Jesus.

Edward J. Thomas makes a helpful observation in an appendix entitled "Buddhism and Christianity" in his book *The Life of Buddha as Legend and History*:[4]

> The Gospel stories all belong to the first century *A.D.* They were all written down at the time when a living tradition and memory of the events may have existed. For one school this tradition did exist. The story of the Samaritan woman, of the choosing of the disciples, was told because there really was a Samaritan woman and disciples who had been fisherman.

Unlike the Christian tradition, Buddhism does not have the benefit of authoritative writings penned by the witnesses or those who interviewed the witnesses. But the Buddhist Suttas also do not bear the same burden of proof borne by the New Testament writings, especially the Gospels. In Christian theology, the reliability of the historical account is necessary for the truth of the Christian mes-

1. Corless, *Vision of Buddhism*, xix.

2. Ibid., xx.

3. For a discussion of the issues regarding reconstructing the Buddha's life, see Yandel and Netland, *Buddhism*, 10–11.

4. Kalupahana comments favorably about this book in his annotated bibliography: "Another work of great erudition, critically evaluating the scanty historical material and the vast collection of legends relating to the life of Buddha." *History of Buddhist Philosophy*, 304.

sage. Many in the last two centuries have challenged the accuracy of the Gospels themselves, compartmentalizing the truth claims of the Christian faith to a little room with white padded walls called the realm of "the phenomenology of religious experience," where anything can *sort of* be "true." However, the first century church believed that the truth of the Gospel depended on the facts of history. They also believed that the Christian message gave meaning to the events of history.

The Buddha, on the other hand, saw his message as only personally verifiable. Buddhism has no grand story to tell. There is no need for witnesses external to one's self. No one needs to consult any chain of temporal events to walk the path to one's own liberation. The practitioner makes his own story, or, even better, puts an end to his own story of pain and suffering. Many of the stories of the Buddha within the different sects of Buddhism exist to communicate some truth about the path to liberation. As such they are often parables for "deeper" truths, which the new student seeks to incorporate into his life. These illustrative stories cannot be harmonized into one cohesive account. The several different conflicting accounts of the Buddha's life present the scholar with problems, but do not necessarily harm the message of Buddhism in the same way that a lack of accurate historical content in the four Gospels would undermine Christian doctrine and faith.

What follows is more or less the common story of the life of Siddhārtha Gautama and how he became the Buddha.

THE LIFE OF THE BUDDHA

When the powerful Suddhodana, king of the Śākya clan, learned that he would have a son, he consulted his wise men who could predict the future. He was told that his son would be a great king or a great religious leader. At this time, religious leaders were filthy men who renounced normal life and lived in the forest off food they would receive from begging. These men wore few clothes and some even put dung in their hair. Of course it was a tough choice, but as he held his baby boy Siddhārtha, he knew which life he wanted for his son!

Taking the most radical measures, he guarded his son from wanting to go into the forest. He gave his son every pleasure and isolated him from the world. The king prohibited anyone to speak to his son of old age, sickness, or death. Siddhārtha would never see anyone with such attributes. And never would he hear of the religious men in the forest. That was his life—a life of luxury. Later in life, Siddhārtha would tell his students:

> I was delicate, O monks, extremely delicate, excessively delicate. In my father's dwelling lotus-pools had been made, in one blue lotuses, in another red, in another white, all for my sake. I used no sandalwood that was not Benares, my dress was of Benares cloth, my tunic, my under-robe, and cloak. Night and day a white parasol was held over me so that I should not be touched by cold or heat, by dust or weeds or dew.
>
> I had three palaces, one for the cold season, one for the hot, and one for the seasons of rains. Through the four rainy months, in the place for the rainy season, entertained by female minstrels I did not come down from the palace; and as in the dwellings of others food from the husks of rice is given to the slaves and workmen together with sour gruel, so in my father's dwelling rice and meat was given to the slaves and workmen.[5]

Siddhārtha was insulated from the world's pain and given every pleasure he could want. Even the slaves ate well. He took a wife, named Yasodharā, who bore him one son, Rāhula.

But Siddhārtha could never leave. When he did travel from palace to palace, all the old, sick, and dead were removed from the path. The aged were removed from the palace. When people around him became ill, they would "go on a journey" and return when well. All this security made Siddhārtha suspicious. He craved to know what was beyond the walls.

Finally, he could stand it no longer. He summoned his charioteer, ordering him to take him into town. The charioteer believed that the king would kill him if he did this, so he refused to take Siddhārtha. Siddhārtha told him that if he did not, he would be killed anyway. So the charioteer took him into town where he saw a man "worn out with old age, with broken teeth, gray hair, bent, with a broken-down

5. *Auguttara-nikāya*. I. 145 quoted in Ibid., 47

body, with a stick in hand, trembling."[6] Siddhārtha asked what was wrong with the man.

The charioteer told him, "Sir, that man is old."

Siddhārtha asked, "How did he get this way?"

The charioteer said, "This happens to everyone. It will even happen to you."

Siddhārtha looked at the old man for a pensive moment and then requested the driver to take him home. He stayed up much of the night considering what he had seen. The king discovered that Siddhārtha had seen the effects of old age and ordered dancing girls to come and entertain his son, hoping that he would forget. The guard on the palace was also increased.

However, Siddhārtha evaded the increased security and again put pressure on his charioteer to take him from the palace. On his second trip into the city he found a man racked with illness. Siddhārtha had never seen a man like this. Sanitary conditions in the palace were far superior to the villages. He asked his charioteer why the man was like this.

The charioteer told him, "Sir, that man is very sick."

Siddhārtha asked, "How did this happen?"

The charioteer said, "Everyone gets sick. Some suffer more than others."

"Not me. I won't get sick"

"Even you will get sick."

Siddhārtha thought for a moment. "Take me back, chariot driver, this is enough for today." And he returned to the palace.

The next day he went out again. He saw a man lying in the street, stinking and circled by flies. As the chariot came upon the man he appeared to be sleeping. He wanted to wake the man to move him. Surely if he knew he were covered with flies he would not be pleased. The charioteer told Siddhārtha that would not be possible, for the man was dead. Once again the charioteer made clear that this, too, would happen to him. Once again Siddhārtha requested the chariot driver take him home.

He again went out into the villages and saw a religious man begging for food. He learned that men go to the forest to put an

6. Ibid., 52.

end to suffering and understand the nature of ultimate reality. That night he left the palace forever. This event Buddhists call the Great Renunciation. Siddhārtha told his wife that he was leaving and kissed his sleeping son. His family would always have physical provisions. As he made his way out of the palace under the cover of night, he left behind his place of service to his clan, his wife, and his son. He had experienced all the pleasures of life and found them lacking when confronted with the reality of pain. Swapping robes with a beggar, he entered the forest. He was twenty-eight.

Gautama's Ascetic Life

As Siddhārtha fled the palace, he had no desires for power or fame. Instead, he wanted clarity on the issues of suffering. As a brilliant and earnest young man, he quickly found his first teacher, Ālāra Kālāma. Kālāma trained Gautama in ecstatic practices and meditation (yoga). After several years of study, Kālāma informed Gautama that he was now ready to be an instructor as he had mastered all the knowledge of his teacher. Gautama knew that he had not yet understood the origins of suffering (*dukkha*); the spiritual techniques of insight he had learned were inadequate for the task. He found a new teacher, Uddaka Rāmaputra. He mastered everything taught him by this new teacher and realized that it, too, was lacking.

In time, Siddhārtha came to know five other men who had similar dissatisfaction. They banded together and in an effort to push through to enlightenment, find clarity, and put an end to suffering (*dukkha*), they began to meditate. After meeting with repeated failure, they decided that this radical purpose required extreme measures. They adopted a stringent fast with the most severe austerity. Each of them separated into different places in the forest with the goal of enlightenment or death.

Enlightenment

This extreme action took its toll. Gautama, emaciated and near death, was found by a beautiful young girl. She gave him food and water, returning his strength to him. The other five friends found him with this girl and shunned him, thinking him weak for the task. They left him, but he pressed on, finding a *ficus religiosa* (a tree) in

Bodh-Gayā. Under the Bodhi Tree in 531 B.C.,[7] the Buddha "woke up." Here he formulated the Four Noble Truths, the discussion of which I will leave for following chapters.

He continued meditating for about seven weeks. Finally, he traveled to tell his five fellow monks who had joined together in a "strenuous effort" (*mahāpadāna*) to break free. He proclaimed what he discovered. They also became enlightened. This began a ministry that would last about forty-five years, till the Buddha's death at the age of eighty.

The Buddha remained in the region of the middle Ganges. He ordained his first five disciples, the men to whom he first preached, and then set out on a mission to teach anyone who would listen to him. With the conversions of some larger Indian religious orders, the ranks of the new faith swelled. The new order began to grow specifically in the monastic community. The movement acquired many monasteries and the Buddha himself became publicly recognized as a religious leader, which even led to intrigue and attempts on his life.

Often the Buddha would visit Kapilavastu at the base of the Himalayas to see his father Suddhodana, Yasodharā, and Rāhula. Eventually a wave of conversion swept his homeland. Through the forty-five years of his eventful ministry, he was known for his pleasantness, warm smile, and brilliance in debate. The Buddha was arguably the sharpest Indian mind of his time, and his clarity was combined with winsome rhetorical effectiveness.

Siddhārtha also knew how to think strategically. At times he would be asked about the positions of others and decline to answer.[8] Sometimes he was attacked for this single-minded devotion to the teaching of how to end suffering. To those attacks he responded, "The ascetic Gotama roars his lion's roar, in company and confidently, they question him and he answers, he wins them over with his

7. The precise history of the Buddha presents several problems. The dates in this biography of the Buddha are from Lamotte, *History of Indian Buddhism*. For discussion of emerging evidence that the Buddha may have lived a hundred years latter than Lamotte suggests see Williams, *Buddhist Thought*, 17f.

8. *Dīgha-nikāya* 2.150–151.

answers, they find it pleasing and are satisfied, they are on the path of truth, and they are satisfied with the practice."[9]

At the age of eighty he became violently ill after receiving a "tasty dish of pork." As a monk who had left society to pursue enlightenment in the forest, he found sustenance by begging for food. Sometimes people gave substandard or spoiled food, which the monks ate with gratitude. This particular meal caused the Buddha to have bloody diarrhea. Although he was weak, he continued to teach, but eventually the sickness overtook him. The Nirvāṇa—that is, his death—came in 486 B.C.

The Buddha's followers carefully remembered his words and eventually began writing them as "sutras" (in Pali, *sutta*). The moment grew and flourished. Several hundred years later, Buddhism split into the Mahāyāna (large cart) and Hīnayāna (small cart) sects, which eventually became fully developed traditions. The Mahāyāna tradition tended to believe that Buddha was divine. The Hīnayāna group, being more conservative, wanted to hold onto the original views of the Buddha.[10]

CONCLUSION

An accurate history of the Buddha is a difficult scholarly task. Scholars of Buddhism have long known that the problem of rendering an accurate history of the Buddha's life stems from the view of history presented within Buddhism. History itself is a Western, Abrahamic discipline that assumes a linear view of time.

Nevertheless, there is a general consensus, based on the evidence, that the Buddha lived and flourished in the sixth century B.C. in what is now southern Nepal. Siddhārtha Gautama was born into great wealth and privilege as a member of the Śākya clan. He came to see the lofty pleasures of his high estate as vanity when viewed in the context of human suffering. He left is own wealth and pleasure to devote himself to discovering the causes of suffering and to putting an end to them. In his mid-thirties, while meditating

9. *Dīgha-nikāya* 1.175. Quoted from Walshe, *Long Discourses*, 156.

10. This last sentence is controversial, but I am taking the side of Pali Buddhism, not only because this section should present early Buddhist philosophy sympathetically but also because I think the early texts best represent the Buddha's philosophy.

under the Bodhi tree, he discovered the Four Noble Truths, which explain how human beings can end their suffering. He spent the next forty-five years teaching these truths and their rich implications to his followers. Even though his teaching was heterodox from Vedic religion, his doctrine earned many converts. After the Buddha's death, his followers continued preaching and teaching the Buddha's message of how to end suffering—a message which has now made its way to nearly every region of the world.

5

The Beginning of Knowledge

Something may be accepted fully out of faith, yet it may be empty, hollow, and false.... [Under these conditions] it is not proper for a wise man who preserves truth to come to the definite conclusion: "Only this is true, anything else is wrong."

Cankī Sutta, Majjhima-nikāya 2.171–172

Shall the potter be considered as equal with the clay, That what is made should say to its maker, "He did not make me"; Or what is formed say to him who formed it, "He has no understanding"?

Isaiah 29:16

As I explained in the introduction, this work is a Christian assessment of early Buddhist philosophy, reflected in the earliest Buddhist scriptures, the Pali Canon.[1] I intend to go back to the source, back to the rich philosophical outlook of the Buddha himself. Before critically examining Buddhism, we must understand it on its own terms. The following five chapters will explain the Buddha's view of knowledge, causality, personality, karma, ethics, and *nirvāṇa*. In this chapter we will look at the Buddha's epistemology.

1. The Pali Canon is the group of scriptures used by the Hīnayāna sect of Buddhism. Pali was the original language of their composition. Dates for the writing of the texts range from 400 B.C. to A.D. 100. For a more detailed discussion of a history of the Buddhist Scriptures, see Mizuno, *Buddhist Sutras*.

Epistemology is the discipline of philosophy that studies how we know what we know. The term can also refer to the particular system or theory we use to explain what knowledge is. The Buddha had a distinct epistemology, which provides the basis for his claims.

When people think of Buddhism on the popular level, they usually think of the Four Noble Truths, which the Buddha developed under the Bhodi Tree. We ought to acquaint ourselves with them first since the Buddha's epistemology tries to establish them as reliable.

- The first noble truth is that life is suffering (*dukkha*). *Dukkha* is the word that the Buddha used to describe the unsatisfactory quality of life. It refers to anything from torture to having a coke machine take your coke without giving you a soda. "Suffering" is a bit of a strong word for *dukkha,* but it is a good English equivalent for now.
- The second noble truth is that *dukkha* has causes. The Buddha saw causality as the ultimate explanatory principle that described the operation of the universe. So this second noble truth is an expression of the highest truth of Buddhism, denoted by the Pali word *paṭiccasamuppāda* (Skt: *pratītiasamupāda*). This word is translated many ways: "codependent origination," "interdependent coorigination," "interdependent causality," or "dependent arising." The idea is that for any event there are several causes and that each of those causes also has several causes. When traced to the end, every event is caused by every other event in the universe.
- The third noble truth is that if you understand the causes of your suffering, you can put an end to them and thus end your suffering. This is the truth of *nirvāṇa* or liberation. We can put an end to *dukkha* and "wake up."
- The fourth noble truth is the Eightfold Noble Path. This is the path to clarity about the Buddha's doctrine. It involves various ethical standards that allow the one pursing enlightenment to work out their end to *dukkha.* Buddhism is all about ending suffering. The understanding and appropriating of these truths is enlightenment.

These are the Four Noble Truths. How do we know they are true? That is a tough question. It must be answered against the backcloth of the Buddha's philosophical context in this period of history. During the fifth century B.C., the Buddha encountered three major schools of thought that offered their own answers to the question of knowledge: the Traditionalists, the Rationalists, and the Experientialists. Each had a distinct epistemology. Those who held to scriptures or some other form of handed-down revelation were the Traditionalists. Jayetilleke and Kalupahana present the Traditionalist epistemology as arguments from mere authority.[2] The Buddha, however, rejected revelation, including supposedly divine insights into the nature of *Brahman*. Rejection of revelation naturally meant rejection of any ideas accepted on the basis of revelation.

The Buddha required any revelation claim to be verified by another source of knowledge. He believed that when one makes a claim to know based on revelation it is appropriate to ask why one accepts the content of the revelation. To accept revelation simply because it was revealed is to reason in a circle. A faithful devotee may have strong convictions, but mere strong convictions do not prove something to be true.

The Buddha did not want a tautology; he wanted an answer to why a revealed claim should be accepted. Revelation not only demands a place in our epistemological method but also demands to be the arbiter and verifier of truth, and itself requires no authentication. If revelation must first be verified, it ceases to have authority as revelation. But if it cannot be verified, then in what sense should we call it knowledge? Hence the Buddha knew that if revelation must first be verified apart from itself, then it is rendered useless. Thus, the Buddha called all revelation into question.

Some Vedic teachers held to the Tradition of the *Vedas* because these books were part of their sacred religious tradition. The Buddha criticized this Vedic tradition on several points. First, though the Vedic texts may have been part of an assorted canon of scripture, the Buddha claimed the texts were simply the writings of men. "The original seers are constantly described as 'the makers and utters

2. See Jayatilleke, *Early Buddhist Theory*, 192–204; Kalupahana, *History of Buddhist Philosophy*, 30–31; and *Buddhist Philosophy*, 16–17.

of the hymns' "[3] These hymns were criticized as having exclusively human authorship. If the writings carry no quality of revelation, then claims based on the continuity of tradition are meaningless since the texts would contain no revelation in the first place. The Buddha treated these texts as being no better than rumor. And rumor was also rejected as a form of knowledge. With the Buddha's attitude toward revelation, we can see how he treats arguments arising from conformity with scripture as ridiculous.

Second, the Buddha argued that testimony of a qualified person is only as reliable as that person is qualified. Knowledge based on testimony requires prior proof before someone can place confidence in the one giving testimony. If the one offering testimony has to provide some type of proof or accreditation, then they cannot be the final authoritative source of knowledge—some other credential is. Belief in them would be actually based on something else. The requirement that a person justify their own claim to authority was used by the Buddha to critique another type of testimony claim, that of omniscience. Some religious leaders, such as the Nigaṇha Nātaputta of the Jainas, claimed to have the potential to know anything, and, therefore, they were to be trusted. The Buddha rejected Nātaputta's claim on the basis of common sense, showing that Nātaputta's claim to knowledge could not be justified beyond the mere fact that the revered Jaina leader said so. Since anyone can get up and make a metaphysical claim, the Buddha wanted outside empirical verification of testimony, some reason to believe it before it could be accepted.

Some texts suggest the Buddha was omniscient, but omniscience texts show up no earlier than the last strata of the Pali canon.[4] Theravāda scholars, who naturally reject that Buddha ever claimed to be divine, argue that the Buddha's disciples only said this to keep up with the Jainas. Those who do not take this tactic argue that the Buddha did believe he could know any particular fact. Since they believe we acquire knowledge empirically, the Buddha would merely need the opportunity to examine the issue empirically.

At any rate, the Buddha held that:

3. See *Dīgha-nikāya*. 1.242, *Majjhima-nikāya*. 2.169 and Jayatilleke, *Early Buddhist Theory*,193.

4. For a detailed discussion, see Ibid., 376–81.

> There are five things that have a twofold result in this life. What five? [Knowledge based on] faith, likes, tradition, reflection on form, and delight in views. . . . Even if I know something on the basis of best faith, that may be empty, hollow, and confused, while, what I do not know on the best faith may be may be factual, true, and not otherwise. It is not proper for an intelligent person, safeguarding the truth, to come categorically to the conclusion in this matter that such alone is true and whatever else is false.[5]

Faith, desire, tradition, reflection on form, and the contemplation and debating of different views may result in true beliefs, but tripping over truth and possessing knowledge are two different things altogether. Also, faith may be placed in an unfaithful knowledge claim. We may still be wrong no matter how great a faith we have. Something is not true merely because we believe it.

From this text, we also see that the Buddha rejected the epistemology of the second group, the Rationalist. The Rationalists based knowledge upon rational inferences. He rejected their position because he believed that views formed on mere reasoned arguments were speculation, and he viewed the Vedic tradition as speculation compounded on speculation.[6] Arguments were presented for different metaphysical views; however, since the debates rarely focused on testable pheno-mena, conclusions could never be reached. For these reasons, the Buddha rejected the epistemic approaches of both the Traditionalists and the Rationalists.

Rupert Gethin appears to take issue with the kind of characterization of the Buddha's teaching on faith that Kalupahana offers and that I have presented here.[7] With the support of Edward Conze, Gethin argues that the hostility to religious faith is a Western phenomenon. Gethin makes the case that the Buddha supported religious faith, making his case from the *Kālāma Sutta*.[8] This choice is problematic, because the faith which the *Kālāma Sutta* describes is the trust in the Buddha which the Buddha has earned based on how

5. *Majjhima-nikāya* 2.170–171. Quoted from Kalupahana, *History of Buddhist Philosophy*, 31.

6. Translated above as "delight in views," *Majjhima-Nikāya* 2.170.

7. Gethin, *Foundations of Buddhism*, 165–169.

8. *Aṅguttara-nikāya* 1.189

he is proven that he is enlightened. If one is to find enlightenment, one must be able to trust one's teacher and what that teacher is teaching. The better faith text to consider is the *Cankī Sutta*, the source of Kalupahana's quotation, which specifically addresses faith as an epistemological foundation for belief.[9] It is clear from this text that the Buddha is repudiating faith as an epistemological foundation, while the Buddha does encourage faith in a teacher who had demonstrated competance in the *dhamma* and has put an end to the causes of his own suffering.

SENSE EXPERIENCE

The Buddha rejected Traditionalist authority and Rationalist speculation, but he did accept the epistemology of the Experientialists. He claims to be one of the brahmans or ascetics who has access to the higher knowledge, which means there must have been others who took a similar epistemic approach. Thus, the Buddha turned to a detailed analysis of sense experience:

> Depending on the visual organ and the visual object, O monks, arises visual consciousness; the meeting together of these three is contact; conditioned by contact arises feeling. What one feels, one perceives; what one perceives, one reflects about; what one reflects about, one is obsessed with. What one is obsessed with due to that, concepts characterized by such obsessed perceptions assail him in regard to visible objects cognizable by the visual organ, belonging to the past, future, and the present.[10]

Here the Buddha begins his description of perception by acknowledging mutual dependence (*paṭiccasamuppāda*) of the organ and the object being sensed. While *Ātman* does not account for the unity between the inner and outer world, dependence (causality) does. The sensing organ is part of a physically identifiable person. Sense perception does not give us a world apart from our experience. Every experience is conditioned by both the senses and the object sensed. The resulting experience is the causal product of both items. We never objectively know an object in itself. And, according to the

9. *Majjhima-nikāya* 2.170–171

10. *Majjhima-nikāya* 1.111–112, quoted from Kalupahana, *History of Buddhist Philosophy*, 32.

Buddha, we do not need to. The Buddha's theory of perception is *almost* Kantian, but not quite (more in chapter 6).

Kalupahana comments on the phrase 'What one feels, one perceives."[11] Regular contact with certain perceptions develops feelings, emotions. Kalupahana connects these feelings with ethics. We place value on those things to which we develop attachments, and, therefore, our ethics have an empirical source (more in chapter 8). The Buddha thought human discussions of right and wrong tend to leave the tangible world and ascend into in metaphysical speculations. Then strife begets strife, and the solutions to our ethical problems escape our reach. If we do get a finger hold, they will slip through our fingers as if we were grasping oil. The Buddha attempted to make ethics more empirical by showing human emotions condition human perceptions. Emotions seem to reign as tyrants in the mind, yet he believed meditation could triumph over them.

Nevertheless, knowledge begins with experience. Of the three schools of thought on knowledge present within the fifth century Indian philosophical scene—the Traditionalists, the Rationalists, and the Experimentalist—the Buddha accepted the third approach, that of Experimentalism.

How was the Buddha's approach to knowledge different from that of the *Upaniṣads*? The Upaniṣadic teachers sought to put themselves in states where they could gain direct access into the nature of the universe. In these states they 'experienced' that *Ātman* (Self as individual) and *Brahman* (the Creator) are one and the same. These passionate pursuers of impersonality stopped at what they perceived as clear metaphysical perception. The Buddha discerned this halting as futility. In fact, he left Rāmaputta for this reason. The Buddha believed he had reached the meditative state where the distinction between 'oneself' and 'other' dissipates. This state has no linguistic descriptions because language presupposes distinctions. Although the Buddha reached this state of consciousness, he also thought he surpassed it. Kalupahana thinks the Buddha was able to exceed the achievements of his predecessor because, unlike Rāmaputta, the Buddha was not looking for some state of

11. Ibid., 33–34.

personal cognitive *experience*. He was able to pass the early stages of meditative experience and bring an end to perception itself. The Buddha met the end of the meditative road, the cessation of perception altogether, in a non-cognitive state.

The Buddha recognized that nothing could be done in this state. Once perceptions have ceased, the gate to understanding the causes of suffering also closes. The techniques of the Upaniṣadic thinkers gave no knowledge as to the problems of existence. They brought no end to suffering, nor could they ever.

The Pali Canon claims that the Buddha developed extra-sensory powers. Moderns tend to redact these "supernatural" abilities from the Buddhist texts. If they are sympathetic to the Buddha's doctrine, they will expound a perspective consistent with modern naturalism and reject the miraculous. However, consider that the question of whether the Buddha had these abilities, miraculous by our standard, is harmless to the epistemic case for Buddhism. Extrasensory perception is only an embellished empiricism. In fact, "extrasensory" is a poor word to describe these abilities of the Buddha. Perhaps *heightened* or alternative sensory perception would serve us better.

The heightened forms of empirical knowledge accepted by the Upaniṣadic thinker are:[12]

- Psychokinesis (*iddhividha*): exhibiting the power of will in the world. This is not a source of knowledge but more of an ability.
- Clairaudience (*dibbasota*): a faculty of awareness regarding distant sounds way beyond the range of normal hearing. This allows for the direct perception of events normally inferred.
- Telepathy (*cetoparityañāṇa*): ability to apprehend the contents of another's thoughts as that person is thinking them.
- Retrocognition (*pubbenivāsânussati ñāṇa*): the ability to access one's memory of past lives.
- Clairvoyance (*dibbacakkhu* or *cut' ūpapātañāṇa*): awareness of the death and further states of beings on the wheel of *saṃsāra*, experiencing the results of their moral actions (karma).
- Knowledge of destruction of defiling impulses (*āsavak-*

12. Kalupahana, *Buddhist Philosophy*, 21–22.

khagañāṇa): This source of knowledge coupled with the others gives insight into the Four Noble Truths (discussed below).

The Buddha found the last three very useful. He believed these perceptions to be empirical, thinking that man has such faculties to interact with these corresponding sensible items. The mind (*mano*) without concentration can grasp concepts (*dhammā*). The Buddha believed that the concentrated mind—the mind cleared by meditation—can understand former lives, the thought processes of others, and even the causal process of defiling impulses.

We must be clear on this more "miraculous" side of the Buddha's theory of knowledge. These are merely elaborations on empiricism. The Buddha believed that we have senses which apprehend certain existing perceptible objects in the world. There is no other way to gain knowledge. Even if one receives knowledge in the form of testimony, that testimony is just a string of words, words that must point to sense experience. So testimony refers to perceptions only. Any knowledge claim may only be justified in this empirical, positivist manner. Even knowledge claimed by the gods must be justified in the same manner. Reliable knowledge only comes through sense perception.

These the basic truths of Buddhism, especially Buddhist epistemology, are found in all sects because the Buddha pointed to empiricism as the means for verifying his method and ending suffering. Even in Mahāyāna Buddhism, which emphasizes the divine, the divinities have no greater insight into the nature of the universe than what their senses provide. In a Buddhist understanding of the divine, appeals to such beings provide no clarity to the nature of the universe. Who are the gods? They may be able to sense more than we can, but they have no greater epistemic authority due to their being. Even if they did, the Buddha would want them to comply with the rules of his epistemology. He would grant their claims if they first verified them through sense experience. Incidentally, this is why a Buddhist still can piously worship the Hindu gods, yet a practicing Buddhist cannot at the same time be a faithful Christian. The Buddhist can believe that there are powerful beings in this world, but power neither equates to enlightenment regarding the causes of *dukkha* nor is the means to end it.[13]

In addition, the views of the Buddha need not be established by extraordinary sense perceptions. In fact, we *ought* to verify the highest truth of Buddhism, the truth of "interdependent causality" based on common experience (more in chapter 6). In *Sutta-nipāta* 1122, one of the Buddha's followers tells him, "You do not have (or recognize) something that is not seen, heard, conceived, or cognized in this world." The Buddha believed the average, everyday man with normal perceptions could rid himself of suffering apart from faith in things not seen.

Experience cannot provide us with certain knowledge, but the Buddha did not want certain knowledge. He wanted to understand causal relations (see chapter 6) for the purpose of ending suffering. He believed we cause our own suffering by attempting to make things permanent when in reality everything is in constant flux. This is why the sixth and highest form of knowledge is the knowledge of the destruction of defiling impulses. For the Buddha, knowledge relates to the here and now—not grand, mystical, insensible claims. Understanding of the causes of suffering and the means to end it is right before our eyes.

JUSTIFYING CAUSALITY

For the Buddha to remain consistent, causality—his all-encompassing explanatory principle—must be empirically justified. If the Buddha cannot account for his own theory of causality through his theory of knowledge, then his epistemology and causal theory are at war with one another.

David Hume believed that the empirical justification of causality was impossible. Hume presents an argument that threatens to undermine the Buddha's epistemology:

> Before we are reconcil'd to this doctrine, how often we must repeat ourselves, *that* the simple view of any two objects or actions, however related, can never give us any idea of power, or of a connection betwixt them: *that* this idea arises from the repetition of their union: *that* the repetition neither discovers

13. See my discussion of regulative concepts in chapter 8.

> nor causes any thing in the objects, but has an influence only on the mind, by that customary transition it produces: that this customary transition is, therefore, the same with the power and necessity; which are consequently qualities of perceptions, not of objects, and are internally felt by the soul, and not percieve'd externally in bodies?[14]

In other words, we associate two events which occur in sequence and *assume* that there is a causal relationship between them. So causality is a judgment call, or worse, a matter of faith. We assume that the future will be like the past, but the future is always in the future and, therefore, not yet available to experience. Any statements about connections between the future and the past depend first on the existence of a connection. Yet that causal connection is exactly what must be proved. So Hume accuses the defender of causality of practicing circular reasoning. To causally connect the future and the past first requires that there be a causal connection.

The Buddha believed that our senses had no access to the past or future, only the present. Intentions toward the future and our memories of the past are concepts (*saṅkhā*), not perceptions. In the modern period we relate a trustworthy observation to our ability to make scientific prediction. To the Buddha, prediction is just a guide. It does not establish truth. Humans seek permanence. One expression of this today is the scientific mindset of belief in objective laws of nature describing the regular operations of the universe at any time. The Buddha thought that "Beings dominated by prediction (*akkheyya*), established upon prediction, not understanding prediction, come under the yoke of death. However, having understood prediction one does not assume oneself to be a foreteller."[15] The Buddha saw a place for prediction but rejected predictability as a solid basis for knowledge. However, he did not jump to Hume's extreme, that of unpredictability. He thought he was walking a middle path between them.

Kalupahana defends the Buddha's approach in arguing that in an essentialist philosophy (that brand of philosophy most common in Western history, where truths are based on such things as universals,

14. *Treatise of Human Nature*, 166; Hume's emphasis.

15. *Saṃyutta-nikāya* 1.11, cited in Kalupahana, *History of Buddhist Philosophy*, 45.

the character of God, or permanence in a regular universe) such criticisms make sense. If certainty is a necessary component of knowledge, then the concept of causality turns into a guess within a strictly empiricist epistemology.

This is why the Buddha rejects essentialist philosophy (which for him was Upaniṣadic thought) tying knowledge directly to experience. Instead of seeing experience as a collection of discrete, separate perceptions, he viewed experience as a continuum. The mind freezes perceived experiences into moments. But there are no moments separate from the causal flux of reality. Once we reject the ontological separation of cause and effect, then (the Buddha would have argued) the Humean criticism evaporates.

Kalupahana contends that causal connections are established not by deduction but by induction. Some experiences show us the causal connections between other experiences:

> However, in a system that repudiates such [essentialist] rational distinctions and *recognizes that relations between events are often revealed in experience, these experienced relations themselves serve as guides for possible future experiences.* Uniformities are thus abstractions and imagination functions more in the formulation of such uniformities than in the experience of relations themselves. *Inductive inference thereby turns out to be an explanatory extension of sensible continuity into the obvious past and the future.*[16]

He views induction then as an extension of experience but not a truth founding experience in itself. Here Kalupahana is showing the Buddha's consistency since the strength of inductive reasoning is its ability to stay close to particulars, in this case the particulars of experience. And it is these particulars, and only these particulars, which give meaning to any inductive argument.

In the following chapter we will discuss the Buddha's view that nature is nonsubstantial. However, something should be said here about what nonsubstantiality in nature holds and how it affects human knowledge. The doctrine of nonsubstantiality is that nothing has any fixed, permanent, immutable essence. All of reality—knowledge, people, things, feelings, whatever one can think of—can neither be pointed to as a permanent reality nor be isolated as an

16. Ibid; emphasis mine.

identity that one can accept as an object of knowledge. There is no bedrock of reality or knowledge, and no regular structure that we can point to that maintains the permanent integrity of knowledge and the perceived world we see around us. So our knowledge can never be ultimately true according to the Buddha. Contingent truth or possible truth is all we have. This presents the Buddha with the interesting question of how he accounts for logic and truth:

> If the search for the ultimate objectivity is to be abandoned in the analysis of the data of sensible experience, there seems to be no reason why it should be retained in the evaluation of other sources of knowledge, such as inference. *Thus the Buddha's theory of non-substantiality applies equally to all data of human thought and experience—objects of experience and relations among events, as well as uniformities.*[17]

The consequences of the Buddha's epistemology do not stop with his claims about causality and suffering. They extend to every area of human life. There is no aspect of life that does not feel the careful poke of the Buddha's epistemological finger.

Truth and Logic

The favorite definition of knowledge for many contemporary philosophers (unless your name is Edmund Gettier!) is *true, justified belief.* Any epistemology must account for both the truth and justification of knowledge claims. Buddhism presents no exceptions. However, the Buddha did qualify "truth" and logic to match his own perspective. So far in this chapter, we have examined the different competing epistemologies contemporary with the Buddha. The Buddha himself was an Experimentalist requiring empirical justification for all claims. Even the gods (if there are any) must be empiricists. There are no absolute statements that anyone can make about the universe. Since all knowledge must be verified empirically, then *perception that depends on sense organs* is the only possible content of a truth claim.

This means that there can never be a "timeless" and "tenseless" statement. As a result, there can never be absolute truths. Since truth is tied to an ever-changing, contingent realm, no statement can

17. Ibid; emphasis mine.

always be true. Yet to function or even stay sane, one must be able to discern some things as true and others as false. Thus, regarding truth the Buddha said, "Truth is one. There is no second."[18] The Buddha believed a truth can be distinguished from what is false.

However, to prevent the deterioration of this truth into an absolute truth, the Buddha also refused to recognize the statement "This alone is true, everything else is false" (*idam eva saccaṃ mohgaṃ aññaṃ*).[19] We must recognize the empirical difference between "This is true" (*idam saccaṃ*) and "This alone is true" (*idam eva saccaṃ*). The word "this" (*idaṃ*) makes the statement particular, pointing it to particular instance. Kalupahana links the demonstrative use here to the Buddha's empiricism. However, when the word "alone" (*eva*) is used, the statement might be misconstrued to refer to an essential, timeless truth. When a statement is qualified with such precision, it moves towards becoming an absolute truth. For this reason the Buddha rejected such a statement. The truth provided by experience is final truth. There is no other.

The Buddha's understanding of truth clarifies his lower view of logic. He rejects ultimate true/false distinctions. This passage from the *Aṅguttara-nikāya* delineates the Buddha's position:

> *I know* what has been seen, heard, thought, cognized, attained, sought, and reflected upon by the people, including the ascetics and brahmans. If *I know* what has been seen. . .by the people. . .and if I were to say, "I do not know it," that would be confusion (*musā*) on my part. And if I were to say, "[It is both that] I know it and I do not know it," that too would be confusion on my part. [However,] if I were to say, "[It is both that] I neither know it nor do not know it," I would be committing a sin (*kali*) on my part.[20]

In this passage, the Buddha presents an understanding of truth in the traditional four-cornered logical system. His outline may be summarized as follows:

18. *Sutta-nipāta* 884.

19. *Majjhima-nikāya*, 1.169. Quoted by Kalupahana, *History of Buddhist Philosophy*, 46.

20. *Aṅguttara-nikāya*, 2.25. Quoted in Ibid., 47.

A. I know *p* (truth, *sacca*)

B. I do not know *p* (confusion, *musā*)

C. [It is both that] I know and do not know *p* (confusion, *musā*)

D. [It is both that] I neither know nor do not know *p* (sin, *kali*)[21]

If knowledge has come to us via perception, then we know the truth. A contradiction of statement B is not false in the sense of *kali* (sin). Instead, the Buddha saw it as muddle-headed confusion (*musā*). Intriguingly, he also includes statement C in the category of "confused," though, in the West, statement C is a blatant contradiction, if both uses of *know* have identical meanings. The Buddha was thoroughly opposed to the final statement D, so much so that he viewed it as an epistemological sin (*kali*).

Historically, the Western mind tends to consider of a priori statements as timeless in some sense. "All aardvarks eat ants" and "Some aardvarks eat ants" seem opposed to one another because one is universal (all) and the other is particular (some). "Some," when placed in the context of "all," seems as though something has been left out. The Buddha, however, qualifies the logical quantifier "all" (*sabbaṃ*) with the word "this" (*idaṃ*). He makes concrete what would be an absolute statement. Now "All aardvarks" must taken in terms of "All these aardvarks." Or to give an example directly from the Buddha, he never says, "All is suffering" (*sabbaṃ dukkhaṃ*). He only says, "All this is suffering" (*sabbam idaṃ dukkhaṃ*).

The Buddha, believing that all knowledge must be inherently empirical, built his categories for rational understanding from the speaker's experience. If a speaker experiences something and communicates that experience or inductively reasons from that experience, he can give a true statement. If he denies his experience (statement B in our outline of the passage from the *Angutara-nikāya*), he is merely confused. The Buddha will not call the man's action a blatant contradiction. Nor will he call statement C a contradiction. Statement D, labeled "sin," is a direct attack on the traditions of the *Upaniṣads* and Jainas for even allowing such a statement to the table of discussion. "For the Buddha, a truly contradictory statement implies not only indescribability as this or that but also the absence

21. Ibid., 48.

of any possibility of knowing."[22] The Upaniṣadic view of being made ultimate knowledge incommunicable and unintelligible (see chapter 3). Empirical statements, however, cannot be contradicted without first abandoning the entire enterprise of knowing and communicating. The Buddha thought he had a sure thing.

So now we come to the great question: *What is the standard by which a true statement can be distinguished from contradictory or contrary statement?* Statement C prevents us from adopting a coherence theory of truth.[23] But it also keeps us from adopting a correspondence theory of truth[24] since a correspondence theory not only requires logical consistency but also claims of existence/nonexistence. Correspondence theories of truth link true/false claims with the alternatives of existence and nonexistence. As we will see in later chapters, the Buddha rejects questions of existence and nonexistence since they only lead to metaphysical speculations.

Therefore, the Buddha embraced a "pragmatic criterion of truth."[25] The truth of a thing depends on whether or not it is useful. With this in mind, statements B and C are not contradictions since they do not deny the possibility of knowledge. They are confusion (*musā*), but not epistemological sin. Violations of the Aristotelian excluded middle would fall under statement C. So we can see how Western logic runs into considerable culture shock when confronting the Buddhist system.

In the following chapter, we will examine the way that things come into being in the world. As we close this chapter, recall that in the Buddha's eyes we are to think of 'truth' in terms of "what has come

22. Ibid., 49.

23. A coherence theory of truth holds that a truth-bearer (a thought, a sentence, etc.) is true because it is logically constant with other truth-bearers. Adherents of this theory tend to see truths as forming a great web of belief. A belief is accepted as true if it is consistent with other beliefs in the web. Obviously, there are many philosophers who would hold this theory but then add their own nuance to it. For a clear introduction to the coherence theory of truth, see Scruton, *Modern Philosophy*, 101–4.

24. A correspondence theory of truth holds that a truth-bearer (a thought, a sentence, etc.) is true because in correlates in some way to some thing in the world. For example, the statement "The snow is white" is true if in fact the "snow" being referred to is in fact "white." For a clear introduction to the correspondence theory of truth, see Scruton, 99–101.

25. Kalupahana, *History of Buddhist Philosophy*, 50.

to be." "The best epistemological criterion for distinguishing what has come to be and what has not come to be is simply usefulness or utility."[26] We must recognize that even though the term 'true' (*sacca*) is related to 'become' (*bhūta*), the term 'not become' (*abhūta*) does not equate with 'false' (kali). The Buddha connects 'not becoming' with confusion (*musā*). So the Buddha's system of logic is not absolutist, but instead "allows for change and creativity."[27] Utility is thus free to guide our development of logic. Whatever becomes, *that* is useful to us. If it has not yet become, then it is fiction, and useless.

CONCLUSION

We have covered a great deal of important ground in this chapter. We first examined the Traditionalist and Rationalist epistemologies, coming to understand why the Buddha saw benefits in the Experientialist position. He based his theory of knowledge on radical empiricism[28], proving causality through inductive inference. But radical empiricism leads to the abandoning of metaphysical claims. For this reason, the Buddha's empiricism also led to a new conception of truth and logic, cast in terms of pragmatism. The goal of that pragmatism, we shall see later, is the end of suffering (*dukkha*).

26. Ibid., 51.
27. Ibid., 52.
28. Radical empiricism is Kalupahana's own term. See Ibid.

6

Causality: The Heart of Buddhism

And what, bhikkhus is dependent origination? 'With birth as condition, aging-and-death [comes to be]': whether there is an arising of Tathāgatas [or enlightened ones] or no arising of Thatāgatas, that element still persists, the stableness of the Dhamma, the fixed course of the Dhamma., specific conditionality. A Thatāgata awakens to this and breaks through it. Having done so, he explains it, teaches it, proclaims it, establishes it, discloses it, analyzes it, elucidates it. And he says: 'See!

Saṃyutta-nikāya 2.25

And in the generations gone by He permitted all the nations to go their own ways; and yet He did not leave Himself without witness, in that He did good and gave you rains from heaven and fruitful seasons, satisfying your hearts with food and gladness.

Acts 14:16–17

INTRODUCTION

In the previous chapter, we saw that through radical empiricism the Buddha inferred that everything arises from previous causes. This chapter will explore what 'causality' entails within the Buddha's perspective. Causality is Buddhism's central doctrine and the backbone of the Four Noble Truths. We learned in the last chapter that this highest truth the Buddha called *paṭiccasamuppāda,* "dependent arising." Most books on comparative religion begin their exposition of Buddhism with the Four Noble Truths. But we are examining the philosophical structure of Buddhism and how it developed in its own dependent arising, so we must step back into the philosophy that the Four Noble Truths presuppose. We begin with the Buddha's view of *nonabsolutist causal uniformity.*

Once we have a right understanding of causal law in the universe, we will naturally grasp the three marks of existence (see chapter 7), namely: impermanence (*anicca,* Sk. *anitya*), the lack of a soul (*anatta*), and suffering (*dukkha*). The Four Noble Truths that end ignorance and bring enlightenment follow from an understanding of these three marks of existence, and so the Truths hinge on the principle of causality. The Buddha believed his rigorous empiricism would protect those who wanted to end their suffering from speculations that gave no help.

THE BUDDHA'S CAUSAL THEORY

Buddhist causal theory involves two concepts: (1) the principle of causality (*paṭiccasamppāda.* Skt. *pratītiasamupāda*) and the product of previous conditions, and (2) the causally conditioned phenomena themselves (*paṭiccasamuppanna dhamma*).[1] These two principles, according to the Buddha, explain the arising of all phenomena and are the key to understanding all reality.

Before we embark on understanding the Buddhist view of causality, we should grasp the three competing theories of this era. These theories were: (1) self-causation (*sayaṃ kataṃ*), (2) ex-ternal causation (*paraṃ kataṃ*), and (3) a combination of both self and external causation (*sayaṃ katañ ca paraṃ katañ ca*).

As was already explained in chapter 3, the Brahmanists held that the 'Self' (*ātman*) was the unifying causal principle, immanent in everything. Since everything is ultimately *ātman,* the Brahmanist had little choice. The 'Self' was the final explanation of all causal process since *ātman* underlies all reality—not just personal consciousness, but everything as a whole (*sarvaṃ*). Since this school

1. Kalupahana, *Buddhist Philosophy,* 93.

did not admit to any type of causality outside of the 'Self', causality within this system is an internal relation.[2]

The second group, the Naturalists, held to an external theory of causality. Rejecting Upaniṣadic speculations, the Naturalists believed that phenomena has an 'inherent nature' (*svabhāva*) and that this 'inherent nature' was the regulating factor behind the operations of nature. Man himself is governed and directed by this physical principle so that he is ultimately not responsible for his choices as we saw in chapter 1. The Naturalists envisioned causality as a strictly external relation[3] between particulars with a fixed essence.

The Jainas held the third view, combining the self and external causality and maintaining the metaphysical assumptions of both views.

Though close to the Naturalist theory of causality, the Buddha saw enough of a difference to coin a new term to describe his view of causality (*paṭiccasamuppāda*). The differences between the Buddha's view and the Naturalists' are twofold. First, the Buddha's view applies to more than physical causation. Later scholastics, looking at what the Buddha said, classified five realms[4] in which the law of causation accurately accounts for arising and cessation. They are: (1) the physical organic order (*utu-niyāma*), (2) the inorganic physical order (*bīja-niyāma*), (3) the sphere of thought or mental life (*citta-niyāma*), (4) the social or moral sphere (*kamma-niyāma*), and (5) the higher spiritual life (*dhamma-niyāma*).

Note that in the West we see the interaction of these realms as a problem. Take as examples the mind-body problem, or the problem of accounting for moral value within materialistic naturalism. The Buddha viewed causality as exerting influence from one realm to

2. 'Internal relation' refers to a situation where what a thing is depends on what another thing is in itself. In other words, the essence of one item is what it is because of the essence of another item. Josiah Roice, F. H. Bradley, and others held this view regarding the world. In xRy, the relation R connects x and y in such a way that they must really be the same item since their essences can not be separated while still remaining the same things. Therefore, this view leads to a strong monism.

3. An 'external relation' is a relationship between items where the essence of the items is unaffected. Atoms were at one time thought to be the irreducible components of nature. At that time, their interaction was considered an external relation.

4. Kalupahana, *Buddhist Philosophy*, 30.

another. Another note about these five realms or spheres: If causal law accurately accounts for all relations within and between each realm, then the truth regarding causal relations in one order must also be a truth that applies to another order. What is true of causality in the physical organic order must also be true of mental life, or the social or moral sphere. If this is not the case, then the claim of causal law accounting for each of these realms becomes unintelligible.

The second difference separating the Buddha from the Naturalists is Buddha's rejection of 'inherent nature' that predetermines the resulting causal nexus leading to a fixed determinism. Instead, the Buddha thought of causation more in terms of conditionality, recognizing the multiplicity of causes bearing on any one event.

The importance of the Buddha's conception of causality cannot be overstated. It is the central philosophy of Buddhism and its highest truth. This highest truth of causality, *paṭiccasamuppāda*, is the empirical claim that every event arises from causes. As noted previously, this term receives many translations, including "interdependent co-origination," "co-dependent arising," "dependent arising," "dependent origination." It is the Buddha's doctrine of dependent orginination which permits him to drop any need for a divine being. A "talk of God" is not necessary for him to explain any particular event in his worldview.[5] Each event is the sum product of all events in the cosmos.

In the "Discourse on Causal Relations,"[6] the Buddha gives four characteristics of causation:

1. objectivity (*tathatā*),
2. necessity (*avitathatā*),
3. invariability (*anaññathatā*), and
4. conditionality (*idappaccayatā*).[7]

'Objectivity' refers to the status of causal relationships as descriptive of the phenomena presented to us. Causality does not refer to a subjective state or a projection we place on the world,

5. Williams, *Buddhist Thought*, 47.

6. *Paccaya-sutta*, *Saṃyutta-nikāya*, 2.25 ff.

7. For a detailed discussion of the characteristics of causality, see Kalupahana, *Causality*, 90–96.

as possible in Upaniṣadic thought. At one point the Buddha was asked who fashioned this theory of causality. He responded, "It was neither made by me nor by another. Whether the Tathāgatas (or Buddhas) were to arise in this world or not, this pattern of things (*fa chieh* = *dhammadātu*) is eternally existent."[8] So the Buddha did not consider causality to be a product of the mind but, instead, a real trait of the world. In fact, the word *tathatā*, translated here as 'objectivity', refers more to 'correspondence' in the early Buddhist texts.[9] So causality must not be seen as a disconnected theory, but as a notion that directly corresponds to our findings in nature.

Regarding the second characteristic of the causal nexus, namely necessity, the fifth century Buddhist systematizer, Buddhaghosa said, "Since there is no failure, even for a moment, to produce the events that arise when the conditions come together, there is said to be 'necessity.'"[10]

'Invariability' also characterizes causality but in a different way. Everything that arises has multiple causes. In fact, the same event can never happen twice since the identical causal situation never occurs twice. 'Invariability' in Buddhist texts does not refer to the nature of causes and effects but instead refers to the regular relationships between causes and effects. A constant relationship stands between causes of a certain type and effects of a certain type.

With necessity and invariability, no event could possibly fall outside the pattern of causality. "Events that appear to follow no causal pattern, events that are generally called accidental occurrences, are not really so. Merely our ignorance of the causal pattern prompts us to consider them accidental."[11]

The fourth characteristic, 'conditionality', Buddhaghosa defines as, "From the condition or group of conditions that gives rise to such states as decay and death there is said to be conditionality."[12] This means that a thing or event will only be if the conditions are

8. *Taishō Shinshu Daizōkyō* 2.85 b-c (*Tsa a-han ching* 30.16) in Ibid., 92. Here I break my normal policy of citing only the Pali canon because "This short but very important sutra does not appear in a Pali version." Kalupahana, *Causality*, 210.

9. Ibid., 93.

10. *Samyutta-aṭṭhakathā* 2.41, quoted in Ibid.

11. Kalupahana, *Buddhist Philosophy*, 28.

12. *Samyutta-aṭṭhakathā* 2.41, quoted in Kalupahana, *Causality*, 94.

right for its arising. While strict determinism involves a direct and necessary connection between cause and effect, it neglects the sense of 'conditions' that are helpful to those of us who live in the world, face decisions, and make plans. The Buddha tries to avoid the two extremes of fatalism and accidentalism, the first removing the freedom to choose and the latter assuming an arbitrary view of the will.

These characteristics describe the Buddha's view of causality, which he expounds through this formulaic refrain that appears in the early discourses:

> When this is present, that comes to be;
> From the arising of this, that arises.
> When this is absent, that does not come to be;
> On the cessation of this, that ceases.[13]

We began the chapter by looking at the causal theories at the time of the Buddha. Though close to the Materialists, he believed that causality referred to more than just physical events and he also rejected inherent nature. Codependent-origination (*paṭiccasamuppāda*), the Buddha believed, accounts for all relationships between the five spheres of reality. Objectivity, invariability, necessity and conditionality characterize the application of this causal law.

THE MIDDLE WAY OF PHENOMENA

The Buddha believed his understanding avoided the extremes of annihilation and immutability. On the one hand, by forming our concepts in light of experience we see that things are changed rather than ultimately destroyed. Yet no item or idea remains unaffected by the changing world, so our empiricism leads us to the rejection of immutability (existence). The Buddha's empiricism collapses the absolute distinction between sensations produced by an "objective" external world and the perceptions of one's own private inner being. Buddhism leads to a middle path between the two opposite poles.

The Buddha maintained this middle path by adhering to the radical empiricism discussed in the previous chapter. This Buddhist proto-positivism rejects metaphysical speculations. In the centuries

13. Kalupahana, *Buddhist Philosophy*, 28.

following the Buddha, questions arose among the followers of the Buddha's teachings as to what actually was the fundamental nature of causality. A scholastic side of Buddhism developed called *Abhidharma*, which pursued debates over the "mechanics" of causality and impermanence. They postulated that reality was comprised of staccato moments or flashes (*dhammā*) in which reality (*dharma*) would arise. Reality continually changes and demonstrates impermanence since each new moment of reality arises to take the place of the old. Theodore Stcherbatsky presents this view of staccato moments as the actual Buddhist theory of reality, but Kalupahana argues that the early texts do not suggest this view of causation.[14] In fact, the eighth century Hindu philosopher Śaṅkara criticized this view:

> Those who maintain that everything has a momentary existence only admit that when the thing existing in the second moment enters into being the thing in the first moment ceases to be. On this admission it is impossible to establish between the two things the relation of cause and effect, since the former momentary existence ceases or has ceased to be, and so has entered into the state of non-existence, cannot be the cause of the later momentary existence.[15]

Early Buddhism did not isolate the elements involved in causal relationships into discrete moments. Instead, the Buddha attempted to prove causal conjunction empirically, dissuading his followers from metaphysical investigation. The Upaniṣadic effort to unite *ātman* and *Brahman* did nothing to alleviate suffering. This is why the Buddha advocated that his own students test his words to see for themselves if his understanding of the operation of the world was correct, thus, breaking the Vedic epistemic stalemate.

In considering our own mental and external perceptions, we realize that certain states tend to associate themselves with prior conditions. The Buddha did not look for some common substance underlying reality. Indeed, his epistemology does not permit that type of knowledge. So the Buddha's view of causal relations does not claim an insight into the fundamental nature of things in themselves,

14. Kalupahana, *Causality*, 70.

15. *Śaṅkara-bhāṣya* on *Brahma-sūtra* 2.2.20 quoted in Ibid., 72.

per se, or in Pali, *svabhāva.* Our senses never give us insight into things in themselves.

Knowledge is comprised of two things: sensation or name (*nāma*) and material body or form (*rūpa*). *In The Great Discourse on Origination,*[16] the Buddha designates reality as *nāma-rūpa,* which is translated as 'mind-and-body.' The discourse discusses the *nāma* and *rūpa* components separately.[17] But it does not use the term *components.* Maurice Walshe renders the phrase *nāma-kāya* as mind-factor and *rūpa-kāya* as body-factor. The mental component that makes up phenomena cannot be separated from the physical. Here 'body' refers to all that we would think of in terms of material form, extended in space. These two aspects of phenomena are seen more as factors of consciousness.

In the West, one's cultural common sense tells the westerner that she or he has a mind that is not quite the same as the material we sense around us. The Buddha wants us to think of the surrounding world in terms of sense perception thought about by minds. Consciousness results from the contact that the senses make, but that contact itself is conditioned by the mind and the material form of what we call the world. As *rūpa* (material form) seems to go through the changes of 'becoming' and 'not-becoming' so does *nāma* (mind or name).

The great German philosopher Immanuel Kant took a somewhat similar approach. Kant tried to explain the underlying causes of the appearance of the world, what he called *phenomena.* He described phenomena as the result of the noumenal mind (the mind as it really is) and the noumenal world (the world as it really is) working together. He thought that the underlying "real" world did not *really* "look like" what it looks like to human beings. However, in the end, Kant's philosophical outlook demands the conclusion that it is ultimately impossible to understand the noumena, the real. Many philosophers after Kant drew from his philosophy a warrant for skepticism. Now, the Buddha's perspective is comparable to Kant's while also being quite different. It is comparable in that *nāma-kāya* and *rūpa-kāya* are the two factors of phenomena (*nāma-*

16. Quoting the *Mahānidāna Sutta,* in Walshe, *Long Discourses of the Buddha.*

17. *Dīgha-nikāya.* 2.62

rūpa). Nevertheless, the Buddha differed strongly with Kant in that he rejected absolutism and would, therefore, never postulate a noumenal mind or noumenal world. Since Rene Descartes, Western philosophy had aimed at a goal: the high standard of Cartesian certainty. But the Buddha did not share this goal. Instead, he wanted to end *dukkha,* which he believes is an immediate empirical reality. He did not demand that knowledge be built on certainty, only utility. In his view, understanding the nature of *Nāma-rūpa* (phenomena) will not lead to skepticism, but only to the realization that trying to make an ever-changing world permanent is chasing after the wind.

The Buddha differs not only with Kant's essentialism but also with his view of causation. Kant held that what we call 'causality' was a mental category. But the Buddha believed that *nāma-rūpa* was conditioned by consciousness and vice-versa.[18] Since he believed consciousness was the result of contact with the senses, that awareness of sensation cannot be separated from the interactive factors of mind-and-body (*nāma-rūpa*). However, this interaction of the mental and physical factors of phenomena involves conditionality. Every event has prior causes called conditions. In the Buddha's view, causality is not a mere product of consciousness, but, in fact, the very account of the origin of consciousness. *Paṭiccasamuppāda* is not a product of our minds. *It describes the way phenomcna really are.*

NO METAPHYSICAL SPECULATIONS

I hope my last sentence seemed a bit strange. When we in the West hear "phenomena" we tend to think of something less than real. We have a strong absolutist tradition, going back thousands of years. In considering the Buddhist position, we approach it through our own categories, and, if done carelessly, we may suspect the Buddha of throwing away reality all together.

Remember chapter 3 discussed the Upaniṣadic view of the 'Self' (*ātman*). As the Upaniṣadic-influenced Indian examined the world, he saw that everything in his life was an aspect of the 'Self'. Think of it. Everything! The capacity of his cognitive faculties and tree bark are each an aspect of the one. Western philosophers may take the phrase "all are one" as an anti-logical proposition. But the

18. *Dīgha-nikāya.* 2.56.

Upaniṣadic sages saw it with their eyes, touched it with their hands; it interpreted their going out and their coming in. They understood those words in terms of their own experience of life and cognition. Many Western minds want to reduce all knowledge to the categories of physics. Well, imagine if we reject the idea of distinct matter. To what categories would we reduce the world then? The Upaniṣadic thinkers did not have a two thousand year old scientific culture behind them. They had an understanding of the 'Self' that extended into the world and unified all reality and knowledge.

The Buddha casts off this theorizing in search of the end of *dukkha*. When he deduced that *dukkha* had causes, he felt no reason to justify connections between matter, mind, and spirit. If his opponents held that all these are expressions of *ātman*, why should he not feel perfectly justified in examining them all as phenomena governed by causal law? When a thing causes suffering, the question of its ontological status in regard to other realities does not matter to the Buddha. Whether real or appearance, this life is still *dukkha*. The things that cause suffering stay close to us.

The Buddha believed his epistemology broke the stalemate of Vedic-Upaniṣadic thought. His epistemology leaves no opportunity to know anything outside of that described by *paṭiccasamuppāda* (dependent arising). Whether something exists beyond *nāma* and *rūpa*, we cannot know. Questions about *ātman* or *Brahman*—or the deity of Christ—cannot be considered since they cannot be verified by radical empiricism. No one can observe any pattern of causal conjunction that provides a criterion of falsifiability for metaphysical claims.

CONCLUSION

Doctrines, as linguistically expressed beliefs, assume the use of language. If phenomena are the only knowable thing, then phenomena are the only thing we can name. But if we understand *paṭiccasamuppāda*, we recognize that words often trick us since every time we use a word we assume that its referent has not changed since the last time the word was used. Whenever we try to create permanence, we postulate something beyond our experience, and lead ourselves into greater suffering. Even the concepts behind our words are not absolute. Our next chapter will explore the Buddhist understanding of existence. To recap this chapter we close with an appropriate summary, the last paragraph from Kalupahana's own analysis of Causality:

> Rejecting an Absolute (such as the *Brahman* or *Ātman* of the *Upaniṣads*) or a transempirical reality, the Buddha confined himself to what is empirically given. Following a method comparable to that adopted by the modern Logical Positivists, he sometimes resorted to linguistic analysis and appeal to experience to demonstrate the futility of metaphysics. As a result of his empiricism he recognized causality as the reality and made it the essence to his teaching. Hence his statement: "He who sees causality sees the dhamma."[19]

19. *Causality*, 185.

7

The Three Marks of Existence and the Five Aggregates

Therefore, bhikkhus, any kind of material form whatever, whether past, future, or present, internal or external, gross or subtle, inferior or superior, far or near, all consciousness should be seen as it actually is with proper wisdom thus: "This is not mine, this I am not, this is not my self." Any kind of feeling whatever. . . . Any kind of perception whatever. . . . Any kind of consciousness whatever, whether past, future, or present, internal or external, gross or subtle, inferior or superior, far or near, all consciousness should be seen as it actually is with proper wisdom thus: "This is not mine, this I am not, this is not my self."

Alagaddūpama Sutta, Majjhima-Nikāya 1.139–40

I know that everything God does will remain forever; there is nothing to add to it and there is nothing to take from it, for God has so *worked that men should fear Him. That which is has been already, and that which will be has already been, for God seeks what has passed by.*

Ecclesiastes 3:14–15

INTRODUCTION

We have come a long way. We have covered the Buddha's epistemology and his account of causality, *paṭiccasamuppāda* (dependent arising). The three marks of existence—impermanence (*anicca*, Sk. *anitya*), its unsatisfactory nature (*dukkha*), its non-substantiality, or lack of 'self' (*anatta*)—naturally follow from *paṭiccasamuppāda*, so we should see this chapter as a continuation of the last. Our journey is not yet over.

IMPERMANENCE

No sane man can doubt the impermanent and transitory nature of life. Babies grow up. Men get old and die. Companies that seemed so secure lay off workers. Banks that seemed so secure one day implode the next. Marriages that seemed so secure, so full of happiness, end in divorce or death. These examples of impermanence are like the big 'E' on the eye chart—obvious examples of impermanence that directly follow from the constant causal flux of life.

However, the Buddha took impermanence beyond the daily grind of life, recognizing that if *paṭiccasamuppāda* accounted for all phenomena, then it accounted for the five realms of existence (chapter 6): the physical organic order (*utu-niyāma*), the inorganic physical order (*bīja-niyāma*), the sphere of thought or mental life (*citta-niyāma*), the social or moral sphere (*kamma-niyāma*), and the higher spiritual life (*dhamma-niyāma*). All existence arises and diminishes in constant causal conjunction. Things and people come into being and pass away.

DUKKHA

This leads to the second mark of existence, *dukkha*. In the brief summary of the Four Noble Truths at the beginning of chapter 5, we learned that *dukkha* refers to that unsatisfactory quality of life. Now we see that the lack of satisfaction comes from the impermanent nature of the world. "Suffering" in some ways is too strong a word, in other ways too weak. *Saṃsāra*, the perpetual cycle of reincarnation, is the 'wheel of suffering' where you can once again relive the pains of this life. All the torture and shattered dreams are yours again. So *dukkha* has a range of meanings, all unpleasant.

Dukkha results from our own "grasping" of existence, trying to make things permanent. Human nature tends to grasp onto or put faith in things to acquire hope, safety, satisfaction, or whatever the case may be. But *paṭiccasamuppāda* (dependent arising), which brought that item into "being," will also dissolve in our grasp. That empty clutching hand of the soul is craving (*taṇhā*).[1] 1 We will grasp onto many things—other people, objects, ideas, nations, and memories—but all of them will dissolve. We will want them back, but they will never come back. And if something similar returns, by necessity it arose into existence by different causes so it must by causal origin be a different item. A man's wife may die, leaving him with a little daughter to parent alone. Yet the maturing of the daughter into the likeness of her mother does not replace his beloved wife. She may even remind him of the woman he lost.

NO SELF OR SUBSTANCE

One may say, "At least *I* am still myself. *I* suffer the loss." But the causal principle necessitates that our own person is also subject to arising and cessation, hence the third mark of existence, no self (*anatta*). The Buddha went further than the obvious fact that all the born will die. He argued that no one could ever prove the existence of a permanent 'Self' (*ātman*). Anything we may try to point to, he thought, would fall into the five spheres of existence. Causal law applies to them all, a law that he believed he had proven empirically. This causal law describes the constant change of existence. Therefore, even perceived mental moments are arisen phenomena that will cease at some point.

Our physical body changes as it ages. So the primary evidence that one has for one's personal identity over time is one's personal memories. In fact, it is through one's memories that one makes sense of photo evidence and other external evidences that a person retains his or her personal identity through time. The Buddha argues that the notion of a 'permanent soul' is a non-referring concept, a concept that has no pertaining reality in the world. But even if there were a soul we could never know it since it cannot be empirically verified. To what permanent thing could one point showing that we have a changeless aspect to our being? Even our beliefs change over time, along with the gaining and forgetting of different memories. Even our appearance changes a little each day.

1. Thomas, *History of Buddhist Thought*, 59.

All this led the Buddha to conclude a position of no 'self' (*anatta*). Instead he explains the individual as composed of five aggregates (*khandas*, literally "heap" or "bundle"): body or material form (*rūpa*), feeling or sensation (*vedanā*), perception (*saññā*), dispositions (*saṅkhārā*), and consciousness (*viññāṇa*).

Body or material form (*rūpa*) is the physical personality—what we commonly use to distinguish one person from another. Clearly, the body comes into being through conception and birth and ceases to be at death. (Interestingly, the early discourses mention nothing of an immaterial personality.) *Rūpa* refers to the sense organs and also the external physical sources for their stimuli.

Feeling or sensation (*vedanā*) denotes the emotional factor resulting from sense contact with the *rūpa* perceived as external to us. All things sensed are pleasurable, painful, or neutral. Ethical needs result from these feelings (more in chapter 8).

Perception (*saññā*), the act of perceiving, like the feeling of sensation, affects all the person in that our perception provides the content for our consciousness. Kalupahana writes, "Each of our perceptions is a mixed bag of memories, concepts, dispositions, and material elements. The Buddha or any subsequent Buddhist psychologist who has remained faithful to the Buddha does not recognize a pure percept, undiluted by such conditions. *A pure percept is as metaphysical as pure* a priori *category*."[2]

Dispositions (*saṅkhārā*), the volitional "bundle" of the individual, put the mind in action. Resulting from dispositions, we commit acts of *Karmic* value and perpetuate our stay on the wheel of *saṃsāra*.

Finally, consciousness (*viññāṇa*) results as the activity of contact between the senses and the external world. Six types of consciousness arise, each coterminous with the eye, ear, nose, tongue, body, and mind. Consciousness means awareness of the outside world, not identification, which is a function of perception (the third aggregate).

The aggregates ought not to be thought of as interactive substances. Instead, they are categories of phenomena. In the end they all may be reduced to *nāma* and *rūpa* (name and form, or mind

2. *History of Buddhist Philosophy*, 71; emphasis mine.

and body). Remember that *nāma-rūpa* is the Buddhist term for phenomena.

Nonsubstantiality not only describes the individual person but also the substance of the universe. Returning to radical empiricism, the Buddha believed that the content of knowledge is only sense experience. Even when people communicate knowledge, the meaning of their words must connect directly to sense impressions of the world. We can never separate the world as it is from the way it funnels into our own particular senses. Therefore, we must understand the six elements, earth (*pahavi*), water (*āpo*), fire (*tejo*), air (*vāyu*), space (*ākāsa*), and consciousness (*viññāṇa*), as phenomena—not as though we have a concrete understanding of essences outside ourselves. The Buddha defined the six elements in terms of human experience.

CONCLUSION

In this chapter we applied the Buddha's doctrine of causality to the rest of life. Dependent arising (*paṭiccasamuppāda*) necessarily concludes the impermanence or existence. Any attempt to find satisfaction in this impermanent whirl of phenomena leads to *dukkha* (dissatisfaction). We cannot even take confidence in a permanent self or a permanent world. The Buddha accounted for non-substantial existence with the five aggregates and interpreted the elements of the universe in terms of personal experience.

8

Karma and Ethics

[K]amma *is the field, consciousness the seed, and craving the moisture for their consciousness to be established in an inferior realm.*

Aṅguttara-nikāya 1.223

[I]t is appointed for men to die once and after this comes judgment . . .

Hebrews 9:27

INTRODUCTION

The Buddha knew what he wanted. He knew his goal. Because he wanted to end suffering, his goal naturally led him to a search for the causes of suffering. We cannot hope to understand his goal without examining his view of karma and the possible foundation for a nonabsolutist ethical system based within a world characterized by dependent arising (*paṭiccasamuppāda*).

KARMA

The Buddha believed that the karmic cycle of birth and death explained the cause of suffering. In our historical introduction, we saw how the Vedic tradition viewed karma. They considered it a kind of morality money; the inescapable earnings which curse one to live incarnation after incarnation. Being an aspect of *ātman* means consciousness and volition, two concepts that quickly lead to a need to weigh the moral value of a person's chosen actions. Without a God figure to distribute final judgment, they accounted for justice as the direct result of the recipient's own actions.

The word karma literally means "deed" or "action." What we call theories of karma are simply theories that account for justice in the world on the basis of our actions without the need of a personal being passing judgment.

Karma sounds to us like a metaphysical concept. If a Western philosopher considers the proto-positivist position held by the Buddha, he or she might be puzzled as to why the Buddha ever embraced it. As we have discussed, original Buddhism held that there was no 'self' (*anatta*). E. J. Thomas and many others have taken the Buddha's defense of karma as a cultural blind spot.[1] Kalupahana believes that the Buddha did not assume karma blindly: "A college student may take certain scientific theories to be true because he finds them in a textbook on science. But a competent scientist does not do this."[2] Apparently the Buddha empirically verified the existence of karma through inference based on extrasensory perception.

Be this as it may, by drawing an analogy between the Buddha and a learned scientist, Kalupahana opens himself to Thomas Kuhn's criticism in *The Structure of Scientific Revolutions*. The "competent" scientist receives his adjudication from textbooks and papers published at the time. The community of scientists makes their living based on what is recognized as responsible science. Scientists regularly take for granted the content of textbooks; in fact, they must. How can anyone possibly verify all the "facts" in even a beginning chemistry textbook? This is impossible, which is why the chemist must stand on the shoulders of Democritus, Aristotle, Roger Bacon, Lavoisier, and Bohr. Each of these men would not necessarily have agreed with each other.[3] Each had to challenge the good science of his day in some particular way. Jayatilleke and

1. "Buddhism in Modern Times," 216.

2. *Buddhist Philosophy*, 45.

3. Bacon did not agree with Aristotle although he should have. See Collender, "Complexity and Hermeneutic Phenomenology."

Kalupahana both argue that the Buddha must not have assumed karma without question. Yet their arguments seem weak in light of the overwhelming evidence that previous paradigms influence subsequent thinkers, especially in the sciences. The Greek rejection of infinity prevented Archimedes from discovering calculus in the third century *B.C.* Aristotelian science stunted the development of an elliptical heliocentric solar model. Chapter 3 demonstrated how the Brahmanist doctrine of karma arose out of previously held assumptions about the relationship between God and creation. There is plenty of evidence for this trend. One must work very hard not to be influenced by hidden assumptions. One of our modern foibles is the propensity to think the contemporary outlook better than the perspective of previous generations and this outlook leads us to forget our history.

In the same way, Jayatilleke and Kalupahana show themselves to be men of their century. The modern period has propounded the meme of the daring, autonomous scientist who somehow empirically verifies all truth apart from assumptions. Jayatilleke and Kalupahana buy into this meme, something easy and fashionable to do in the twentieth and early twenty-first centuries. Could not the Buddha have done the same thing by accepting the perspective of his own age?

Even though the idea of karma without *ātman* seems strange, we can still investigate its purpose in the Buddha's scheme of things. In *The Shorter Exposition of Action*[4] and *The Greater Exposition of Action*[5] the Buddha presents his view that good and bad actions have a necessary causal result in conditioning favorable and unfavorable incarnations. *The Greater Exposition* shows that the Buddha did believe that meditation cleared the mind to 'see' how certain individuals would reincarnate depending on their choices. These texts give no causal account as to the mechanism that connects our actions with our future fate.

Though confident in the doctrine of reincarnation, the Buddha gave no account of what connects one incarnation to another. He also did not explain what actually is reincarnated if there is no 'Self'

4. *Cūḷakammavibhanga Sutta*, from *Majjhima-nikāya* 3.202–206.

5. *Mahākammavibhanga Sutta*, from *Majjhima-nikāya* 3.207–215.

(*ātman*). The Buddha believed that the continuity of the psycho-physical personality must be understood in terms of the continuity of perceived moments and, therefore, the continuity between a person's incarnations are memories of the past life. Yet the karma that the previous life produced still affects the "whatever it is" that receives the previous memories.

One can see that the doctrine of no "self" (*anatta*) makes the explanation of karma much more difficult. However, since the Buddha wants to end suffering, the kind of suffering produced by the wheel of *saṃsāra*, therefore to do that he must find a way to keep from committing actions that have *karmic* value. Even though he does not hold the same metaphysical concepts as the Vedic thinkers, he still held a similar notion of karma as the value of volitional actions. By our own dispositions (the fourth of the five aggregates), we cause the development of karma. Therefore, actions that involve Self and craving must be abandoned to halt the generation of karma. If one knows the causes of suffering, one can stop them. Karma is a cause, and the Buddha says we can put an end to it.

Even though karma without *ātman* is a huge problem in Buddhist metaphysics, In my view, one can still make Buddhism work without the doctrine of karma. The idea of understanding the causes of suffering and putting an end to them does not necessitate that suffering be related to *karmic* effects. Even though I have been somewhat critical of karma, it is safe to say such things in this sympathetic exposition section because I believe Buddhism can be discussed intelligibly without karma if it is modified as a secular system of ending the causes of pain in one's life. In my view, this problem does not necessarily defeat or destroy Buddhism.

ETHICS

Ideology and agenda inevitably meet in ethics. Certainly Buddhist ethics present no exception. The Buddha's philosophical approach aids his goal of ending *dukkha*. However, the 'truths' he has discovered need feet. They must be put into practice. If causality (*paṭiccasamuppāda*) describes everything, then we can act on the causes of our suffering to bring an end to dissatisfaction.

Apprehending the teaching (*dhamma*), though first realized in a moment, will involve the exercise of one's entire life.

The Buddha's theory of karma retained reincarnation and the causal connection between the individual's actions and his future fate. Therefore, his solution to *dukkha*'s causes must also apply to *karmic* theory. He believed the individual's own acts of craving were causally connected to the quality of incarnation he would enjoy. So putting an end to suffering meant putting an end to suffering in this and the next life. John Dewey thought that morals seek escape from the hazards of existence.[6] The hazards, in the Buddha's view, are all the various causes of dissatisfaction.

In much of ancient philosophy, morality and the good life seem intrinsically connected, though not the same. The biblical Book of Proverbs presents the fear of Israel's God as the beginning of even moral knowledge (Proverbs 1:7a). This knowledge required instruction in Torah (Proverbs 1:7b). Proverbs is clear in advocating the life of dependence on divine counsel as the one that brings the greatest satisfaction and pleasure. No one can read through the Book of Proverbs and conclude anything else. Aristotle also recognized this connection between moral law and the good life, in that happiness guides the Golden Mean.[7] Even though the ethical systems of the Book of Proverbs and Aristotle approach ethics from different worldviews, they both accept that morality and the good life cannot be divided.[8]

The Buddha's goal-oriented empiricism also makes the connection between morality and the good life, but, unlike Aristotle, the Buddha has a distinct goal in mind that motivates all ethical formulas. The Buddha's goal in terms of *karmic* theory is the attainment of freedom from birth and, thus, the avoidance of death and decay as part of ending *dukkha*.

For a man to free himself from *dukkha* and rebirth, he must live a life that has constant causal influence on the causes of his *dukkha*. This means the creation of a self-culture of moral rectitude that perpetually works in bringing freedom, a goal that one achieves

6. *The Quest for Certainty*, 3.

7. In Aristotle's corpus, compare 1104a 10–25 with 1097b 21.

8. They assume this because both of their philosophies emphasize particularity.

gradually because of one's own trailing *karmic* baggage. Since the goal of Buddhism is this personal liberation (*nirvāṇa*) from *dukkha*, Buddhist ethics serve this personal goal. In other words, the good life goes before morality, qualifying the meaning of morality.

As we saw earlier, perceptions have a component of emotion that arises as our senses contact the nonsubstantial world. This emotional content is pleasurable, painful, or neutral. Kalupahana, at the beginning of his own ethical treatise, says that people "experience difficulty in accounting for certain feelings and aspirations, especially those relating to freedom, the latter being the foundation of all moral philosophy."[9] Thus, ethics deals with the phenomena of feelings that arise from sense contact.

The Buddha took feelings a step further, seeing a connection between the emotions and the dispositions. By our own choice, our dispositions crave things that we find satisfying or pleasing. However, as mentioned earlier, nothing in this world is permanent. The Buddha's ethical formula seeks to preserve the wellbeing of the practitioner. The system "lives" for him, not he for the system. The Buddhist ethic rests on nothing beyond the man or woman who chooses to adopt it. Its goal is *nirvāṇa*, which one can only attain as an individual. No one can bring *nirvāṇa* to another.

Since the Buddha's ethical system works for the betterment of the individual, we may consider it a utilitarian ethical system with one proviso. Philosophically speaking, when we think of Utilitarianism we think of Jeremy Bentham, John Stuart Mill, and phrases like "the greatest happiness for the greatest number of people." We tend to think of happiness in terms of a refined and respectful pleasure. We see happiness in terms of how we treat one another, justice, charity, etc. However, external conditions do nothing to serve the cessation of *dukkha*. *Dukkha* comes from within as we hanker for satisfaction from the ever-changing, nonsubstantial phenomena that results from sense contact. The Buddha taught that we must learn to control our own internal desire to grasp and make things permanent, for this action itself is the cause of karma. Believing the struggle for *nirvāṇa* to be an internal one, he abandoned strict asceticism,

9. *Ethics in Early Buddhism*, 3.

thinking it profitless for ending *dukkha*, choosing a 'middle way' between asceticism and the decadence he had once known.

The terms 'right' and 'wrong' in Buddhism correlate to the earlier discussion of epistemology. The Buddha rejected the absolute of 'true and false' for 'true and confused', since he developed a pragmatic system of logic. In the same way, he did not view 'right' with the same vibrant absolutist ethical force that it retains in the West. He saw it in a more contextual pragmatic sense. The Buddha's word for 'right' (*Sammā*) has more the sense of "complete," while the word for 'wrong' (*micchā*) has more the sense of the partial, of the confused. Right and wrong, then, are dependent on inter-personal context as the true and confused are dependent on empirical context.

The Buddha gave as the Fourth Noble Truth the Eightfold Noble Path. Like the Ten Commandments, the Eightfold Path is a collection of "file tabs." Buddhist ethics is not just the summary of the path, but each of the eight categories is gateway to a wealth of ethical insight and centuries of further commentary. The Eightfold Path consists of:

1. Right view (*sammā dihi*): One must have a complete perspective on morality, not the absolutist objectivity of the *Upaniṣads* or the subjectivity of the materialist. "The right view, according to the Buddha, is a middle perspective that avoids the excesses of subjectivity and objectivity."[10]

2. Right conception (*sammā saṅkappa*): A meaningful conception must reference an object that a community can agree upon, and, therefore, right conception anticipates Wittgenstein's Private Language Argument. "In this sense, the difference between a conception and a convention is reduced to a great extent."[11]

3. Right speech (*sammā vācā*): In short, don't lie! But for the philosopher who must understand and qualify his truth claims, this means making statements that are empirically verifiable. In everyday terms it means avoiding slander, falsehood, mindless chatter, harmful words, and the like. All speech should be directed toward the edification of one's 'self' and others. Edifi-

10. Kalupahana, *History of Buddhist Philosophy*, 104.

11. Ibid.

cation means speech directed toward enlightening the hearer.

4. Right action (*sammā kammanta*): What makes actions right cannot be determined by an absolute law. So the goal of happiness of one's self and others should be the goal of all actions.

5. Right livelihood (*sammā ājīva*): If we desire to end the suffering of others, then our occupations must also take compassion and consideration of others seriously. We will promote fair business, economic benefit, freedom from debt, and freedom from blame.

6. Right effort (*sammā vāyāma*): We pursue the application of the teaching (*dhamma*) and apply it to our lives. Nevertheless, an absolute law does not govern this effort. "While denying a mysterious 'ghost in the machine,' the Buddha reduced the universal and objective laws to linguistic convention, thereby accommodating an element of skepticism."[12] In ending our own grasping, the Buddha considered four types of effort:

    1. Preventive effort: not attempting to grasp conceptions of qualities and substances when sense contact occurs.
    2. Effort at relinquishing: letting go of what we have already grasped.
    3. Effort to develop: cultivating wholesome attitudes consistent with the goals of enlightenment.
    4. Effort to maintain: continuing the cultivation of what good one has already developed.

7. Right mindfulness (*sammā sati*): Retrospection, the function of the mind reconsidering what it has already perceived, aids in understanding the Buddha's teachings. By this action we can see that experience is not a series of staccato moments but a continuum of change. Retrospection involves consideration of physical personality, feelings, thoughts, and ideas. However, we ought not pursue such an inquiry to make dogmatic views about the past.

8. Right concentration (*sammā samādhi*): This involves the con-

12. Ibid., 107.

> centration upon what we have learned previously, to check what we think to be the case, so we can revise former beliefs. This way we can keep from being caught up in healthy ideas. Kalupahana adds to this analysis that, "The above analysis of concentration would mean that there is no absolutely true or real event, state, or process on which the wayfarer may focus. In the absence of absolute knowledge, constant revision of our understanding and behavior becomes inevitable."[13]

If one walks this path, he will gain the clarity and take the action necessary to end his own suffering.

REGULATIVE CONCEPTS

The Buddha's understanding was heterodox to Vedic views, which held to an objective standard for ethics and emphasized the place of divinities in the care of moral norms. Yet the Vedic gods were subject to the moral constraints that contributed to karmic debt. As such, they provided no explanation for the nature of ethics. In fact, their pursuit of sensual pleasure gives the Buddha a sermon illustration for the vanity of success within the karmic system.

The Buddha seems to have rejected belief in gods, demons, or hell *per se*. However, it is nearly impossible to completely remove the discussion of gods and demons from the Buddha's teaching. They are conceptually entangled with the Buddha's teachings.[14] It must be kept in mind though that the Hindu gods provide no real insight into the means to end suffering. As Paul Williams observes, "Buddhists have no objection to the Hindu gods. . . . Nevertheless, one cannot as a Buddhist take refuge in Hindu gods, for Hindu gods are not Buddhas, that is they are not enlightened. What this means is that Hindu gods, for all their power, do not see the final way that things are, the final truth of things. They do not see it as it is. Power does not necessarily entail insight, and for the Buddhists the Hindu gods, unlike Buddhas, do not have that insight. Thus, because they are not liberated Hindu gods too ultimately suffer." Demons are those who will suffer from their own wickedness. And ultimately 'hell' is

13. Ibid., 109.

14. See Gethin excellent discussion of this point *Foundations of Buddhism*, 130-132.

a metaphor for unpleasant feelings (*dukkha*). Thus, the Buddha saw concepts such as 'gods', 'demons', and 'hell' as *regulative* concepts. Only an uneducated ordinary man (*assutanā puthujjano*) believes in or trusts in them.[15]

CONCLUSION

This chapter presented the Buddha's teaching on karma and ethics.

Regarding karma, the Buddha taught that our actions willed from self-interest cause the karma that keeps one reincarnating. He believed that if we understood that there is no permanence and no self, we would cease self-interested grasping and end the causes that keep us suffering through each incarnation. But the Buddha could not account for a mechanism that connected our actions to the production of future *dukkha*. He also could not account for an individual's continuity to the next incarnation.

The Buddha's philosophy not only reshaped the doctrine of karma but also the ethical theory held by his followers. The ethics of early Buddhism reflect radical empiricism and pragmatism. No ethical norm can be justified beyond the Buddha's epistemology, so deontological ethics—ethics based on duty—are meaningless. For these two reasons, he views ethics in terms of lessening the *dukkha* of one's self and others. Bringing people happiness does not lend itself to absolute laws; instead, it helps people to discover what will end their *dukkha*. Now we can understand what he means when he says that even "what is good has to be abandoned, let alone evil."[16]

15. For a more detailed discussion, see Kalupahana, *Buddhist Philosophy*, 65–66.

16. *Majjhima-nikāya* 1.135. Quoted from Kalupahana, *History of Buddhist Philosophy*, 101.

9

The Big Picture: Four Noble Truths and *Nirvāṇa*

Therefore, Mālunkyaputta, remember what I have left undeclared as undeclared. And what have I left undeclared? 'The world is eternal'—I have left undeclared. 'The world is not eternal'—I have left undeclared. 'The world is finite'—I have left undeclared. 'The soul is the same as the body'—I have left undeclared. 'The soul is one thing and the body another'—I have left undeclared. After death a Tathāgata [enlightened one] exists'—I have left undeclared. 'After death a Tathāgata does not exist'—I have left undeclared. 'After death a Tathāgata both exists and does not exist'—I have left undeclared. 'After death a Tathāgata neither exists nor does not exist'—I have left undeclared.

Majjhima-nikāya, Cūḷamālunkya Sutta 1.431

It is the glory of God to conceal a matter, but the glory of kings is to search out a matter.

Proverbs 25:2

INTRODUCTION

We have gathered the appropriate blocks to finish the building. Here the Buddha will take us through to his logical conclusion, a path to a personal eschatology. His conclusions are both logically consistent with his own perspective and unspeakable.

THE FOUR NOBLE TRUTHS

Having now worked through epistemology, causality, existence, karma, and ethics, we can grasp the meaning of the Four Noble Truths. Without understanding these concepts, Buddhism becomes just another pop-psyche, self-help fad. The Buddha constructs an approach to knowledge, life, and reality that one must accept before appropriating his moral teaching. His teachings have epistemological consequences. The Buddha's words may sound like good advice, but the Buddha himself would be the first to say that his words must all be taken together to affect the ending of *dukkha*. Before discussing *nirvāṇa*—the goal of the Theravāda Buddhist practitioner—it is important to review the Four Noble Truths and put the philosophical concepts into the popular structure used to teach Buddhism.

First: Life is dukkha: We all know that this is true. From the four-year-old disappointed by what is not under the Christmas tree to the wealthy and powerful Howard Hughes who has everything and shoots himself, all men seem to see that during our lifetimes we encounter dissatisfaction. We see the hurt and suffering around us. The Buddha presented this noble truth first. As a brilliant rhetorician, he understood how to connect with the mass of humankind. Anyone can identify with dissatisfaction.

Second: Dukkha has causes: This is the great doctrine of *paṭiccasamuppāda* (dependent arising). Though not the first doctrine preached, we can now see its philosophical priority as the view, which makes suffering intelligible. As we have covered in previous chapters, the Buddha places a priority on causality (*paṭiccasamuppāda*) because he believes it holds the answer to ending suffering and dissatisfaction in life. To account for the arising of *dukkha*, which culminates in death and rebirth, he isolates the twelve factors, a chain of causality from ignorance to suffering. In the Buddha's discourse with Kaccāyana (the *Kakkāyanagotta-sutta*), he describes this chain of causality:

> Dependent upon ignorance arise dispositions; dependent upon dispositions arises consciousness; dependent upon consciousness arises the psycho-physical personality; dependent upon the psycho-physical personality arise the six senses; dependent upon the six senses arises contact; dependent upon contact

> arises feeling; dependent upon feeling arises craving; dependent upon craving arises grasping; dependent upon grasping arises becoming; dependent upon becoming arises birth; dependent upon birth arises old age and death, grief, lamentation, suffering, dejection, and despair. Thus arises this entire mass of suffering.[1]

So we can trace a pattern for the causal arising of suffering through these factors:

1. Ignorance
2. Dispositions
3. Consciousness
4. Psycho-physical personality
5. The six senses
6. Contact
7. Feeling
8. Craving
9. Grasping
10. Becoming
11. Birth
12. Old age and death, grief, lamentation, suffering, dejection, and despair. Thus arises this whole mass of suffering.

Note that these factors cross over the five spheres from our discussion of causality. They are the physical organic order (*utu-niyāma*), the inorganic physical order (*bīja-niyāma*), the sphere of thought or mental life (*citta-niyāma*), the social or moral sphere (*kamma-niyāma*), and the higher spiritual life (*dhamma-niyāma*). The Buddha applies the law of causality across the board in accounting for the origination of *dukkha*.

Third: If we know the causes of dukkha, we can put an end to them and, thus, end dukkha: Here the Buddha explains *nirvāṇa* (liberation), called *nibbāna* in the early texts. He traces the causal chain from ignorance to consciousness and so on, showing that if we cease ignorance, dispositions will also cease and so on all the way to the end. "[F]rom the ceasing of becoming, there is ceasing of birth; from the ceasing of birth, there is ceasing of old age and

1. Kalupahana, *History of Buddhist Philosophy*, 58.

death, grief, lamentation, suffering, dejection, and despair. Thus, there is the ceasing of this entire mass of suffering."[2] The resulting state, nirvāṇa, is the final subject of this chapter.

Fourth: the Noble Eightfold Path: In the previous chapter on Buddhist ethics, we sketched the path. Buddhism does not view the cessation of ignorance as merely a one-time event but instead as a constant struggle. Since life moves in perpetual change, our discipline must confront the daily challenge of our own suffering.

NIRVĀṆA

The goal of the Buddhist practitioner is nirvāṇa. We have seen that the Buddha rejected reincarnation of a permanent soul (*ātman*). Instead, somehow the process of the aggregates appears again, or at least the memories and karmic burden are somehow transferred to another individual. The Buddha used the illustration of a forest fire leaping over an interposing river to show how one can incarnate without the transfer of an essence.

With this in mind, consider that the literal meaning for *nibbāna* (Pali for *nirvāṇa*) is "blowing out." *Nibbāna* is the snuffing out of our *karmic* fire. The Buddha refused to offer speculation about this state, which has frustrated Buddhist scholars. The texts treat *nibbāna* enigmatically. In this short conclusion to our exposition of early Buddhism, we shall try to understand what he means by "blowing out."

The highest goal of the Theravāda practitioner means becoming an *arahant*, which can be rendered "Worthy One" or "Slayer of the Foe," depending on the etymology. An *arahant* is one who has reached *nibbāna*. The *arahant* then lives out the rest of his life and dies. We will try to ascertain the quality of his *nibbāna* in life and death.

To understand the change in the human who has reached liberation, we must look back to the twelve factors mentioned above. In the third noble truth, we saw that the practitioner reversed the causes of *dukkha*. The first step to this cessation requires an end to ignorance. The teaching (*dhamma*) now informs how one shapes one's dispositions.

2. Ibid.

According to the Buddha, *karmic* "baggage" forms from actions stemming from our own sense of individuality. When one gains insight, one no longer see oneself as a discrete, self-important being. Therefore, the sense of self dissipates and with it the idea that one's own distinct consciousness, or anyone else's for that matter, has priority.

From this alteration of consciousness comes an alteration in perception. The *arahant* still has sense contact from which follows feeling. Feeling, in the Buddha's perspective, refers to the emotive factor resulting from sense impression. Now even though one feels pleasurable, painful, and neutral sensations, one is not affected by them. What was once an aggregate of personhood has now come under the individual's control. With the slavery to pleasure and pain ended, craving need not arise. Without craving there is no motive to grasp onto existence, trying to make things certain or permanent beyond what *paṭiccasamuppāda* provides.

Grasping (*upādāna*), which of necessity presupposes the priority of one's self as the grasper, leads to rebirth within the *karmic* scheme. Without grasping there is no becoming, no birth and death, lamentation, or suffering.

So the consciousness of the *arahant* is markedly different from the consciousness of the ordinary man. The same alterations within the mind of the *arahant* make it possible for one *arahant* to know another *arahant*. Yet the mind of the man who reaches *nibbāna* is somewhat of a mystery in the same way that the Buddha claimed that anything metaphysical must be unknowable. Buddhist texts tell of how the Buddha was able to enjoy a restful meditative state where he shut off perceptions altogether. Nevertheless, in this life such a state must be temporary.

The *arahant* reaches a freedom (*nibbāna*) that we can classify into three areas of application: epistemology, behavior, and psychology.[3] Epistemologically, the *arahant* no longer thinks in ways that lead to grasping. He is free from the compulsion to hold concepts as eternal truths. Regarding behavior, the *arahant* feels the freedom to pursue wholesome, non-*dukkha*-causing actions, without the often *dukkha*-causing restrictions, which show no sensitivity for particular

3. For more, see Ibid., 90–100.

situations. Finally, the psychological freedom is a clear happiness, unclouded by pain or cravings for pleasures. This happiness only lasts while the causes of suffering have been ended. This means that the benefits of *nibbāna* seem only to be "experienced" while the five aggregates are conjoined.

So what happens to the *arahant* at death? The Buddha called the dead *arahant* by the term *tathāgata*, the "thus-gone-one." We can see how many would speculate about where he might have gone. However, remember the Buddha's epistemology. If we keep in mind the Buddha's epistemology of radical empiricism, we must conclude that the condition of the dead *arahant* is unknowable. When a person dies, their physical personality ceases along with the senses from which contact arises. Contact results in consciousness, as we saw in the *nāma-rūpa* (name-and-form or mind-and-body) discussion in chapter 7. So when the physical personality ceases, we can only reason that the rest of the aggregates also cease. Therefore, we have no grounds for speculation about the post-mortem quality of the *tathāgata*'s existence. If we assume an absolutist view of the aggregates, we will conclude that the *tathāgata* must no longer exist. On the other hand, if we conclude that the *tathāgata* must exist in a transcendent realm, we have misunderstood everything the Buddha has taught about the rejection of metaphysical claims (claims not directly testable by our or another's experience).

The middle path in regard to the *tathāgata's* afterlife is a reverent silence. The Buddha was silent as to the accuracy of these six statements:

1. The soul is identical with the body.
2. The soul is different from the body
3. The *tathāgata* exists after death.
4. The *tathāgata* does not exist after death.
5. The *tathāgata* both exists and does not exist after death.
6. The *tathāgata* neither exists nor does not exist after death.[4]

Nibbāna then is not a metaphysical state as so many interpreters of Buddhism have tried to suggest. They concede metaphysical status to this state despite the clear epistemological qualifications,

4. Ibid., 97–98.

upon which the Buddha will not waver. We ought not attack the Buddha for his silence. Instead, he should be commended for his logical consistency. The Buddha allowed for no trans-empirical reality in his diagnosis and cure of suffering. Certainly it would seem strange if he smuggled it back into this teaching as a final goal for the practitioner.

CONCLUSION

As we draw our exposition of Buddhism to a close, we should keep in mind some of its big themes. The Buddha stressed a radical empiricism, a pragmatic theory of logic, and a proto-positivist view of language. Regarding metaphysics, he taught to abandon the project altogether and focused on the intimacy and concrete quality of sense perception. Dependent arising (*paṭiccasamuppāda*) describes his empirically-based theory of causality. His goal is to end *dukkha*, and at the end of *dukkha* is *nirvāṇa*. Thus we blow out the candle.

Part III

A Christian Critique of Buddhist Philosophy

10

The Logic Problem

"Householder, if you will debate on the basis of truth, we might have some conversation about this."

"I will debate on the basis of truth, venerable sir, so let us have some conversation about this."

Majjhima-nikāya, Upāli Sutta 1.376

You shall not bear a false report; do not join your hand with a wicked man to be a malicious witness. You shall not follow a multitude in doing evil, nor shall you testify in a dispute so as to turn aside after a multitude in order to pervert justice; nor shall you be partial to a poor man in his dispute.

Exodus 23:1–3

INTRODUCTION

FOR MANY PEOPLE, LOGIC causes pain. Logic can be defined as the art and science of correct reasoning. Mastering it takes work, focus, and patience. Certainly, its homework can be painful. (Perhaps in this way logic is a form of *dukkha*!) However, rational thought is universal, belonging to the ken of all people. So much so that many philosophers throughout history have distinguished humans from animals specifically through the attribute of human rationality.

The next eight chapters will critically examine the Buddha's teaching, particularly, in the areas of doctrine upon which truth claims depend within the Buddha's worldview. These points can be established by examining the criticism that the Buddha levels against his own opponents, which I presented in chapter 3. The first four chapters of this section address the problems that Buddhism has in offering an account of logical reasoning. Then, the next five chapters of this section address the problem of other minds, causal relationships, and Buddha's pragmatic outlook. (Everything in its own time.) This chapter will introduce the logic problem.

THE BUDDHA'S NEED FOR RATIONALITY

Logical arguments enjoin listeners to use reason to evaluate claims. The Buddha engaged in reasoned debate. The third of the Eightfold Noble Path requires Buddhists not to lie. They are to think accurately and represent what they have experienced with logical integrity. The Buddha sought to be consistent and he *rationally* engaged opponents. Many times he says:

> What you said before does not agree with what you said afterwards, nor does what you say afterwards agree with what you said before. Yet you made this statement: "I will debate on the basis of truth, venerable sir, so let us have some conversation about this."[1]

Because of his openness to reason, the Buddha himself provides a warrant for the Buddha's own philosophy. Should we not put the Buddha's philosophy to the test? Ask him whether he agrees to what he himself says? And invite him to debate on the basis of truth?

So let us do just that.

SETTING UP THE PROBLEM

The Buddha's epistemology and theory of causality govern Buddhist philosophy. The Buddha rejects metaphysics. Instead, he wants us to think in terms of *nāma-rūpa* (phenomena). *Nāma-rūpa* is not a substance. Remember, the Buddha rejected substantiality. After all,

1. *Majjhima-nikāya* 1.378 in Nanomali and Bodhi, *Middle Length Discourses.*

nonsubstantiality is one of the three marks of existence. *Nāma-rūpa* describes the result of contact with the senses.

Because of the Buddha's epistemology, causality describes relationships of the world we see, but no supposition should be made about the fundamental nature of what we perceive beyond what is taught by the doctrine of dependent arising (*paṭiccasamuppāda*), the Buddha's view of causality, which describes all relationships within *all spheres of existence. All of them.* Everything is in a state of flux and constant change. Remember the doctrine of the five spheres of existence (chapter 6). *Paṭiccasamuppāda* also describes the arising and operations of the five aggregates (chapter 7), which are different from the five spheres since they specifically describe the human person.

Herein lies the problem: If everything changes, then why do the standards for measuring validity stay the same? The empirical truth of a statement is not the same as the logical validity of an argument. Validity deals with the structure of our reasoning, not the usefulness of its content. When we ask whether one's thoughts display the quality of validity, that is a completely different question from whether or not they are true. *An empiricist can argue that a statement is true because it is empirically verified. However, an empiricist may not say that an argument is valid because its conclusion is empirically verified.*

Take this argument:[2]

All men are mortal.
The Buddha is a man.
Therefore the Buddha is mortal.

We say that these premises are true, and the argument is valid. The conclusion also has the possibility of empirical verification if we were contemporaries of the Buddha. Now, what about this argument:

All men are mortal.
The Buddha is a man.
Therefore the Buddha's parents named him Siddhārtha.

Notice in this second argument that the conclusion is still true. If we had lived back at the time of the Buddha, we could have empirically

2. These examples are simple; that is why I chose them.

verified that the Buddha was named Siddhārtha, in as much as getting testimony from someone can be considered empirical verification. If he would not tell us, we could ask his folks or see if he signed his name somewhere. However, even if all the propositions in the argument are true, the conclusion is still invalid because it does not follow from the given premises. Therefore, the empirically derived premises cannot prove the conclusion empirically.

When we ask for an accounting of validity within the parameters of *paṭiccasamuppāda*, we are asking for an account of the reliability of validity. People at this time in history were not as concerned with the justification of formal logic. In the West, formal work on that project was not taken up until Aristotle. However, both East and West still had in mind the importance of justifying the objectivity of reasoning. For the Brahmanist, *Brahman* accounts for the objectivity of knowledge.[3] In the Christian worldview, God provides the basis for valid reasoning. In strong contradistinction from Brahmanism, God is personal and the creator. The universe is governed by cosmic personalism, not impersonal chance, *ātman*, or *paṭiccasamuppāda*. As Creator, God's thinking organized and planned the world and all that is in it, including human thought. God is the standard for the cogency of human thought and the perfection of moral character. Our cognition must submit to his standards, even though our thinking maintains qualitative and quantitative differences from his thinking. For example, God knows immediately and rationally, without needing a period of time in which to draw conclusions while humans need to reason in a temporal sequence the way we do.

In this regard, the author of Proverbs personifies wisdom and the clarity of thought. Wisdom says of herself:

> The Lord possessed me at the beginning of His way, before His works of old. From everlasting I was established, From the beginning, from the earliest times of the earth. When there were no depths I was brought forth; . . . When He established the

3. Upaniṣadic philosophy attempts to make knowledge objective by postulating the unity of the many in one. However, this perspective, if carried to its final conclusion, makes rational argumentation useless because the distinctions of language can never access this one fundamental reality. With rational arguments abandoned, the only available basis for objective knowledge becomes direct mystical experience. The Upaniṣadic thinkers reasoned consistently, which presents them with an altogether different problem.

> heavens, I was there. (8:22–24, 27)

Wisdom, *one aspect of which is the ability to think with validity*, was present before anything was created. It was present with God, according to the Book of Proverbs. Wisdom was present before anything was made; for that reason, wisdom was capable of comprehending God's creative acts. The Hebrews believed humans to be created in the image of God. Since God presents us with both truth claims and imperatives, clearly he expects us to recognize logically consistent statements. Within the view of wisdom presented in the biblical Book of Proverbs and the cohesive worldview presented throughout the rest of the Bible, we find a story that gives an account for why there are integrity-bearing, sequential chains of thought in the human mind.

In contrast with the biblical story, the Buddha boasts of having no grand ontology of existence, and for good reason. He thinks that attaining the goal of ending suffering is more important than coming up with vast metaphysical infrastructures. The Buddha is in a hurry. However, he does offer *paṭiccasamuppāda* as an explanation for all reality. So how can the Buddha, who teaches *paṭiccasamuppāda*, account for logical validity without assuming it on faith? Recall from chapter 5 that the Buddha repudiated accepting anything based on faith or reasoning about views.

I am not suggesting the Buddha needs some special ontology. Perhaps he does not. However, he has given us nothing to explain what validity is or how to account for it within his perspective. He would need to say it is a process, but the question still remains: What and where is this process? And how and why does it connect some empirically based statements but not others? He cannot point to the five aggregates, the six elements, or the five spheres of existence to answer the question of why his mental acts retain valid connections over time, especially since the content of mental acts (experience) constantly changes. For the purpose of bringing cessation to grasping, the Buddha propounded a philosophy that made all reality vapor in the hands of the one who grasps it. It appears his doctrine of *paṭiccasamuppāda* worked only too well, and that the problem of constant change makes permanent validity structures impossible.

Even if a valid relationship occurred in the mind, what makes that relationship valid? And why would it appear again?

All moments arise from previous causes. Those causes arose from other causes. When one runs this thinking out to the nearly infinite number of causal relationships that work together to bring about each successive moment, clearly no two events can have exactly the same cause. As Kalupahana writes:

> A theory of causation, maintaining that if the same cause is repeated the same effect will result, is said to have the shortcoming of emphasizing the sameness of causes and effects. It has no scope at all "since the same cause never occurs exactly."[4]

Since dependent arising (*paṭiccasamuppāda*) cannot produce the same event twice, what is this validity that shows up in all valid arguments? The Buddha may not point to anything other than *nāma-rūpa.* If he tries to account for the permanent standards of validity with a metaphysical claim, a claim not supported solely by direct empirical investigation, then his epistemology is a house divided, warring against itself..

CONCLUSION

Now that the Buddhist problem of logic has been identified, in the next three chapter, we will look at potential replies that could be offered and actual counter-responses given by Buddhist philosophers. In the next three chapters, I will first give potential counter-arguments that a Buddhist could offer to this Buddhist logic problem. Then I will give my own counter-reply to that counter-argument. One could call it a counter-counter-argument.

4. *Causality,* 93–94.

11

Buddhist Replies to the Logic Problem Part One: Five Possible Objections to the Buddhist Logic Problem

The one who first states a case seems right, until the other comes and cross-examines.

Proverbs 18:17

INTRODUCTION

THIS CHAPTER WILL PRESENT five possible objections the Buddhist logic problem identified in the previous chapter. I will follow each possible response with a reply. Some replies will be direct refutations and some will not. By way of quick summary, these are the five possible replies this chapter addresses:

Objection 1. The Buddhist logic problem explained in the previous chapter is not permitted because transcendental arguments are impermissible in interreligious dialogue. The methodology of this problem is the presuppositional apologetics of Gordon Clark and Cornelius Van Til and is therefore faulty.

Objection 2. The Buddhist logic problem is not a problem because validity does not exist. Rather, logic is only a formal relationship between propositions in an argument.

Objection 3. The Buddhist logic problem is not a problem because logical validity is a natural process like the laws of nature.

Objection 4. The Buddhist logic problem is not a problem because natural selection explains why humans think logically. It helped us survive and evolve into who we are today.

Objection 5. The Buddhist logic problem is not a problem because Quine undermined the notion of logical validity through his notion of radical translation and his application of it to the philosophy of logic.

OBJECTION 1: TRANSCENDENTAL ARGUMENTS ARE NOT PERMISSIBLE IN INTERRELIGIOUS DIALOGUE

In 2006, I presented the Buddhist logic problem at the Gonzaga Socratic Club at Gonzaga University. Professor Quanhua Liu of our philosophy department responded to my presentation and the text of his response is available online.[1] Prof. Liu objects to my use of the transcendental argument in interreligious dialogue. In order to do this, he characterized my position as presuppositional Christian apologetics. According to his interpretation, presuppositional Christian apologists view the Christian faith as the one-and-only logically consistent system while maintaining that all other non-Christian systems are inconsistent. He believes twentieth century Christian apologists Gordon Clark and Cornelius Van Til are intellectual fathers of presuppositional apologetics. In his view, Gordon Clark, in particular, and Van Til think the Christian apologists should treat the Christian worldview as an axiom system that is logically consistent and then point out how other religions are inconsistent. Prof. Liu rejects this view for three reasons. First, it is possible to make a logical framework that is consistent and then make different models from that same framework. So it is possible to have multiple consistent worldviews. Second, Prof. Liu rightly believes that there is more to a worldview than the question of whether or not it is logically consistent. People choose a worldview for many reasons; those who aim only to hold consistent views seem to end up with something other than wisdom, a point that even G.K. Chesterton affirms.[2] Finally, Prof. Liu points to Kurt Gödel's incompleteness theorems, by which

1. The text of Liu's response to my presentation can be found here: http://guweb2.gonzaga.edu/faculty/calhoun/socratic/Liu_resp_to_Collender.pdf..

2. Chesterton, *Orthodoxy*, 175–89.

Gödel demonstrates that any formal system cannot prove itself. On this basis, Liu thinks mere consistency is a bad criterion by which to judge all religions.

Response

Prof. Liu is a gentleman. He fulfilled his tenure as chair of our department with graciousness and efficiency. He has a wonderfully clear mind. However, his case against the use of the transcendental arguments in interreligious dialogue neither addresses the case I presented in 2006 nor the one I present here.[3] Before I explain why, it will be necessary to unravel a number of assumptions in his reply. First, I feel uncomfortable with the use of the term "presuppositional" to describe the kind of argument presented here.[4] I would prefer to call my methodology Augustinian rather than presuppositional. Some treat presuppositional apologetics as though its methodology is wholly opposed to the offering of evidence, as though one must just simply presuppose a position and then berate one's opponent for not believing it. This is not the position represented here. One can argue from evidence to the reliability of a worldview, which the biblical authors demonstrate. Augustine argued that one must "believe in order to understand." However, Augustine did not argue that understanding evidence contributed nothing to belief. He understood that according to the Christian Worldview "In [God's] light shall we see light."[5] Or, as N. T. Wright observes, the reconstruction of historical narratives based on concrete bits of evidence must be done within a worldview that can account for the work of doing historical reconstruction.[6] There is a reciprocal relationship in a worldview between evaluation of evidence and the standards that one uses to

3. Before completing this chapter, I met with Prof. Liu on November 1, 2012, to discuss his views and to ensure that my memory of his opposition to transcendental arguments in interreligious dialogue and his interpretation of presuppositional apologetics were correct. He confirmed that this is what he meant and that his views in 2012 are the same as they were in 2006.

4. My master's thesis, in which I present some of the arguments contained in this book, is titled "Buddhism Reconsidered: A Presuppositional Critique of Theravada Buddhist Philosophy. . . ." Over the last decade, I have come to see that calling this approach "presuppositional" is confusing for the reasons I discuss in this chapter.

5. Augustine, *Exposition on Psalms*, 30.

6. *New Testament and People of God*, 137.

evaluate that evidence. Thus, as Kant observed, an argument that seeks to prove God (i.e. a worldview claim) must itself be logically prior to factual questions related to particular evidence since such an argument aims to prove what must be the ground of all existence and experience.[7] When we aim to prove the preconditions of intelligible experience, we must approach them differently than a simple empirical claim. That is Kant's point.

However, Prof. Liu defines "presuppositional" as something different. In his view, "The concept of coherence or consistence plays a crucial role in [the presuppositionalists'] defense of their views and in their attacks to their opponents' [views] as well." Thus, he attacks presuppositionalism by characterizing it through the methodology of Gordon Clark, who did treat the Christian worldview as though it earns its spurs by being a consistent axiom system.[8] It is true that "presuppositionalists" do think coherence or consistency plays a crucial role. They reason about worldviews. Of course they use coherence and consistency, and they should do so without shame. The problem here is the characterization of presuppositionalism by way of Gordon Clark, as though all presuppositionalists wear his stripes. While his methodology may be that of a child at play with a Tinkertoy set whose only goal is to make sure all the parts of his little structure fit together perfectly, not everyone plays that way. In my 2006 interaction with Prof. Liu, I began my reply to his case by repudiating Clark and Liu's corresponding interpretation of Van Til. In addition, the kind of interpretation that Prof. Liu offers of Van Til is addressed by John Frame in his book *Cornelius Van Til: An Analysis of His Thought* in which Frame shows that Van Til essentially maintained a position closer to the Augustinian position, which supports the use of evidence. It should be kept in mind, though, that Van Til was more the leader of a theological movement than he was a philosopher intent on making subtle distinctions. Frame's *perspectivalism* is a more carefully nuanced position reflecting the tradition of Augustine and Calvin, which I described in chapter 2.[9]

7. *One Possible Basis for a Demonstration of the Existence of God*, 147–59.

8. See Liu, 2.

9. See Frame, *Doctrine of Knowledge of God*. See also Frame, *Cornelius Van Til: An Analysis*, pp. 97-113 for a list of original sources and an analysis of the controversy.

Having made these clarifications, it is now possible to address each of Prof. Liu's objections in turn. Regarding his first point about the possibility of having multiple consistent systems, notice that if we recall the four possible options I described in chapter 2, his caricature of my Augustinian argument turns it into Option 1, which I strenuously argued against in that chapter. If the standard that establishes a religion is actually outside a religion, then the religion that is making a claim to presenting a total truth of the kind that Kant describes in *The One Possible Basis* is already presumed to not be what it claims to be.

Furthermore, Prof. Liu is correct in asserting that if adjudicating conflicting claims between religious worldviews is based on logical consistency alone, it is at least possible that one could invent a religion that is designed to be a set of consistent claims. The absurd criterion of logical consistency alone ends up granting this hypothetical Religious Never-Never Land the same status as Buddhism or Christianity, both of which are rooted in a real, factual history. Adjudicating religious claims requires religions that actually have claims. While one might want to argue that Christianity is the only consistent and, thus, true religion, the God revealed in the Bible must also be the ground of all logical consistency and proof. Or Christianity, even if consistent, must be false. This is the point I made in 2006 when Prof. Liu made his argument. I challenged him to give me the worldview that accounts for the applicability of logic to all areas of human experience and belief, including even hypothetical religious belief models. Prof. Liu was silent on this question for the remainder of our exchange. However, the Bible is not silent on these questions.

Prof. Liu is correct that people choose religions for more than their consistency and that Kurt Gödel's incompleteness theorems cast doubt on the strategy of treating a religion as though it were a consistent axiom system. The world's great religions became great because they offered a corresponding way of life, a "culture[,]. . . religion externalized."[10] This is why I have not focused on trying to point to contradictions within Buddhism. Cheap appeals to contradiction in this case are not fair. Instead, we must give a patient

10. Van Til, *Calvinistic Concept of Culture*, 186.

hearing to the questions that Buddhism asks and engage with those questions faithfully and consistently. For this reason, *To End All Suffering* ends with a discussion of Buddhist pragmatism, but the details of that discussion I must leave for the last chapter.

Kurt Gödel's theorems are also helpful here. They demonstrate the insufficiency of logic as an *ultimate* test. Try as we might to use human reason as an ultimate arbiter of truth, logic itself defies the task, which is why mathematicians after Gödel must choose to make their systems inconsistent or incomplete. They generally choose to make them incomplete, for who wants to be inconsistent? Yet that choice is a subtle rebuke, which we all must take to heart. In what worldview is the human grasp of logic exhaustively applicable to all of human experience, yet also admittedly finite and incomplete?

OBJECTION 2: LOGICAL VALIDITY DOES NOT EXIST

Some have argued that logical validity does not really exist, that it is merely a formal relationship between propositions in an argument.

Response

Well, this objection is not saying much. In philosophy, the term *formal* describes the abstract pattern, principle, or structure of a thing or idea as opposed to its physical parts. The spiral seen in some flower petals and the spiral of a snail's shell both display the Fibonacci sequence.[11] However, one can intelligently speak of the Fibonacci sequence even though one only sees it incarnated in something else. Even though validity is something one can never find wholly isolated unto itself, one can still speak of it existing and arising.[12] In organisms, this beautiful spiral sequence blossoms out

11. The Fibonacci sequence is a mathematical number sequence in which a number is added to the number that preceded it, yielding a new number. This sequence can go on infinitely. An example of a Fibonacci sequence is: 0, 1, 1, 2, 3, 5, 8, 13, 21, 34, 55. This sequence shows up in many naturally occurring structures and is the basis for the Golden Rectangle, which is often used in architecture and as a proper ratio for book covers.

12. This *arising of existence* applies not only to physical things but also mental events. As was discussed in the previous chapter, the five aggregates and the five spheres of existence, which also constitute the mental aspects of existence, are subject to *paṭiccasamuppāda*.

of the organism's structure, but validity in arguments cannot make the same appeal.

Another possible way for a Buddhist to argue against the need for an account of logical validity is to reject the whole question of logical validity pointing to a supposed similarity in mental events. Hypothetically, from these similarities one may draw structures that can be used to infer logically valid relationships. Such an argument will only work if one can first isolate different instances of internal mental cognitive awareness into classes for reasoning. Yet this kind of activity can only transpire meaningfully if classes are things (whatever their nature) that may be evaluated in a valid manner. Thus, this account presupposes that validity already exists and has meaning before the mind works to sort internal mental perception into classes for evaluation. The nature and ability to make valid inferences must first be accounted for before arguments about the similarities of mental events may be brought to the table.

A lesser argument (but one that applies because of the Buddha's claims) is to consider that even if one could account for a moment of validity within the Buddha's view of causality (*paṭiccasamuppāda*), one must still account for why validity does not change over time. If the Buddha makes a valid argument on Tuesday, why is that argument still valid on Saturday?

If one stipulates that composed arguments simply maintain validity over time without any reason for that stipulation, then why not just stipulate that the Buddha is right? Forget, then, empirical evidence. Or the evaluation of causal law. Why all this talk of arguments and empiricism? When we just stipulate a criterion to prove something true, notice we just create a middleman to make our notions seem more palatable.

In a system that disdains appeals to authority, the Buddha must account for validity over time. Again, there is nothing in early Buddhism to account for why the same argument should remain valid over any length of time. If life arises and ceases leaving a body, why does not validity arise and cease, and thus make nonsense out of a concept that previously contained validly related premises?

As name and form (*nāma* and *rūpa*) change, then so must everything except the truth that all things change. If validity is not in one of the five aggregates, then it does not exist. If it is one of the five aggregates, then it, too, is subject to change. Therefore, if we hold the doctrine of interdependent co-origination, we have no reason for thinking that the arguments that the Buddha presented twenty-five hundred years ago were valid then or are still valid today.

OBJECTION 3: LAWS OF THOUGHT ARE LIKE PHYSICAL LAWS

One may say that as certain norms arise out of "physical" experience, so will similar norms arise out of "mental" experience.[13] This objection alleges that physical laws govern the external world such that we can live predictably while logical laws govern the life of the mind such that we can reason and draw conclusions together. Nature definitely has something to say when I attempt to defy physical laws; although it does not prevent me from saying "round-square" or "man-onion," it does nevertheless give strong hints that these things are impossible. Clearly, rational norms can emerge out of the experienced life of the mind.

Response

Though this objection appears strong, it depends on a metaphor equating physical laws of nature and norms of the mind. Metaphorical arguments are fine when the metaphor fits, but the behavior of nature and the life of the mind should not be equated like this. Nature provides us with no evidence that the physical laws, mentioned above, even exist, only that the objects and properties of nature interact in regular patterns, many of which can be quantified. On the contrary, mental events do not occur in regular patterns like the interactions of nature around us. The human capacity to imagine and to change perspective or attitude is what makes human mental life a rich, moldable world constantly open to new possibilities.

Another serious complication this objection faces is the problem that arises in explaining how logical norms "give strong hints" that a "round-square" is impossible. The mind certainly does give strong hints when it "sees" a contradiction. But the "strong hint" depends on

13. Nick Gier, Professor Emeritus at the University of Idaho, first brought this objection to my attention. Even some of the wording of the objection comes directly from him.

the mind's ability to recognize contradictions. In contrast, physical laws do not cause this sensation.[14] Rather, our definition of physical laws is the product of inferences about experience. So rational norms that preserve validity are needed even before we discover physical "laws." This objection clearly turns on itself.

OBJECTION 4: LOGICAL THINKING IS AN EVOLUTIONARY PRODUCT

When I have raised the Buddhist logic problem to Buddhist philosophers, I have often encountered the objection that we simply think this way because we are naturally selected to. These Darwinian Buddhists believe they can wiggle out of the problem of justifying rational norms by assuming that humans have developed rational thought to help them survive. Their proposed solution can turn into a pragmatist account of validity, but we will save that discussion for the next chapter. First things first.

Response

Keith Lehrer criticizes epistemology by natural selection, and his comments apply directly to our discussion here on the evolutionary Buddhist account of validity:

> Yet another way of saving observation statements, by appeal to the theory of natural selection, is equally faulty for similar reasons. To argue that beliefs about what we observe must be completely justified because they have survival value in the process of natural selection will leave one epistemologically bankrupt. First, the form of survival theory that currently appears most tenable is one recognizing that many factors bear little weight in the struggle for survival and consequently, may be retained even though they have almost no survival value. Hence, one cannot argue from the existence of beliefs to their survival value. Second, and more important, even if this inference is allowed, the epistemic leap to the conclusion that such beliefs are completely justified is totally unwarranted. Beliefs that are neither true nor completely justified may have considerable survival value. Perhaps the truth would destroy us.[15]

14. Perhaps they do if you are a hyper-rationalist.
15. Lehrer, *Theory of Knowledge*, 101–2.

We can apply Lehrer's comments directly to the argument that the rational structures of the mind were adapted by natural selection. First, what we perceive as validity may simply have nothing to do with truth. For the Buddhist, this means that he has no reason to conclude that he can soundly infer the causes of his own suffering. From natural selection one cannot be sure that what we call validity developed as a survival-causing property. Perhaps this particular way of thinking is an accidental property that tagged along, like male pattern baldness. This means that on such a platform as natural selection, one could never have confidence in arguments defending natural epistemic selection. This story of natural selection lacks the explanatory power to answer the Buddhist logic problem. Thankfully, Buddhists have come up with more formidable counterarguments than this one.

OBJECTION 5: W. V. QUINE AND "TWO DOGMAS OF EMPIRICISM"

Some may want to point the to the Harvard logician W. V. Quine's attack on the Kantian division between analytic and synthetic sentences found in his essay "Two Dogmas of Empiricism."[16] For background, Kant argued that some statements are analytic in that all the information, which appears in the predicate, is actually contained in the subject. However, in a synthetic statement, the predicate adds something to the subject.

Quine concludes, based on what he calls "radical translation,"[17] that a statement's logical structure is somewhat determined by

16. Quine, *From a Logical Point of View*, 20–46.

17. Radical Translation (hereafter RT) is a term coined by Quine. Because of the broader audience for this work, it is appropriate to include a short digest defining RT. For a longer introduction, see Martin, *The Meaning of Language*.

RT refers to what a man, born and raised in the West, does when he attempts to communicate with a people who have always been isolated in some distant corner of the earth. When you make RT you must assume that: (1) the natives are not trying to lie to you, (2) most of the natives' beliefs about themselves and their surroundings are true, (3) the environment stimulates the natives the same way it stimulates you, and (4) you make assumptions about the inner workings of their language. As you learn more, these assumptions may be revised.

Context always affixes meanings. Meanings cannot be learned as isolated particulars. Since the discernment of meaning is a scientific process, it is conceivable that one could develop two internally consistent paradigms of interpretation for uttered sounds. The two theories might score equally well on the criterion of grammar. Kalupahana seems to agree with Quine. In his discussion of the sixth factor of the Eightfold Noble Path he writes: "While denying the mysterious 'ghost in the machine,' the Buddha reduced the universal and objective laws to linguistic conventions, thereby accommodating an element of skepticism."[18] Kalupahana, in the next sentence, points to "dependent arising" (*paṭiccasamuppāda*) as the reason why we must see "objective laws" as conventional.

In some languages, the lines for what functions as a predicate and what functions as a subject can get blurry. Quine believes that in many ways the difference between analytic and synthetic must be seen in terms of what is easy to overthrow by experience. Something that is easily overthrown is more synthetic while something more difficult to overthrow is put in the category of analytic.

---

coherence with observable fact. Quine, therefore, holds that observed facts might not determine that one theory is preferable over another. Our theories are underdetermined by the facts.

Quine believes that RT also applies to one's own language. In daily life, we believe that others who make the same kinds of noises as we do are speaking our same language; that someone else's word "money" should be translated into our word "money." Quine calls this *identity translation*. He argues that our understanding of our language is still a theory that we personally test scientifically through personal RT. When trying to figure the meaning of any term spoken in one's own language, one generally accepts the best theory.

Quine claims that the question of whether one is correct or not in the conflict between meanings is irrelevant; in fact, one cannot possibly know who is ultimately right. We can have a good theory and a good translation manual and that is all. The better theory is the one that better fits the criterion of a good translation manual, not the one that "fits the facts." No meaning, only good theories, or put another way, meaning is not in heads but in interpretive theories.

Experience, then, interacts with one's sentences as a whole, not on an individual basis. Like Kuhn's theory of paradigms, the sentences we accept or reject are also tied to a system of previously accepted sentences. What we judge to be "truth" is tied to the rest of these sentences, and the true now may be false later depending on the shift of our commitments to certain sentences. True and false distinctions, then, are somewhat irrelevant. Experience could possibly overturn any sentence.

The distinction between analytic and synthetic categories also becomes weak because the fact that a statement contains the predicate within the subject is a grammatical and interpretive question. Only comparatively can one say a statement is *a priori* or *a posteriori*. A comparatively *a priori* statement might not easily be overturned by experience. A comparatively *a posteriori* statement just might.

18. *History of Buddhist Philosophy*, 107.

Following Quine's lead, a Buddhist apologist may argue that logical structure must be seen as grammar combined with an extension of empirical verification. If we grant that all grammar is culturally relative and logic itself is a product of grammar, then the authoritative structures of logic are conventional. They are dependent on cultural consensus. According to the second noble truth, meaningful conception "must relate to an object, whether mental or material, that a community of intelligent beings can agree on. In this sense, the difference between conception and convention is reduced to a great extent."[19] Kalupahana tells us that "universal law" type statements have no more ontology than the agreement of a community to use such statements. If grammar is culturally relative, then the conception of logical validity must be in some sense culturally relative. The Buddhist who wishes to borrow Quine's argument may also want to point to some particular sense experience to validate validity. To summarize, the Quinean counter-argument suggests that logical structures are more conventional and represent generalizations that are difficult to overthrow by experience. This way the Buddhist may stick to ever-changing experience in the hopes that it will produce the regularity necessary to make logical validity a reliable norm for reasoning.

Response

As hopeful as the above Quinean counter-argument might appear, it provides no help in answering Buddhism's problem of identifying and preserving logical validity. First, it reduces the laws of logic to conventionally held standards. However, logical norms are guides for intelligibly connecting truth bearing mental acts.[20] Certainly a community of intellects maintains truth statements. It requires members to reason with integrity. It also provides checks and balances, but the importance of a logical community should not lead us

19. Kalupahana, *History of Buddhist Philosophy*, 104.

20. By *rational structure* I am not referring to any kind of particular mental essence. Earlier, I mentioned how the mind cannot accurately establish classes without already anticipating the appropriate way these classes are to be interrelated. In this sense, it is appropriate to see the formal relations of rational structures as prescriptive for the associations of classes that are themselves mental acts (one should hope they are truth-bearing).

to conclude that the rational standards of the language of the community have the same conventional quality as the grammar of the language used by the community. The Buddha's method of debating with his opponents seems to require this.

As previously stated, rational norms are prescriptive, guiding valid connections of truth-bearing mental acts. If minds could not already make these connections, then the goal of communications between minds would seem absurd, and if the measure of rational thought was a body of culturally held conventions, then a community could make anything rational.

Second, the conventional status that Buddhist philosophy places on logical norms does not seem to accord with their regular usefulness in the world. If they were merely conventional, like shaking hands instead of raising the palm of the right hand and saying "Háu" then one should not expect their application to fit so well with the ever-changing contingent realm of experience we daily navigate, let alone help generals plan battles and scientists build rocket ships.

Third, an objection to what I have just argued could never be sustained by an appeal to experience since there is no normative experience to which one might appeal. Take a moment and review the last couple pages. Notice how the domain of study we are examining regarding the nature of logic requires more than simple appeals to experience. No direct experience can refute these paragraphs. *Someone wishing to challenge them must challenge their logic* in terms of their coherence and correspondance with previously presented information that this text assumes.

Empirical explanations of logic could not be reliable for the Buddha's philosophical arguments against the Vedic and Upaniṣadic thinkers. The Buddha raises logical problems within their own metaphysical schemes. He accuses them not only of botching empirical verifications but also of having contradictions,.

Fourth, as we have already noted, if the validity of logical relationships stems from conventions held between people, then logic is culturally relative. Note that once this assertion is accepted, the very fact that the Buddha lived and taught in an ancient foreign culture suggests his philosophy, as well as that of the *Vedas* and *Upaniṣads*, is irrelevant to contemporary culture. I certainly do not hold this view, but it follows from the premises that logic is culturally relative and a kind of grammar.

As I mentioned in the introduction to this section on the Buddha's logical problem, we gain a deeper understanding of rational structures and methods over time. Some of Quine's insights are wise and useful. Yet the Buddha's view of *paṭiccasamuppāda* makes it relevant to ask whether Quine's argument is valid and worthy of consideration or whether it is still valid now even though many years have passed since its writing? If one can raise this question to Quine, how much more can one raise this question to the Buddha? If both of these gentlemen have written arguments that are still valid, then validity must be something that remains untouched by the transient quality of dependent arising (*paṭiccasamuppāda*).

Finally, Quine's argument itself is a perfect example of why we need validity. If the Quinean culturally relative logic argument is presented, then it offers itself to be judged either valid or invalid. If people accepted it because it was a valid argument, then *the presentation of the argument assumes rational norms.* Presenting this as an argument about the structure of logic assumes that authoritative standards of inference and validity should still constrain our acceptance of propositions. Therefore, before one can ever accept the Buddhist/Quinean argument, one must first account for the rational structure necessary to make the presentation of an argument meaningful.

In other words, this argument seems to presuppose a view of logic that does not necessitate that we embrace its conclusion.

CONCLUSION

This chapter offered responses to five potential objections to the Buddhist logical problem; namely: (1) transcendental arguments are not permissible in interreligious dialogue; (2) validity does not exist; (3) logical validity is somehow a natural, organic process; (4) natural selection explains why humans think logically; and finally (5) Quine undermined the notion of logical validity through his theory of radical translation. I replied to each in turn.

Nevertheless, more objections remain. The next chapter will continue to nuance the Buddhist logic problem by reflecting on the problem of 'this' and 'that'.

12

Buddhist Replies to the Logic Problem Part Two: The Problem of 'This' and 'That'

When this exists, that comes to be,
with the arising of this, that arises....
When this does not exist, that does not come to be;
with the cessation of this, that ceases.

Majjhima-nikāya 2.262–264

INTRODUCTION

THE RELATION BETWEEN 'THIS' and 'that' in Buddhism presents a further problem with Buddhist philosophy worthy of its own chapter.[1] This problem is significant and its consequences so devastating because it eliminates both the Buddha's account of logic and causation at once.

Recall that chapter 5 demonstrates how the Buddha escaped absolutism by employing a four-cornered logic rooted in experience. The four corners of the Buddha's system can be outlined as follows:

A. I know *p* (truth, *sacca*)
B. I do not know *p* (confusion, *musā*)
C. [It is both that] I know and do not know *p* (confusion, *musā*)

1. I am indebted to Peter J. Leithart, Senior Fellow of Theology and Literature at New Saint Andrews College, for persuading me of the importance of this argument against early Buddhist philosophy.

D. [It is both that] I neither know nor do not know *p* (sin, *kali*)[2]

Recall also that the Buddha did not want to talk in absolute terms as Aristotle did in developing his own, very different, four-cornered system. Aristotle hinges his own four corners on the concept of 'all' and 'none'. In three of his four corners in the Aristotelian Square of Opposition, Aristotle uses what David Kalupahana calls 'absolutism' to make it possible to affirm or negate a 'some' statement about a thing by refering to 'all' or 'none' of that thing. In Aristotelian logic, this action of speaking about 'all' or 'none' of a term is called 'distribution'. Buddhist logic attempts to get around the absolutism of 'all' or 'none' statements by making 'this' statements. The Buddha did not use the logical quantifier 'all' (*sabbaṃ*). Instead, he used the word 'this' (*idaṃ*). By using 'this' instead of 'all', he distributes his subject term in a concrete and particular way, referring to something specific, rather than making an encompassing, absolute statement. As I explained in chapter 5, the Buddha never says "All is suffering" (*sabbaṃ dukkhaṃ*); he only says "All this is suffering" (*sabbam idaṃ dukkhaṃ*). This change makes it possible for the Buddha to talk as though he is using an Aristotelian A or E statement (i.e. All A is B, No A is B) from Aristotle's Square of Opposition, but he does so only after translating them into Aristotelian I and O statements (i.e. Some A is B, Some A is not B). This is the true genius of Buddhist logic, especially given the Buddha's goals. He gets his followers to stop thinking in terms of universal categories and focus on what is in front of them instead: 'this' and 'that'.

Now, regarding causality: for the Buddha's theory of causality to work, there must be a 'this' and a 'that', two items that relate to one another in some way. Nevertheless, we must ask: Are these items (events, states, things, etc.) objects with boundaries particular to themselves or particular to us? Just to clairify, consider the following question: When we conceptualize an orange and place a name to the orange (i.e. the linguistic token "orange"), have we named the object in its own limits or our conception of where its limits should be?

2. Kalupahana, *History of Buddhist Philosophy*, 48.

THE PROBLEM

Here lies the problem. For the causal law to be objective, as the Buddha says it is, the boundaries of 'this' and 'that' must be particular to the objects ('this' and 'that') in question. Otherwise 'this' cannot cause 'that'. In some way there must be a 'this' that causes 'that', else the word 'causality' is unintelligible. However, if the boundaries of 'this' and 'that' were particular to the objects, such a situation would seem to suggest some kind of set structured metaphysics external to the individual. Obviously, a metaphysical way to solve this type of problem is to posit the existence of substances, but Kalupahana recognizes the fault with that option and the conundrums that type of thinking manufactured in Buddhist scholasticism.

Kalupahana barely addresses this problem in his chapter appropriately titled "The Object."[3] The Buddha taught that humans cannot separate perception and cognition. In the act of perception, humans receive sense data, but humans cannot help but conceptualize objects in that sense data.

Herein lies the rub. Is the 'this' and 'that': (A) in the sense data (B) in our conception of the sense data, (C) in both, or (D) in neither? We will consider all of these briefly, following this outline:

A. In sense data
B. In the mind
C. In the mind and sense data
  1. Present in both individually
  2. Present in the meeting of both
D. Neither in the mind nor in sense data

First let us consider sense data.

In the Sense Data: It must be in the sense data, otherwise one not could claim to have empirically perceived a causal relation, something Kalupahana argues for in his book *Causality* (discussed in chapter 6 and also in greater detail in chapter 15). If this is the case, then something must be causally relating, which leads to the notion of substances underneath what we observe.

3. Ibid., 78–84.

The ancient Buddhist logician Dignāga, standing on the Buddha's shoulders, dispelled this perspective by pointing out that when one considers an object, one can conceptualize it in such a way as to make it metaphysical. One might see a color, but it is a "metaphysical construction that assumes the color to be a characteristic or property (*lakṣaṇa*) of a real existing object."[4] Since all is in constant causal change, it makes little sense to be a stickler about boundaries and the limits of an object or an event, As Kalupahana writes:

> Extreme analysis can thus fix the boundaries so sharply that the fringes can no longer remain to account for possible relations. Avoiding such an analysis eliminates the need for grounding them in substance. Thus the objects of experience are without fixity (*appaṇihita*), without substance (*animita*), and therefore empty of substantial existence (*suññа*).[5]

This outlook may help to guard against some potential philosophical problems, but not the problem of relating 'this' and 'that'. Let us grant that the Buddhist can have fuzzy edges on 'this' and 'that'—that one's 'this' and 'that' can have a fudge factor. Our question here is: Why do 'this' and 'that' apply—*period*—in an ever-changing contingent realm of experience? Also, on what basis are the terms 'this' and 'that' assigned?

Let us make this concrete. Take a box of oranges. How do we count how many oranges are in the box? The simple answer is that we number each little, round orange. However, if a knife were used to trace what the mind calls an orange (a 'this'), and the knife included "fuzzy edges"—whatever those are—would we end up with a whole orange or just sundry orange parts? For causality to be objective, then 'this' and 'that' must designate objects or events in the non-substantial world. "Orange" must be able to designate an orange. If the box is merely full of orange pulp, there are no oranges to number. If the world is just a box full of orange pulp, then the boundaries (even fuzzy boundaries) are not there and then there is no causality between 'this' and 'that'.

In the Buddha's teaching, there is no way to distinguish between 'this' and 'that' except from experience. But are there actual

4. Ibid., 197.

5. Ibid., 83–84.

boundaries on the world between 'this' and 'that' such that terms may be assigned? The Buddha provides no way of accounting for how this is possible. The anti-metaphysical position of the Buddha (thus, ambiguity on the nature of object boundaries) is meant to be an aid in helping the Buddhist practitioner gain enlightenment. Yet without clarity on this point, his causal formula is unintelligible.

The Buddhist will object to this line of reasoning. He might say, "Clearly, we all know what the boundaries of objects and events are. We live in the world and to reject that there are boundaries would mean death. I merely suggest that we cannot affix absolute boundaries." Fine. All the oranges in the box can either come with peels or without. However, such a Buddhist response would not address the question in the slightest because the question is: Are the boundaries of things in the sense data, in the world, in both or in neither? In our specific example regarding the oranges, if the boundaries are in the oranges, even with the fudge factor, they do not conform to Buddhism, which holds a world empty of substances (also see the discussion of Nāgārjuna's philosophy in the following chapter). Peels or not, the point for the Buddha is *there are no oranges.*

In contrast with the Buddhist worldview, the Bible teaches that the world is created by a being who is both one and plural. If we numerically qualify the question What is God? God is One. If we numerically qualify the question Who is God? God is Three. The beauty of Trinitarian unity and plurality is reflected in creation. The universe is made in 'kinds' where within a 'kind' can be diversity while at the same time unity is maintained. Take maple leaves. One can identify the form of the maple tree leaf though each maple leaf is completely different from another if its three-dimensional fractal structure is examined mathematically. This slight apparent "randomness" contributes to the beauty and order of the world. And this is exactly what one should expect in a world created by such a being. (I offer this as an illustration, not a proof.) We are surrounded by a world that may readily be categorized and enjoyed. We should expect that boundaries apply precisely in one sense and not in another sense. In fact, this is exactly what we find in the Trinitarian nature of God. "Three is One" is not a contradiction in the nature of God because these are numerical answers to different questions. The Trinitarian option is not available to the Buddhist. The "Christian world" is full of presence. For each person, there is a real creation that exists "out there" and in the internal world of human life. There is lots of interesting stuff. Joyful, bountiful, metaphysics galore. Many things for which one can be thankful. Unfortunately, the Buddhist cannot revel in such things.

Instead, the Buddha must dodge the horns of a miserable dilemma. He held that the universe was 'empty' (*suṇṇa*). Humans tend to crave and hold onto things. If phenomena are empty, as the Buddha said, we have no reason to crave them. Yet this empty world must still have objects or events, which cause other objects and events. Without this relationship of conditionality or cause and effect, one could never discover the causes of one's own suffering or put an end to those causes and, therefore, end suffering. The Buddha must convince the craving part of human nature that objects, in some sense, do not exist. At the same time, he must persuade the suffering part of human nature that a knowledge of how stuff works will lead to an end of suffering. Hence, the Buddha retreats into his own special psychology to talk about the world, which is his attempt to dodge these problems of suggesting that boundaries are in the sense data. This brings us to our second option.

Only in the Mind: If Buddhism cannot account for the boundaries of objects or events, maybe the mind can make the world into objects and events. Maybe 'this' and 'that' are in our minds. As I mentioned before, this will not work since it makes causality subjective and the Buddha cannot allow this to be the case. (I have already discussed why in chapter 6; this is a theme I will return to again in chapter 15.)

Both in the Mind and Sense Data: The third option is that 'this' and 'that' are both in sense data and our conception of the sense data. This is probably the best option. Under this option there are two possibilities that need to be addressed: either (1) they are present in both the sense data and the conception of the sense data or (2) the meeting of conception and sense data contain 'this' and 'that', and it would be impossible to have one without the other.

Option 1: As to the first, if 'this' and 'that' are not present in sense data, then the mind's action of conception does the Buddhist no good in accounting for causality. In this case, we may bring to bear all the problems associated with arguing that 'this' and 'that' are presented in sense data.

Option 2: The better option for the Buddhist is the second. The Buddhist should argue that conception and sense data cannot be separated. Since we wrap phenomena in concepts, we must understand that the two are not intrinsically separated. Consequently, it is irrelevant to speak of separating them; it is a false dichotomy and a foolish question to raise.

However, the relevance of my criticisms against the Buddhist problem of 'this' and 'that' may still be seen even under option 2. Let us ask the question: If the mind that conceptualizes causal relationships did not exist (or the Thatāgata, as this question came up in the *Samyukta-āgama*), would interdependent co-origination (*paṭiccasamuppāda*) still be the case? Of course. Answering the question this way puts the answer back into the category of option 1. In option 1, all the problems of identifying 'this' and 'that' and their causal relations still apply.

Neither the Mind nor Sense Data: If 'this' and 'that' are not present in the phenomena of the mind or in sense experience, then we cannot know them and they are irrelevant. If 'this' and 'that' are not present in either sense data or the mind, then there can be no Buddhism.

CONCLUSION

It seems, then, that the Buddhist cannot even begin to intelligibly discuss the relationship of 'this' and 'that' in the flux of interdependent co-origination (*paṭiccasamuppāda*), even when granting 'this' and 'that' some fuzzy boundaries.

If this argument holds, then *paṭiccasamuppāda* is not an intelligible concept within the Buddha's theory of knowledge. Additionally, there are more problems with *paṭiccasamuppāda* that will be examined in chapter 15, a chapter that will pretend as though the problem discussed in this chapter does not exist.

13

Nāgārjuna

So, because all entities are empty,
Which views of permanence, etc., would occur,
And to whom, when, why, and about what
Would they occur at all?

I prostrate to Gotama
Who through compassion
Taught the true doctrine
Which leads to the relinquishing of all views.

Mūlamadhyamikakārikā 27.29–30

We are destroying speculations and every lofty thing raised up against the knowledge of God, and we are taking every thought captive to the obedience of Christ.

2 Corinthians 10:5

INTRODUCTION TO NĀGĀRJUNA

THE SECOND CENTURY *A.D.* Buddhist philosopher Nāgārjuna, the founder of the Mādhyamika School of Mahāyāna Buddhism, presents a considerable threat to my arguments in the last three chapters. If Nāgārjuna is correct, then scrupulous thinking itself may lead to *dukkha*. Logic truly would be a useful fiction from which I am asking too much. Nāgārjuna is one of the greatest philosophers of world history. While his work may be less familiar to Western philosophers, the impact of his work on Eastern philosophy and religion was shattering.

In the hundreds of years following the Buddha, Buddhist philosophers wrestled with the philosophical problems that seemed to be implied by the Buddha's theory of causality. Out of this struggle, the theory that reality is a whirling continuum of staccato moments (explained in chapter 6) came to be, and, thus, a form of Buddhist scholasticism called *Abhidharma* was born. Nāgārjuna found himself in a complex maze of debated questions within Buddhist scholasticism, and he would become famous for shaking this philosophical school to its core—so much so that he became the stuff of legend. We can be fairly sure he authored the *Mulamadyamikakārikā* (hereafter the *Kārikā*). In this great treatise, Nāgārjuna attacks his philosophical opponents on all fronts: epistemology, causality, and any other issue in Buddhist philosophical debate.

Nāgārjuna's philosophy had a powerful influence in the history of Eastern philosophy. Hsueh-li Cheng argues in *Empty Logic* that Zen Buddhism's rejection of concepts finds its source in Nāgārjuna's thought. Also, Śaṅkara, the eighth century philosopher whom some Western philosophers consider the best systematic presenter of Indian Philosophy, actually borrows from Nāgārjuna to solve several key problems within the relationship of *Ātman* and *Brahman*. The dependency is so strong that many of his contemporaries accused him of being a closet Buddhist.

Before analyzing Nāgārjuna's philosophy, we must look at the context of his thought. Nāgārjuna wrote his profound treatise six hundred years after the Buddha, in a tradition that invested great energy in trying to understand how the world can have patterns of consistency while still being *paṭiccasamuppāda*, (dependent arising). Everything that exists does so because previous events have made it to be. Different philosophers in the Buddhist tradition struggled with the question of causality, the question of the soul, the question of the uniqueness of some perceived moments or of their similarity with other perceived moments. Nāgārjuna finds himself standing in a whirling mass of concepts. Attempting to return to the Buddha's teaching by means of logical critique, he demolishes all claims about "fundamental natures" by demonstrating that all conceptual systems are ultimately self-contradictory. By letting go of concepts, one no longer experiences *dukkka* and finds *nirvāṇa* (a ceasing of *dukkha*). Nāgārjuna sees the forming of concepts as a way of trying to make things permanent. The Buddha taught that our desire for permanence is one of the causes of our suffering; the self wants to hold onto something constant. Ultimately, one must learn that one is not a "self," but a process. Thus, Nāgārjuna's end goals are soteriological, not epistemological. He claims his understanding is a method, not a theory.

NĀGĀRJUNA'S METHOD

Though he is presented as not having any metaphysical claims, he does have a starting point. Nāgārjuna's method begins with the world and the observer—the one who is trying to understand the world. The observer is part of the process. There is no third point of reference. Douglas D. Daye, who holds a perspective similar to Kalupahana, explains why the Buddhists begin here.[1]

> [C]onsider that to be able to answer the question of either the uniqueness or non-uniqueness of momentary experience presupposes first that there be a position independent of both the world as it is and our knowing it, from which we might compare. This obviously seems impossible without further and equally weak appeals to assumptions, which lead one to a circular argument.[2]

Dependence on a third party would lead to a circular argument since the third party would be the foundation of proof. Yet to prove the foundational third party's reliability would require another party—some additional foundation or point of leverage outside this original foundational third party; hence, the foundation is no longer the foundation, or the third party is the justification *just because* it is the third party. The second case would seem to be an inescapable tautology.

1. By saying Daye's position is similar to Kalupahana's, I am only referring to Kalupahana's later rejection of Nāgārjuna as a transcendentalist. Kalupahana maintains a minority position, which is why I am illuminating this section with the work of other scholars.

2. "Major Schools of the Mahāyāna: Mādhyamika," 80.

As I explained in chapter 5, the Buddhist epistemology is a radical empiricism holding that the only available knowledge comes from experience. Experience presents itself either as first person experience or third person experience, which results in language: a set of culturally agreed-upon conventional symbols that stand for experience that have been generally categorized by the society. Thus, members of a society can communicate with each other through language because they share common experiences. People segregate experience into categories useful for communication and for understanding the experiences they perceive. *Paṭiccasamuppāda* (dependent arising) has no innate categories. Humans impose categories on phenomena they observe.

However, the Buddha also believes that causality is empirically demonstrable. One of the Four Noble Truths is the causal origin of *dukkha*. Causality must be a real quality of the world. This one claim by the Buddha motivated many Buddhist religious teachers to try and explain causality over the centuries following the death of the Buddha. These scholastic Buddhists thought they had found the answers to the philosophical problems of causality.

When Nāgārjuna's contemporary philosophers offered their answers to philosophical conundrums, Nāgārjuna would easily shoot them down. Since they presented arguments, they had to assume logical consistency. Nāgārjuna would use their own commitment to reasoning to demonstrate that their view lacked logical grounds. One example of this is his analysis of change. When one argues for change, one must argue that something goes from being one thing to another. Nāgārjuna pointed out the age-old philosophical problem that if something becomes a different thing, then it becomes what it is not. If it becomes what it is not, then how can it be the same item and, therefore, an example of change? In the West, Parmenidies, because of his love of abstraction, accepted this as proof that change did not exist. Aristotle took a different approach, introducing the concepts of potentiality and actuality. Nāgārjuna held the problem was not in the world or in the concept of change but merely in the assumption that the world should be like our concept. Today we call this reasoning error *reification*.

In the Buddhist tradition, we find an example of reification in the Abhidharmist theory accounting for the perceived moments we experience. Each of these perceived located moments they called a *dharma* (This use is different from teaching "*dharma*"). These *dharmas* arise into being and then cease. There is nothing behind *dharmas.* A *dharma* is what one perceives—that is all. That is all. Yet people can look around and see that the phenomena of experience have patterns. I am typing this book on a computer. This machine runs more computations that any mathematician ever could. If there is no pattern in the world, then why does my computer act regularly? As you read this page, why does your mind stay in the condition it does so that you can follow the flow of my arguments? To account for the connectedness of *dharmas*, the Abhidharma scholastics postulated the meta-*dharma*, a sort of "*dharma* glue," holding all these punctilinear instances of reality together. This idea offered the constancy needed to explain the seeming regularity of *dharma* action.

However, when considered further, some Abhidharma scholastics realized that no amount of evidence could ever prove that meta-*dharmas* did not exist. They were just postulated to plug a hole in a system, like Ptolemy's epicycles. Hence, the concept was not falsifiable. It merely served to explain what we perceive. Once Buddhist philosophers realized this, they leveled the same criticism at *dharmas* as well. *Dharmas* were just extraneous concepts verification could never prove. They were just speculations. Many thinkers rejected *dharmas* because their only function was to make sense of language.

Reification also takes place, according to Nāgārjuna and other Buddhists, when we talk about the self. Each arising arises dependently based on everything else. What is it we will call the 'self' since all is process? Where does the self-process begin and end? What part of us is unchanging so we can name it 'self'? If there is no unchanging part, then why do "we" still seek to be named? "We" should abandon this desire for permanence, which causes suffering, and realize that the stream of perceived moments we call a mind is just a process, too.

As Nāgārjuna attempts to stay faithful to the Buddha's perspective, he does not seek to explain logic in relation to anything constant and permanent in the universe. In fact, my alleged Buddhist logic problem some might label reification.

According to Buddhism, reification is something we do all the time. Nāgārjuna points out that it happens when we make up words to talk about words.[3] It is true that "walk" is a verb, but when we think that verbs exist in the same way that a walking man exists, we commit reification. A language that talks about another language is called a metalanguage. When we then talk about how language relates to reality we have abstracted even further from the original concrete referent of words and are speaking in a meta-metalanguage. That last sentence you just read is an example of meta-meta-metalanguage because it was a commentary on meta-metalanguage and so on, *ad infinitum*. By analyzing concepts instead of the world, we are going beyond experience, which is the foundation of our concepts, and reading more into the world than is there.

Nāgārjuna gutted concepts, laboring to show that at some point they are empty of content. Take existence. If something does not exist, then how are these appearances we see there? However, if our only observation of reality is appearances, then we are in big trouble because how can appearances be real? Through these types of arguments Nāgārjuna developed the Fourteen Antinomies: One cannot say whether the world is (1) finite, (2) or not, (3) or both, (4) or neither; or (5) permanent, (6) or not, (7) or both, (8) or neither; or conclude that, after nirvāṇa, the Buddha is (9) existent, (10) or not, (11) or both, (12) or neither; or be certain about whether mind and matter are (13) identical (14) or not. He presents his objective in the opening dedicatory verses, where he sets out what the "Perfect Buddha, the best of teachers" teaches himself:

> I prostrate to the Perfect Buddha,
> The best of teachers, who taught that
> Whatever is dependently arisen is
> Unceasing, unborn,
> Unannihilated, not permanent,
> Not coming, not going
> Without distinction, without identity,
> And free from conceptual construction.[4]

3. Here I am offering my own summary of what Nāgārjuna is doing in the *Kārikā*. For a more detailed treatment, see Garfield, *Fundamental Wisdom*.

4. Ibid., 2.

Conceptual constructions about what is underneath what we observe are just words about words about words. In the end, words are a raft to get you to the other side of the lake of this world. They are useful but no more. When one adds to them a reality they do not have, one creates problems. Meta-metalanguage on language. Once language loses its usefulness, it can be cast aside like a raft one no longer needs once the far shore is reached. (Unless you are in California; then you will have to pay a fine!) There is no truth in concepts, only in experience, since words are symbols for experience. In the end, all statements that are true are both empirical and tautological. A teacup is a teacup. Love is love. Experience is just that, experience. As Daye writes:

> "[A]ll ontological descriptions are merely pragmatically useful but provisional fictions. They guarantee only that what is known is simply (and tautologically) consistent with what *is* known. That is, no conclusions about the transcendental or ultimate nature. . . are authorized by statements verified by public or private observation."[5]

What is left is *śūnyatā* (emptiness). Human categories lack internal meaning because phenomena do not come divided up into categories. Phenomena come to us devoid of conceptual meaning. Instead, the observer allows conceptual meaning to be filled by having the concept point to something in phenomena. This means that the "world" is emptiness devoid of meaning, substance, and permanence. And emptiness is not a word we can grab onto. It is only *our* category for a lack of categories. As Daye puts it, "Emptiness is a nonreferring word *about* referring words; it has nine letters!"[6] Nāgārjuna would accuse anyone who felt they needed absolute certainty of grasping, of coveting, in a way that brings on suffering.

Logic, as a metalanguage, may describe relations between our conceptions, but it does not describe anything in the universe itself. In Nāgārjuna's philosophy, this type of thinking must be thought of as a "pragmatically useful but provisional fiction."[7] The laws of logic are not empirically verifiable. Instead, we use them to evaluate

5. "Major Schools of the Mahāyāna," 93; Daye's emphasis.

6. Ibid., 92.

7. "Major Schools of the Mahāyāna," 93.

whether or not something has been, in fact, empirically verified. If the laws of logic did not work for our purposes, then we would throw them away.

Nāgārjuna's perspective then makes logic a fiction that individuals perpetuate to live in the world and nothing more. Thus, my argument shows the work of an unenlightened mind that is still looking for permanence. My objection is not wrong, just empty.

TWO OBJECTIONS TO NĀGĀRJUNA'S METHOD

Criticizing Nāgārjuna's philosophy presents us with a difficult task, second only to understanding Nāgārjuna's philosophy. Over the course of his career, even David Kalupahana, one of the most learned scholars of Buddhist philosophy, has changed his own position on Nāgārjuna.[8] Certainly some may read this and think that Nāgārjuna has not been given a fair shake. Unfortunately, the nature of this topic makes that response inevitable.[9]

Beginning with a Tautology: A First Reply

Nāgārjuna would like us to think his method holds no assumptions—that it simply applies to an opponent's assumptions and dismantles them pointing the opponent away from hope in concepts like normative logical validity, and toward liberation from suffering. However, this is not the case.

Daye, representing Nāgārjuna's position to modern minds, presents two alternatives for understanding the relationship of knowledge. He suggests that we consider knowledge as either the interaction between the world and the individual who perceives the world or as something justified by a third party beyond merely the individual and the perceived world. Daye rejects this second situation, accusing it of being tautological. As quoted earlier, he writes:

> [C]onsider that to be able to answer the question of either

8. Kalupahana's early view of Nāgārjuna as a transcendentalist is represented in Kalupahana, *Buddhist Philosophy*, 129–41. The view of Nāgārjuna represented by this chapter may be found in Kalupahana, *History of Buddhist Philosophy*, 160–9.

9. For an excellent and brief summary of standard interpretations of Nāgārjuna's position, see Yandell and Netland, *Buddhism*, 42–46.

> the uniqueness or nonuniqueness of momentary experience presupposes first that there be *a position independent of both the world as it is and our knowing it*, from which we might compare. This obviously seems impossible without further and equally weak appeals to assumptions which lead one to a circular argument.[10]

Now, according to the Christian Scriptures, God is in "The position independent of both the world as it is and our knowing it." Following Daye's argument, the ability to know the way the world is apart from the Buddhist view of phenomena ends in circular reasoning. This would imply that Christian appeals to the Bible or God himself would be treated just like claims in the *Vedas* and *Upaniṣads* if we view them through the lens of a Buddhist epistemology. Many opponents of the Christian faith have attempted to establish that assuming God in one's epistemology and then proving God or a claim in the Christian worldveiw from that epistemology is arguing in a vicious circle.

Daye attempts to avoid such a problem for Buddhism by eliminating the help of any appeals to a third perspective. He then follows this notion through to its end, concluding that knowledge of what underlies experience is impossible. Meaningful statements directly refer to experience. Such statements are tautological. When we go beyond experience we reify:

> [A]ll ontological descriptions are merely pragmatically useful but provisional fictions. They guarantee only that what is known is simply (and tautologically) consistent with what *is* known. That is, no conclusions about the transcendental or ultimate nature . . . are authorized by statements verified by public or private observation; rather, what can be known (explicitly) *is* to be known. Language and its correct consistent use guaranties nothing except itself; it is empty.[11]

So language has no special content apart from what can be verified by experience. Meaning starts and ends with experience, and language adds nothing new to experience. This move is supposed to provide Buddhist epistemology an escape from making tautologies.

10. "Major Schools of the Mahāyāna," 80; emphasis mine.

11. Ibid. 93; Daye's emphasis.

However, this move really just substitutes one tautology for another. Suppose, for a moment, that trusting authoritative testimony from a third party is circular, even if that being is a god. And circular reasoning, tautological reasoning, is bad. Really bad. No being can be *more* authoritative, and no epistemologically authoritative statement can come from the testimony of a divine being. Discourse can *only* refer to back to the content of experience. Knowledge is experience—or more clearly—experience is experience.

Notice what Daye has done: he has merely exchanged circles. With one hand, he rejects a third perspective to provide insight into metaphysical relationships. With the other, he embraces the "pragmatically useful but provisional fictions" of concepts, which, due to radical empiricism, "guarantee only that what is known is simply (and tautologically) consistent with what *is* known."[12] What is the warrant for switching from one tautology to another? Is it because tautologies are bad? If so, then switching makes no sense. If tautologies really are the problem, then one is a fool if one picks either one.

One might say, "See how right Nāgārjuna is! We can't trust sense experience or divine revelation. Yes! Brilliant!" Yet that conclusion is not acceptable because we are looking at the basis for Nāgārjuna's own views. We are asking: why *his* methodology and not another? Notice that the tautological quality of concepts within the Nāgārjuna's epistemology builds firmly upon his presupposed starting point. Nāgārjuna may think metaphysical concepts (any concept not verified by sense experience; therefore, the laws of logic fall under this category) are useful provisional fictions that may be abandoned when they get in the way. However, his conclusion seems to be the outgrowth of an assumption, which we may freely contest. Maybe Nāgājuna's posited problems could be solved by third-party arbitration.

Later I will argue that the place of a third perspective may be justified in a way that goes between the horns of this dilemma. For now, it is sufficient to show that both the third perspective and the assumption that the only two factors in knowledge are the knower

12. Ibid.

and the object of knowledge (the world) result in tautologies. So the choice to reject this third perspective is arbitrary.

Nāgājuna's Enthymeme: A Second Reply

Now a second objection. The following is a very simple argument against Nāgārjuna that some might consider inadequate. However, we must keep his main objective before us. Nāgārjuna presents a host of arguments in the *Kārikā*, but he is working to accomplish a very simple project in the mind of his reader. Some may object to my simple and straight-forward argument against Nāgārjuna's project, saying that I must work through all twenty-seven chapters of the *Kārikā*, refuting every quatrain. Nevertheless, the author of the *Kārikā* would understand my strategy. After all, it is his own! He wrote his great text for a simple purpose: to drive the lover of views to enlightenment. Why should not a simple goal be honored with a simple response?

Here is my argument: Nāgārjuna's method is dishonest because he is not reasoning. He appears to be reasoning, but he is actually *just* practicing rhetoric. What is more, he is practicing the worst kind of rhetoric—sophistry. The journey we must take to prove this will require us to take a few twists and turns. Stay with me.

Nāgārjuna views concepts as useful fictions. Why? Because the logical norms that might apply to the proper handling of concepts are at least a metalanguage, if not a meta-metalanguage. From Nāgārjuna's perspective, my discussion about justifying logic is speaking in a meta-meta-metalanguage; therefore, the very posing of my objection receives, and has received, the nasty label of "reification." This nasty name-calling tries to elude the question of why reasoning is trustworthy against the flux of interdependent co-origination. Nevertheless, when interpreters of Nāgārjuna press logic into the category of "useful fiction," we must ask how Nāgārjuna wanted to *use* logic. "Usefulness" makes no sense without a goal. Useful things serve a purpose. As we have already said, Nāgārjuna wanted to create a method to enlighten men trapped on the gerbil-wheel of philosophy. His analytical logical method is intended to show how conceptual thinking is just shuffling 'emptiness' (*śūnyatā*). Emptiness has no substance. Think of it like the conclusion to

Wittgenstein's *Tractatus,* "Whereof one cannot speak, therefore one must be silent."[13] Once we understand the Buddha's radical empiricism, it drives us to this. So Nāgārjuna's clever arguments attempt to make us let go of clever arguments. We cause ourselves suffering by holding onto concepts as though they are permanent entities in themselves. They are not. They change like the rest of phenomena. When we put strong confidence in logic, it will also disappoint us.

Nāgārjuna offers sixty-three views with which he disagrees. The first sixty-two views suffer obliteration under his dialectical method. However, in a shocking, plot-twist ending, the last view to suffer obliteration is. . . his own view. He concludes the *Kārikā* with these two quatrains:

> So, because all entities are empty,
> Which views of permanence, etc., would occur,
> And to whom, when, why, and about what
> Would they occur at all?
> I prostrate to Gotama
> Who through compassion
> Taught the true doctrine
> Which leads to the relinquishing of all views.[14]

Nāgārjuna advocates the rejection of all views, even his own. Some disagree with this interpretation. Jay Garfield argues convincingly that Nāgārjuna clearly draws this conclusion. It would seem, then, from Nāgārjuna's perspective, that answering our question of how Buddhism justifies logic is futile. Buddhism does not justify anything—it ends suffering! Nāgārjuna makes this clear in *Kārikā* 13.8:

> The victorious ones have said
> That emptiness is the relinquishing of all views.
> For whomever emptiness is a view,
> That one will accomplish nothing.[15]

If one thinks through Nāgārjuna's method and makes the final step, then no way remains to return and heed any views at all. The notion of worldview then is completely antagonistic to Nāgārjuna's philoso-

13. Wittgenstein, *Tractatus Logico-Philosophicius.*.
14. *Mūlamadhyamikakārikā* 27.29–30, in Garfield, *Fundamental Wisdom.*
15. Garfield, *Fundamental Wisdom.*

phy. He claims his is a method with no content save that of direct experience. The method serves a soteriological goal of bringing the man who craves concepts to *nirvāṇa*.[16]

However, let us consider this: Nāgārjuna wants to motivate those concept-craving fellows to abandon concepts. He does this by attempting to generate consistent arguments, for if the arguments were inconsistent, then Nāgārjuna would not advocate we embrace them (nor would he). Right? If we are to heed his valid arguments, then we should heed them because they are *good* arguments, which require that they be *valid*.

Now let us examine, in a terse form, Nāgārjuna's main point:

> By my logically consistent arguments you ought to relinquish all views.
> My view is also a view.
> Therefore you should relinquish my view.

If one accepts his perspective and, finally, rejects his view, then it has been accepted. This argument runs into a serious problem: If it is true, that makes it false, which makes it true, which makes it false, which makes it true.[17]

If one accepts Nāgārjuna's perspective on concepts, one may not see this as a problem. It is no wonder the history of philosophy has shown a strong link between logic and metaphysics. In his survey of the scope of logic, Mortimer Adler notes the similarity between the breadth of subjects covered in metaphysics and the breadth of subjects touched by the study of logic:

> In the words of Josiah Roice, [logic] is "the science of order" and it is applicable to the order of things as well as the order of thought. So conceived, the science of logic is sometimes regarded as having the same type of generality which is traditionally assigned to metaphysics; as for example, by Russell is his essay,

16. I say this even though *nirvāṇa*, in his view, cannot be separated from saṃsāra because of the conventional nature of conceptualization.

> Whatever is the limit of *nirvāṇa*,
> That is the limit of cyclic existence.
> There is not even the slightest difference between them,
> Or even the subtlest thing. (*Kārikā* 25.20 from Ibid.)

17. If the reader thinks that I should have said "confused" instead of "false," I embrace that criticism. But such an objection only pertains if a digital true-false distinction is maintained in regard to the claim that I should have said "confused."

> "Logic is the Essence of Philosophy."[18]

Logic can easily feel the stigma of "metaphysical concept" since it cannot be verified directly by experience. Yet when it gets cast as a provisional fiction, something fun and interesting happens. Take the above summation of Nāgārjuna's final position, that view number sixty-three, which he advocated we reject, was his own. It was demonstrated that his logical argument intended to motivate us to abandon our grasping of concepts, especially metaphysical concepts.

Though the persuasive structure mentioned above looks like a tightly reasoned argument, it is actually what Aristotle called an *enthymeme*, a rhetorical syllogism (1357a). Aristotle gives an illustration of how the enthymeme works:

> The enthymeme must consist of few propositions, fewer often that those than those which make up the normal syllogism. For if any of these propositions is a familiar fact, there is no need even to mention it; the hearer adds it himself. Thus, to show that Dorieus has been victor in a contest for which the prize is a crown, it is enough to say "for he has been victor in the Olympic games," without adding, "And in the Olympic games the prize is a crown," a fact which everyone knows.[19]

Modern commentators present Nāgārjuna as one of the greatest analytical philosophers of history. In actuality, he is one of the greatest rhetoricians of history. His method is a powerful enthymeme, which I summarized above.

> By my logically consistent arguments you ought to relinquish all views.
> My view is also a view.
> Therefore you should relinquish my view.

However, we supply this bit of information:

> Logical consistency determines whether a view ought to be accepted.

If we add this premise to Nāgārjuna's enthymeme, then the argument is remarkably persuasive. The final structure is something like this: (I will letter them for reference)

18. Adler, *The Synopticon*, 799.
19. Aristotle, *Rhetoric*, 1357a 20–22.

A. Logical consistency determines whether a view ought to be accepted.
B. By my logically consistent arguments you ought to relinquish all views
C. My view is also a view.
D. Therefore you should relinquish my view.

Notice that by inserting this premise, one encounters a big problem. Once a person adds the premise, draws the conclusion, and believes that conclusion on the basis of inserting the missing premise (something Aristotle said was psychologically very persuasive[20]), that person can never again embrace the missing premise—namely, that logical reasoning about views guides us to which position we should accept.[21] So Nāgārjuna has essentially proven nothing. He has merely set up a logic bomb, or better, a logic smart bomb. It is targeted to minds that believe logical consistency should warrant whether a view should be accepted or not. When it blows up in such a mind, it has the effect of creating doubt where faith once was in a reasoning philosopher's mind—not doubt regarding claims about the world; rather, doubt regarding the utility and authority of reason itself.

When Nāgārjuna's victim returns to premise A, he can not accept it in the same way he did to make the enthymeme work. If he continually applies the standards of logical consistency, attempting to discover acceptable beliefs, then he has not "relinquished all views." Nāgārjuna was rhetorically brilliant. If someone were to object to his surreptitious argument, he could always say, "My victim did it to himself."

Now we arrive at the crux of the matter. Does Nāgārjuna want us to accept his view because it is logical or not? If we accept it because of its logic, then we abandon logic as a test for truth to which all truth must submit. However, if we accept it for nonlogical reasons, then what is the business of using arguments to persuade?

20. See Book 1, chapters 1 and 2; and Book 2, chapter 22 in *Rhetoric*.

21. Some think that "Logical consistency determines whether a view ought to be accepted" is not a view. However, if Nāgārjuna thought his own perspective was a view and his own perspective had no content at all (being "emptiness"), it seems that my summary of the missing premise must also be a view. At least Nāgārjuna would consider it such.

Nāgārjuna wants to give the appearance that he is practicing honest philosophy. Yet Nāgārjuna does not care about trying to justify the validity of logic. He does not want to show people how to find answers. Rather, *he wants you to stop asking those questions!*

CONCLUSION TO NĀGĀRJUNA

In the end, Nāgārjuna's method does Buddhism little good in answering the objection raised against harmonizing logic with *paṭiccasamuppāda*. As we saw earlier, his method assumes what it tries to prove. It presupposes the circle of radical empiricism's tautological knowledge instead of presupposing a third perspective, which could potentially provide a useful answer to the Buddhist problem of logic. By presupposing an epistemology of radical empiricism, Nāgārjuna leaves no option but a pragmatic criterion of truth for which all apparently "objective" means of proof are arms extending from human goals. Nāgārjuna cannot account for logic. He can only trick readers with various versions of his logic bomb in order to reiterate his own arbitrary pragmatism.

PRAGMATIC ACCOUNT OF LOGIC: CONCLUDING THE BUDDHA'S LOGIC PROBLEM

Two chapters ago, we answered five objections to the argument that Buddhism cannot account for logical validity within the constant change of "dependent arising" (*paṭiccasamuppāda*)—namely, that: (1) transcendental arguments are not permissible in interreligious dialogue; (2) validity does not exist; (3) logical validity is somehow a natural, organic process; (4) natural selection explains why humans think logically; and, finally, (5) Quine undermined the notion of logical validity through his theory of radical translation. Each objection failed to answer the problem.

The previous chapter examined the problem of 'this' and 'that', which arises out of the Buddhist account of logic and the Buddhist doctrine of *paṭiccasamuppāda*. I demonstrated that the Buddha's attempt to not make universal statements but rather only particular statements; referring to 'this', did nothing to help him with his logic problem of accounting for logic within the causal theory of *paṭiccasamuppāda*.

Finally, we considered Nāgārjuna's analysis of concepts. Nāgārjuna believed that concepts were useful fictions to help us navigate through the furniture of the world. Validity would fall into this category. Considering it an actual item that had some control or effect in the world would be reification. Likewise, accounting for it as a method without explaining its connection to phenomena makes it something "with sound and fury, signifying nothing." This is why Nāgārjuna thought of concepts that were not directly connected to experience as "*useful* fictions." Nāgārjuna then does not consider the meta-language of logic to have any foundation for constancy. He gives a pragmatic account of language.

Our counter-argument for Nāgārjuna's objection was twofold. Either his argument is valid, in which case we should listen to it, or invalid, in which case it should be rejected. If Nāgārjuna has no confidence in logic, then his arguments are surreptitious and deceptive. We concluded that his method was an enthymeme with a hidden premise. Application of that hidden premise to the argument then forced the rejection of that hidden premise. Nāgārjuna's method, then, is an empty logic bomb designed to get the one who accepts it to stop asking questions and focus on what is useful for ending suffering.

This brings us to a final Buddhist strategy for addressing the problem of rational norms, and on this one the Buddha gets the last word. Notice that in most of the potential or actual Buddhist responses to the Buddha's logic problem, the subject of *usefulness* seems to appear either in the distance or, in Nāgārjuna's case, up close and personal. Kalupahana points out time and again that the Buddha is a kind of proto-positivist. He separates all claims into statements about the world (facts) and statements about our own internal feelings (values). Yet the Buddha is not a full-blown positivist because he rejects an absolute distinction between facts and values. Perception comes from sense contact. And every instance of contact has feeling involved with it.

I have presented this logic problem to Buddhist philosophers. They answer, again and again, that logical structures are *useful fictions*. Humans have goals and humans think in ways to achieve those goals. If someone wants to build a rocket, that person needs to think in such a way to facilitate building that rocket. They say if one does not think with what we call "validity," then one will be incompetent and not achieve one's goal.

The goal of the Buddha was the cessation of *dukkha*, and the Vedic and Upaniṣadic thinkers did not provide answers that met that goal. Their appeal to sources of knowledge other that empirical verification did not end suffering. So the Buddha's method of reasoning was characterized by pragmatism, and as latter thinkers wrestled through his proto-positivism, they recognized that everything that was not fact or value was a tool.

To illustrate, take the statement:

> All statements are either of empirically verified fact or value.

One can recognize that this statement is self-defeating since it itself is neither a statement of feeling (how the positivists define value) nor does it state something that is empirically verified. The above statement is instead a statement *about* statements. It defines classes. It is a meta-metalanguage, a useful positivist tool.

For the Buddha then, reasoning is useful for the goal of ending suffering. If the structure of human perceptions altered tomorrow so that humans had to adopt a completely different system of logic, the Buddha would advocate that we think in accordance with our own goal to gain the understanding necessary to end *dukkha*. Since the Buddha is goal-oriented, he need not account for absolute truth or absolute validity. We know that we are ending our own suffering when we internally perceive the cessation of our own *dukkha*. If we reason a certain way and, following that, we see that our *dukkha* continues, the Buddha would advocate that we stop and think rightly. In other words, think in a way that will bring about our desired goal. For this reason, Kalupahana writes, "But since he did not believe that there is one absolutely true view, the Buddha could claim that his conception of truth is not confined to any particular time, i.e., that it is atemporal (*akālika*)."[22]

Even though it would appear that Buddhism cannot answer the problem of logical validity, Buddhist philosophers like Kalupahana cast logical operations in terms of pragmatism. We should then

22. *History of Buddhist Philosophy*, 91.

think of pragmatism—Buddhism's epistemological Alamo—as its last stand. We will have to leave Buddhism's last stand for our last chapter.

14

The Buddhist Problem of Other Minds

Even if I know something on the basis of best faith, that may be empty, hollow and confused . . . .

Majjhima-nikāya 2.170

Deceitful is the mind most of all and desperately sick. Who is he that can know it?

Jeremiah 17:9

EPISTEMOLOGICAL CONSTRAINTS

To follow the argument I will present in this chapter, there are a few things we should remember. So far we have established that that the Buddha is a radical empiricist. Everything must be empirically verified. One may not accept something on faith. Like the Buddha said, "Even if I know something on the basis of best faith, that may be empty, hollow and confused."[1] In the chapter on epistemology, we showed that the Buddha does not just accept testimony, but he first has to verify the authority of the one offering testimony. Even testimony must first be supported by experience. Authority can in no way be based on some divine warrant. Instead, it comes from the testifier's proximity to empirical verification.

1. *Majjhima-nikāya* 2.170 quoted in Kalupahana, *History of Buddhist Philosophy*, 31.

In the chapter on the three marks of existence, I also discussed the nonsubstantiality of reality (*anatta*), including both the human person and the world. The Buddha explained the individual person as five aggregates, which are body or material form (*rūpa*), feeling or sensation (*vedanā*), perception (*saññā*), dispositions (*saṅkhārā*), and consciousness (*viññāṇa*). According to the Buddha, these are not substances that interact. These are only categories of the perceived world that one encounters, the "bundle" of phenomena we call the individual.

THE ARGUMENT

The Buddha made it clear that the meaning of one's terms comes from one's experience. One understands material form (*rūpa*), feeling or sensation (*vedanā*), perception (*saññā*), dispositions (*saṅkhārā*), and consciousness (*viññāṇa*) because one experiences them. Yet one does not necessarily experience these with others. One does experience the material form of others. One supposes that the feelings or sensations, perceptions, dispositions, and consciousness which one experiences individually are also present to the material forms of individuals one encounters. Nevertheless, one has no empirical verification of this.[2] One can only have empirical verification of another's physical form (*rūpa*) but not of those things that seem to be associated with the mind (*nāma*).

At first this may seem like I am really reaching, but reflect on what the Buddha actually taught about knowledge. The Vedic and Upaniṣadic thinkers did not provide empirical justification for their claims. For this reason, their claims were not testable since there was no possible situation that could ever prove them false. The Buddha, therefore, would not accept any claim unless it had been verified by the senses.

2. One may wish to say that testimony is a kind of empirical verification. I suggested that strategy earlier when talking about using testimony to support premises in a syllogism. However, the question here is different. Notice that if one were to use testimony as proof, it would presuppose that the individual is already having experiences; thus, to accept testimony from an animated material form begs the question that the testifying individual does already have the shared experiences, which is exactly what is at issue. All claims must be supported empirically first. This counter-argument is tracing through the implications of trying to hold the Buddha's epistemology consistently.

When one experiences what one supposes to be the mind of another, one is actually experiencing the form of another. Keep in mind that material form (*rūpa*) is not substantial. One should not look for an underlying substance, essence, or whatnot beyond our perception. Dignāga, whom Kalupahana describes as "the last of the great Buddhist philosophers of India, who attempted to remain faithful to the original Buddhist tradition,"[3] helps us understand this. Dignāga illustrates how subtle metaphysical distinctions can be. Take the distinction "between cognizing 'blue' (*nīlam vijānāti*) and cognizing something 'as blue' (*nīlam iti vijānāti*). . . . The former is perception (*pratayakṣa*) that involves the conception of color; the latter is a metaphysical construction that assumes the color to be characteristic or property (*lakṣaṇa*) of a reality existing object."[4] Trying to get at underlying substances underneath our perceptions is grasping after metaphysical concepts. Metaphysical claims are, among other things, claims that cannot possibly be empirically verified.

So let's be consistent. If metaphysical claims are claims that cannot possibly be empirically verified, then the claim that *there are further phenomena occurring behind the phenomena we can access* is a metaphysical claim! One looks out into the world, seeing many things and hearing many things. But no one will ever see another person's four mental aggregates. This argument has far-reaching ramifications for Buddhism. If the postulation of other minds is a metaphysical claim, then compassion for other people—or better, the whole project of ethics—becomes an effort based on metaphysical claims.

I wondered if I had understood the Buddha correctly on this, so while I was in Los Angeles working on this book I visited Wat Tai, a Theravāda temple and monastery in order to discuss various matters in Buddhist philosophy with Wat Tai's monks. My lead contact was Sumana Samahita, a monk who had spent years studying the *Dīgha-Nikāya*. He acted as my translator during my conversations with other monks.

3. *History of Buddhist Philosophy*, 194.

4. Ibid., 197.

Through Samahita's kind work of translating, I had the opportunity to ask the head monk of Wat Tai specifically about this problem. I raised the Buddhist problem of other minds and, furthermore, the critical problem this creates for a Buddhist's compassion.

"If one cannot empirically know the minds of other people, then pursing knowledge of other minds is inconsistent with the Buddha's doctrine regarding the kind of knowledge necessary to end one's suffering." Then I asked, "Is not compassion then inconsistent with the kind of knowing that leads one to be able to end one's suffering?"

Samahita translated. There was a long pause.

Then the head monk gave his answer.

Samahita heard the answer but then waited to reply. He himself seemed surprised by it, as though the head teacher had cast a pebble into Samahita's still pond. With calm thoughtfulness, Samahita's eyes saw the ripples and thought through their implications. Then he looked to me and gave the translation. The answer surprised me. He said, "You have correctly understood our doctrine. If someone truly understands the Buddha's teaching, they will see that compassion is meaningless."

The Buddha thought that there were other minds out there, not substantial minds, but minds nonetheless. To make our discussion less 'self' oriented, we will not talk of minds or people out there since all those terms are potentially loaded words for some Buddhists. So let us define an individual as a *location of empirical testing*. Somewhere "out there" other phenomena are resulting from contact of empirical investigation. If metaphysical claims are that which we cannot possibly verify, then the Buddha cannot verify with the phenomena he is privy to that there are any individuals beyond himself. This makes the Buddha's epistemology an enemy of compassion.

OBJECTION 1: WHAT ABOUT LANGUAGE?

The obvious counter-argument to the Buddhist problem of other minds comes from language. Daily life involves constant contact with other individuals through the use of language. We speak words.

When others speak a word, we recognize not only the meaning of the word used but also the action of another individual mentally pointing to a commonly agreed-upon object. Words are products of a community. Words are sounds that have meaning assigned by the community. The second factor of the Eightfold Noble Path reiterates this understanding of the meaning of words. We, as individuals, form concepts guided by the conceptions of others. The forming of our own conceptions is a necessarily linguistic activity.

Philosophical discussion of language's need for community can be traced all the way back to Augustine.[5] Perhaps even further. But Ludwig Wittgenstein, in the twentieth century, famously made a further demand that language only refer to objects that can be identified within a community. This demand he distinctly formalized in his Private Language Argument. In *Philosophical Investigations*, he develops his legendary argument by first suggesting a hypothetical situation that he felt a certain sensation:

> Let us imagine the following case. I want to keep a diary about the recurrence of a certain sensation. To this end I associate it with the sign "S" and write this sign in a calendar for every day on which I have the sensation.—I will mark first of all that a definition of the sign cannot be formulated.—But still I can give myself a kind of ostensive definition.[6]

So Wittgenstein has a symbol that he uses to stand for this sensation with which he is well aquatinted. But can he really point to that sensation?

> Not in the ordinary sense. But I speak or write the sign down, and at the same time I concentrate my attention on the sensation—and so, as it were, point to it inwardly. But what is this ceremony for? for that is all it seems to be! A definition surely seems to establish the meaning of a sign.—Well, that is done precisely by the concentrating of my attention; for in this way I impress on my self the connection between the sign and the sensation.[7]

5. See *Confessions* 1.8 in Augustine, *Confessions.* See also *On Christian Teaching* 2.1–5 in ibid.

6. *Part 1, sect. 258.*

7. *Philosophical Investigations, Part 1, sect. 258.*

Wittgenstein can connect the sensation and the sign of the sensation for himself, but he cannot for someone else.

> But "I impress it on myself" can only mean: this process brings it about that I remember the connection right in the future. But in the present case I have no criteria of correctness. One would like to say: whatever is going to seem right to me is right. And that only means here that we can't talk about 'right'.[8]

Wittgenstein uses this argument to show how one cannot talk with another about the meaning of a sign for a private referent. The hearer has no way to dispute whether the speaker should have assigned that sign and not another. Put into another form the private language argument reads:

> To name you need a rule.
> If you need a rule, you must have a criterion of correctability.
> Therefore, if you have no rule, it is impossible to name.[9]

Wittgenstein believed that being surrounded by a community of judges sometimes supplies the needed contrast between merely seeming to be correct and actually being correct. According to him there can never be a meaningful internal language that has no connection to other judges who can evaluate whether a certain sign should apply to a publicly agreed-upon object. With Wittgenstein's Private Language Argument, the criterion of meaning becomes use, which is consistent with the Buddha's nonabsolutism. Therefore, a *community* is required to judge the meaning of language. Some may want to use spoken language, then, as a way of supporting the existence of a community.

Unfortunately, the Private Language Argument may not be used to support the presence of other *locations of empirical testing*. The Private Language Argument concludes that meanings are only possible within communities. But it does not prove the existence of communities. It only tells us the meaningful language requires a community. Therefore, it argues that language presupposes communities. Now communities may need language, but the Private

8. Ibid.

9. I am indebted to Douglas Jones, fellow of philosophy at New Saint Andrews College, for this clear summary of the Private Language Argument.

Language Argument merely determines what can constitute a language.

Even worse, the Private Language Argument will turn on anyone who tries to use it to justify the existence of minds. If there are not judges, then there is no language. If one's epistemology cannot justify the claim that a community exists, then that epistemology cannot account for the meaning of language.

Though we still have much to learn about language, obviously words have meaning. And there are other people with similar experiences beyond the confines of our own mind. (Anyone disagreeing with this should never marry.) The point of this chapter is to run a *reductio ad absurdum* taking the Buddha's empiricism seriously, applying it as far as it demands to go. The price we pay for the Buddha's radical empiricism is the relegation of anything beyond one's phenomena to the class of metaphysical claim. This should make us a bit suspicious of "metaphysical claim" as a pejorative term. It seems that the Buddha's epistemology, if applied consistently, ruins ethics and language.

OBJECTION 2: WHAT ABOUT ESP?

The insightful reader may be thinking: What about ESP? It seems that extrasensory perception would go along way toward answering this argument. If one could, by some direct act of perception, access the phenomena of another mind, then the other aggregates could be verified. The texts of early Buddhism suggest that the Buddha had the six forms of extrasensory perception. For example, we read in the *Cankī Sutta* that the Buddha used telepathy to understand someone's thoughts so that he might better persuade him.[10]

In *A History of Buddhist Philosophy: Continuities and Discontinuities*, Kalupahana points out some things that anticipate the Buddhist problem of other minds. His discussion of clairvoyance, which for the Buddha is the ability to verify death and rebirth resulting from the influence of karma, attempts to deal with the problem of other minds:

> The recognition of such a form of knowledge [like clairvoyance] appears to be extremely arbitrary on the part of anybody

10. *Majjhima-nikāya*, 2.169.

> claiming to be an empiricist. The question is often raised as to how an empiricist can explain knowledge of other-minds, let alone their evolution through several existences. It seems that doubts about the existence of other-minds are generated more by philosophers who attempt to reach ultimate objectivity in their explanations. In the Indian context, the Materialists, the Ājīvikas, and even the Jainas seem to have been confronted with such problems. In the case of the Buddha, the issue was to a great extent dissolved by his adoption of a philosophical standpoint that simply avoids generating such problems.[11]

Kalupahana points out that later Buddhist philosophers who wanted objectivity in knowledge looked to justify other minds.[12]

Kalupahana answers the problem of other minds by refusing to deal with it. He poisons the well by casting suspicion on those who raise the question by labeling his opponents as those who "attempt to reach ultimate objectivity in their explanations."[13] Seeking objectivity is bad, apparently. He gives no mechanism that explains how the attempt for objectivity necessarily creates the philosophical problem. Odd that objectivity was not a problem when he was proving the law of causality.

Furthermore, Kalupahana mentions that several other philosophical positions, some similar in certain aspects to Buddhism, also had to engage the problem. However, he claims that the Buddha did not have to interact with the problem of other minds because of "his adoption of a philosophical standpoint that simply avoids generating such problems."[14] The problem of other minds raised in this chapter, however, arises out of the Buddha's radical empiricism. It rests on a serious consideration of the Buddha's view of phenomena (*nāma-rūpa*). We are asking how it is possible to justify the presence of another *location of empirical testing*. How can we, while holding to the Buddha's epistemology, claim that there are phenomena beyond the phenomena that we can empirically access? We have already covered how the Private Language Argument and the second factor of the Eightfold Noble Path seem to discount language as evidence

11. *History of Buddhist Philosophy*, 41.
12. Ibid.
13. Ibid.
14. Ibid.

for other minds since discussions of meaning first presuppose a community. On the contrary, it is the Buddha's philosophical approach itself that generates the problem.

Offering ESP as a solution only compounds the problem. Though the Buddha claimed to possess ESP, so did many others. The Buddha rejected the claim of omniscience by the Jaina leader Nigaṇha Nātaputta because the claim could not be justified beyond the religious leader's say-so. Thus, it follows we cannot take the Buddha's word just because he says so. At least we cannot if we want to use the Buddha's epistemology.

I am willing to grant that the Buddha had ESP because I like him, and I want to think the best of him. Nevertheless, my good will is no basis for a truth claim or even close to a proper warrant for belief. We must ask if the Buddha's ESP insights can be trusted. When we look at the different religious groups that claimed insight into the nature of the universe through ESP, we find that different schools held different views on the nature of what exactly they had observed through their higher-sensing abilities. In *The Greater Exposition of Action* (*Mahākammavibhanga Sutta*),[15] the Buddha discusses the results of human actions in the cycle of birth and death. He makes several conclusions about the causal relations of *karmic* actions. More important to our discussion is his rejection of certain claims made by a "recluse or brahmin [who] attains such a concentration of mind that, when his mind is concentrated, with the divine eye, which is purified and surpasses the human."[16] The Buddha goes on to say that this recluse truly *sees*. This recluse clears the mind, with meditation, to be able to see into these things. The Buddha then tells us that some things that the recluse says, the recluse has actually seen. These statements the Buddha affirms. Other claims with which the Buddha disagrees receive no affirmation of having been truly witnessed.

Even though ESP has never been proven in any kind of systematic, repeatable way, let us assume for a moment that ESP is possible. Are we to believe that the Buddha and his disciples are the only ones who can "see" straight? Many of the religious people

15. *Majjhima-nikāya*, 3.207f. in Nanamoli and Bodhi, *Middle Length Discourses.*

16. *Majjhima-nikāya*, 3.210 quoted from Ibid.

of India claimed to have mystically-honed insight into the nature of reality. If this is the case, did these fellows have such poor ESP that they could not accurately perceive? Which ESP-capable witness should we believe?

This brings us to a second criticism of ESP. If the community of recluses and brahmins argue over the meaning of their perceptions, then—according to the first two factors of the Eightfold Noble Path, right view and right conception—we have no reason to place faith in the existence of objects that cannot be "comprehensive [and] "meaningful" when referenced by the community.[17]

Some Buddhists may respond that the small community of the Buddha's followers constitutes the community necessary to make perceptions reliable and meaningful. Answering this objection requires us to look at meditation for a moment. Meditation is meant for many purposes. In fact, there are many different types of meditation. For our discussion, meditation is being used as a means to clear the mind to sense an aspect of the universe not accessible by the five common senses. But in the history of meditation, we also see that a host of contradictory concepts have been experientially verified through meditation. Roger Corless points out that when Mādhyamika Buddhism came to America, Nāgārjuna's philosophy of 'emptiness' was associated with nihilism. People started to meditate presuming this nihilistic insight they called "The Void." Associated with this was the view that "nothing really exists." Some labored to meditate assuming this presupposition. "Alarmingly," he writes, "some people can actually do this and they succeed in experiencing a pervasive nothingness."[18] Meditation then, as well as Buddhist ESP, seems to present to the consciousness something that is imparted or conditioned by the expectations of the practitioner.

Expectation-conditioned ESP presents no problems in a pragmatist outlook. Someone may find it useful to achieve a goal they have chosen. However, both meditation and ESP seem dubious as empirical foundations for knowledge claims, at least if we are to hold the Buddha's epistemology. Too many conflicting doctrines are based on evidence from ESP.

17. Kalupahana, *History of Buddhist Philosophy*, 103–4.

18. *The Vision of Buddhism*, 23.

CONCLUSION

All this said, the ESP argument cannot account for phenomena beyond the phenomena to which we have access. It seems that Buddhism cannot account for the presence of feeling, perception, dispositions, and consciousness beyond the individual—the *location of empirical testing*. Any attempt to justify the common-sense view that other individuals exist seems to put the Buddha's epistemology outside itself. The Buddha's epistemology, then, seems to have serous flaws if it turns other individuals into metaphysical claims, if it ruins ethics and compassion, and if it makes meaningful language absurd.

15

The Causality Problem

It is neither made by me nor by another. Whether the Tathāgatas (enlightened ones) were to arise in this world or not, this pattern of things is eternally existent. Concerning this [pattern of things] the Tathāgata (enlightened one) has insight, is fully enlightened.

Taishō Shinshu Daizōkyō 2.85

INTRODUCTION

THE PROBLEM OF THE underlying nature of causal relations has presented continual scientific and philosophical challenges for both ancient and modern researchers. The investigation into the nature of causal relations is still an open case. Given the current state of inquiry, the Buddha's voice is an important dialogue partner, and his insights are worthy of our attention.

We have already seen that the Buddha's theory of causality (originally *paṭiccasamuppāda,* Sk. *pratītasamupāda*) "dependent arising" follows logically from his epistemology of radical empiricism. The Buddha believed that the Vedic and Upaniṣadic epistemologies did not provide insight into the causes of suffering. The Buddha's proto-positivism requires that any statement be empirical fact, value, or useful fiction. So, if causality actually accounts for all relations of phenomena (*nāma-rūpa*), it must be known empirically by the senses.

Consequently, we should expect that any causal theory presented by the Buddha *must stand solely on the criterion of knowledge offered in his epistemology.* He must justify causality empirically.

The mechanics of the causes of *dukkha* are discussed in the *Abhidharma* material, which I touched on in the chapter on Nāgārjuna.[1] This material seems to be composed later than the material in the *Nikāyas.*[2] Those interested in the philosophical contradictions in Buddhist scholasticism should consult Paul J. Griffiths' excellent book *On Being Buddha.* This chapter will focus on matters that bear on what experience has proved to be more decisive in dialogue with Buddhists. Buddhists who are familiar with the philosophical problems in Buddhist metaphysics can always point to the soteroligical goals of Buddhism and rightly state that abstract philosophical speculations remove one's discourse from the ulimate aim of ending suffering. This seems to be Nāgārjuna's strategy in dealing with the more abstract formulations of Buddhist scholasticism, as I explained in the chapter on Nāgārjuna.[3]

We should keep in mind that the Buddha actually applied his doctrine of causal law to two separate spheres: the cosmological and the psychological.[4] However, as we have already discussed, the Buddha does not separate these spheres completely, a move which would lead the Buddha into a kind of absolutism. This chapter will examine those aspects of the Buddha's doctrine of causal law which enable his teachings to help someone identify the causes of suffering and put an end to them.

A CAUTIOUS PREAMBLE

We must be fair. The questions of causality and the nature of causal relationships are complex. Often, causal relations are not immediately apparent and seem to require interpretation, evaluation of competing evidences, and judgment calls. These three activities are each mental processes; if one must also find a particular sequence

1. For a discussion regarding *Abhidharma* systems and the causal account of *dukkha*, see Gethin, *Foundations of Buddhism,* 112f.

2. Ibid., 204.

3. For a brief introduction to *Abhidharma* that will give the reader a good sense for why Nāgārjuna criticizes its endless speculations as an obstacle to finding enlightenment see ibid., 201–223.

4. Ibid., 112f.

of mental procedures to apply the various processes of inquiry, this makes inquiry into causal relations an even more complex task. This complexity has led some philosophers to frame causality's problematic questions more simply.

Indeed, Descartes attempted to explain all human knowledge and human interaction with the world in terms of the *cogito*, the 'I' who experiences mental events and must take moral responsibility for all thoughts and deeds.[5] Modern philosophy after Descartes followed his lead till Immanuel Kant drove that project into a synthetic apriori tree and parked the wreckage in the phenomenal world, from which philosophy is only now beginning to emerge.[6] It is no wonder that twentieth century philosophers who looked at causal relations attempted to flee the complexity of trying to answer its problematic questions by escaping the mind altogether. The academic philosophy of the last century did just this, the notable exception being the school of phenomenology.[7] The so-called "linguistic turn" was part of this movement in philosophy. Over two thousand years before, Aristotle had defined the meaning of language in terms of a concept in the mind.[8] In his view, human discourse is a set of symbols that stand for mental concepts that stand for experience.[9] Aristotle's understanding of the meaning of discourse strongly influenced the philosophy of language throughout the next two millennia. Given this context, the work of twentieth century philosophers to get language out of the mind demonstrates how powerfully they exerted themselves to get philosophy away from the complex trappings that come with introspection. Some initial movement in this direction can be found in Francis Bacon's repudiation of the use of intuition in science.[10] Nevertheless, in the early twentieth century this general direction dominated the different currents of philosophy. Bertrand Russell thought Platonic

5. See *Descartes: Meditations on First Philosophy.*

6. See Kant, *Critique of Pure Reason* and *Prolegomena to Any Future Metaphysics.*

7. See Husserl, *The Crisis of European Sciences.* See also Merleau-Ponty, *Phenomenology of Perception* and Riceour, *Freud and Philosophy.*

8. See 16a 4–5 in Aristotle, *Categories and De Interpretatione.*

9. See 16a 1–18 in Ibid.

10. See Bacon, *The New Organon and Related Writings.*

Forms, which he called 'universals', accounted for the meaning of almost every word.[11] Once again, we have a twentieth century philosopher, Russell, trying to put the meaning-making work of the mind into an object outside the mind, whereas Aristotle looked for meaning in the mind.[12] Wittgenstein's definition of meaning as 'use' rather than a mental concept is a further example of this trend.[13] The Enlightenment's egocentric predicament makes the mind a scary place. The logical positivist's notions of falsifiability and verification flow directly out of this twentieth century need to get epistemology out of the mind. The positivist sees a verification that occurs outside the mind in experience.

The Buddha also wanted to get out of the mind, but for a different reason. He fled the speculations of the Vedic tradition not merely because they were complex. He fled them because it seemed that they got in the way of ending suffering. In his view, one must verify truth claims for one's self. It appears to be an easy solution to establish the law of causality by simply verifying it by one's personal experience. One can see why he adopted a method somewhat analogous to the positivists.

Unfortunately, causality is a very sticky issue. The history of philosophy has produced many different theories as to how causality works. Usually these theories are tied to a particular metaphor, which works in some cases. However, there are cases where two events are causally related but the metaphor that worked to describe causality in one case does not apply in another.[14] Also, when trying to discuss causality, the examples one chooses will often constrain the discussion.

By attempting to discuss how causality operates, I am opening a can of asps. Yet this must be done since Buddhism is very concerned with knowing causal relations. One cannot become enlightened

11. See discussion in "The World of Universals" in Russell, *The Problems of Philosophy*.

12. See 16a 1–18 in Aristotle, *Categories and De Interpretatione*.

13. See *Philosophical Investigations*.

14. For an extended discussion, see "Events and Causes" in Lakoff and Johnson, *Philosophy in the Flesh*. The discussion in this chapter is useful for identifying the origin of several persistent problems in philosophical discussion of causality. However, the chapter does little to construct a workable theory of causal relations.

without the knowledge of causal relations. The scope of the issues related to causality could fill several books. While I would like to write much more on this topic, for this present work only one chapter is reasonable. I will focus my discussion toward what history has called 'efficient cause'. However, it should be kept in mind that in some situations an absolute distinction between different types of causality, such as Aristotle's four-part classification, could be misleading.

In this chapter, I will first contend one cannot account for causality on the basis of the Buddha's radical empiricism. I will argue that justification for claims of a particular causal event requires an inductive *judgment* based on signs peculiar to the type of situation one is dealing with. *Causal relationships are recognized through inference*. When presented with two or more events, one recognizes causal relationships through a mental process in which one first asks, on some level Are these events connected?

The age-old, canonical, informal fallacy of *post hoc, ergo propter hoc* (after this, therefore because of this) refers to a wrong-headed attempt to infer causal relationships from the conjoining of events based on their sequence in time. The canonization of this fallacy demonstrates that for thousands of years humans have known that a person can experience two events and then mistakenly infer a causal relationship between them. The codification of this inductive mistake into official canons of logic should give us pause for a moment and motivate us to ask the Buddha to produce credentials for what he considers *a perceived causal moment*.

Second, I will contend that a notion of causal uniformity must first be presupposed even to begin the process of proving a causal relationship in the first place. This necessary circularity in proving causality is not a problem. Instead, the recursive character of causal proof requires that we prove causality not by radical empiricism but rather by transcendental argument, something that Buddhist radical empiricism cannot permit. It seems that causality must be proved from the impossibility of the contrary and not by experience.

Now that we have the gist of the arguments, I will examine Kalupahana's works to anticipate his objections to them. Then I will present the arguments in full force while discoursing through

Kalupahana's potential objections (and, thus, keep this chapter from becoming imponderably too long).

WHY KALUPAHANA MUST OPPOSE MY OBJECTIONS

For two reasons, Kalupahana must oppose my objections, which I mentioned above. Namely, (1) that Buddhist radical empiricism cannot account for causality, and (2) that the notion of causal uniformity must first be presupposed in order to show or explain a causal relationship in the first place. First, the Buddha said that causality is not a mere mental concept. Some of the Upaniṣadic thinkers thought that causation was only a creation of the human mind. In the *Samyukta-āgama* the Buddha is questioned as to who manufactured causal theory. Was it the Buddha or another? The Buddha replied:

> It is neither made by me nor by another. Whether the Tathāgatas (enlightened ones) were to arise in this world or not, this pattern of things is eternally existent. Concerning this [pattern of things] the Tathāgata (enlightened one) has insight, is fully enlightened.[15]

So the Buddha rejects causality as a mental construction. If causality were a real thing not perceived by the senses, then it would fall under the class of metaphysical claims. Time and time again the Buddha rejected metaphysical claims.

This brings us to our second reason why Buddhist philosophy must address my two-fold criticism against the Buddha's justification of causality. On the basis of experience, Buddhist philosophy attempts to justify the principle of causality (*paṭiccasamuppāda*) inductively, arguing from specific examples to a general law. I will posit that to try and prove the direct perception of individual causal relations, the general regularity of causality must first be presupposed even before starting such an effort. But if the Buddha's empiricism must first presuppose causality to prove causality, then either the Buddha is making a viciously circular argument or he is making a claim that must be supported by a transcendental recursive argument, following the strategy presented in chapter 2 and at the beginning

15. *Taishō Shinshu Daizōkyō* 2.85 b–c (*Tsa a-han ching* 30.16) quoted in Kalupahana, *Causality*, 92.

of chapter 11. In either case, if the Buddha's proof for causality is either a viciously circular argument or a transcendentally recursive argument, then such circularity would seem to make both the Buddha's epistemology and view of causality (*paṭīccasamuppāda*) completely untenable.

HUME'S STACCATO MOMENTS

To mitigate against these potential objections, in *Causality: the Central Philosophy of Buddhism*, Kalupahana fights against the belief that humans perceive causality through mental inference. Going back to the theory of moments, he first deals with Stcherbatsky's view that early Buddhist thought held to a theory of irreducible momentary point flashes of reality (*dharmas*),[16] showing that this development arose well after the Buddha.

Kalupahana then deals with Hume's arguments against causality. He sees Hume's thought as maintaining that reality is comprised of irreducible moments in time, which pass in perpetual succession. He quotes Hume:

> All this reasoning takes place with regard to time; along with an additional argument which it may be proper to take notice of. 'Tis a property inseparable from time, and which in a manner constitutes its essence, that each of its parts succeeds another, and that *none of them, however contiguous, can ever be co-existent.* For the same reason, that the year 1737 cannot concur with the present year 1738, every moment must be distinct from, and posterior or antecedent to another. 'Tis certain then, that time as it exists, must be compos'd of indivisible moments. For if in time we cou'd never arrive at an end of division, and if each moment, as it succeeds another, were not perfectly single and indivisible, there would be an infinite number of co-existent moments, or parts of time; which I believe will be allow'd to be an arrant contradiction.[17]

So interaction between each successive moment becomes solely a personal hope. Kalupahana rejects Hume's staccato moments as a metaphysical claim since they cannot be falsified.[18] Kalupahana be-

16. Kalupahana, *Causality*, 67–88.
17. Ibid., 102. Quoting Hume, *A Treatise of Human Nature*, 39; emphasis mine.
18. *Causality*, 102–4.

lieves that once fixed, irreducible, homogenous, staccato moments are rejected, then reality can no longer be sectioned into discrete units.[19] Without this idea of discrete moments before our eyes, we can see the world as it is—see the causality perceived in the observable world itself.

Kalupahana contends that the notion of staccato moments arose from seeing causality in terms of constantly conjoined but isolated elements of phenomena.[20] When one sees the stream of our perceptions in terms of constantly conjoined phenomena (*post hoc ergo proper hoc*), concluding fixed units of phenomena is only a short step. To prevent the staccato conclusion, he argues that we include with constant conjunction the notion of productivity.[21] Causes produce their product. Kalupahana looks to the Buddha's causal formula, which we examined earlier. But he emphasizes the notion of production within the formula. "When this is present, that comes to be" is followed up with "From the arising of this, that arises." We are supposed to find it more illuminating that causality involves productivity, and we are told to think of constant conjunction as merely relating two discrete perceptions. "Therefore, the causal connection itself *becomes* an object of experience."[22] He thinks rejecting the staccato moment theory necessitates that causal connection is an object of experience.

Though epistemologically optimistic, Kalupahana makes a critical mistake by assuming that the choice to abandon irreducible staccato moments leaves only the one remaining option of directly

19. "If the objective world is explained in this manner, then it is possible to maintain that we have experience not only of individual objects but also of the causal connections between them." Ibid., 104.

20. "Speculation on the problem of time, which [Hume] considered a necessary condition for the analysis of experience, led him to the view that time consists of indivisible moments, never coexisting but succeeding one another. If experience is analyzed in terms of time, time itself being considered momentary and discreet, the experience of external objects also has to be explained in this manner. Hence, experience of external objects of the outer world came to be analyzed in terms of points, discrete and momentary. Once the experience of the outer world is analyzed in this manner, it becomes difficult to account for the causal efficiency of such discrete and momentary entities or even any kind of relation among them. The connection between them would merely be one of suggestion." Ibid., 102.

21. Ibid., 96.

22. Ibid; emphasis mine.

perceived causality. I will show why this assumption is simply false. Furthermore, he must also show us what causality "looks" like. I have only been able to find one example of a direct experience of causal conjunction given in Kalupahana's work. That example will be dealt with later.

For now, please consider Kalupahana's argument that the simple rejection of irreducible staccato moments leaves only the direct perception of causality. The first line of the Buddha's causal formula reads "When this is present, that comes to be." Hence the causal relationship is between 'this' and 'that'. 'This' and 'that' are not substantive (*anatta*) so they must be phenomena (*nāma-rūpa*). Buddhism claims that nothing is permanent (*anicca*), which means nothing exists forever. So 'this' and 'that' refer to two or more items of phenomena. And we can still ask whether those two or more items of phenomena are causally related.

Suppose a brilliant old Buddhist man confined to a rest home bed at one time held the staccato moment view, and during his time at the rest home he came up with a calibrating system based on his staccato view for measuring the length of certain events. The event he measured most often was the length of time it took for his nurse to answer when he pushed the call button. Then he changed his view to the Buddha's original teaching. After realizing the metaphysical nature of his staccato view, he changes his calibration system now to measure the length of time it takes for his nurse to answer in relation to the flash of an instant it takes for him to push the call button. He calculates that the average ratio is 1 to 500. Even though he does not now hold the staccato view, it still makes sense to talk about the pushing of the call button and the arrival of the nurse as discrete events of a finite length and apply 'this' and 'that', respectively. They may also be seen as discrete phenomena (*nāma-rūpa*) within all the Buddhist categories and qualifications.

If these two elements of phenomena cannot be made discrete, then we have only a 'this' with no 'that'. Without a second event, no causal theory is intelligible let alone possible, as I explained in chapter 12, "The Problem of 'This' and 'That'." So it seems that we have warrant to request Kalupahana to give an explanation as to why denial of the staccato theory necessitates empirically perceived causal relations. He offers none.

His appeal to productivity does not help because causal relationships already suggest that the cause produced the effect. If we assume constant conjunction, the product is just the phenomena that followed the previously arisen phenomena. 'Productivity' simply acts as a synonym for 'causality'. 'Productivity' *feels* as though new content has been added to the term causality, when it only emphasizes the 'that' rather than the 'this' (alluding back to the Buddha's causal formula). He has succeeded in making us look at one side of the causal chain without adding any significant content to the constant conjunction theory.

EMPIRICAL JUSTIFICATION THROUGH NORMAL PERCEPTION AND ESP

So far, we have examined Kalupahana's defense against the staccato moment view of causality. His defense seems weak in that we have yet to see solely empirical verification for the claim that all events are part of a causal continuum. Saying so does not make it so. Nonetheless, Kalupahana believes that the objective validity of a causal proposition is possible.[23] On the basis of perceived causal moments, he thinks that we can inductively derive a general causal law.

Next we will examine Kalupahana's justification for the entire theory of causality (*paṭiccasamuppāda*). Bertrand Russell, who discussed the justification of causality early in the twentieth century, argued that inductive judgments about particular causal relations cannot support an inductive general causal law. He concludes, "To sum up: the strict, certain, universal law of causation which philosophers advocate is an ideal, possibly true, but not *known* to be true in virtue of any available evidence."[24]

Russell believed that one act of assuming a causal relationship could not then be used to prove general causal regularity. To get around this circularity in proving "causal law," Kalupahana distinguishes between causation, the empirically verified causal relation, and causal uniformity, the causal law derived from inductive inference.[25] So his answer to Russell is the difficult proposition that

23. Ibid., 99.

24. *Our Knowledge of the External World*, 226–27.

25. *Causality*, 107.

causality is directly perceived in experience. That way, only the general theory is inductively derived.

Allegedly, one can verify causal law through normal experience and Extra Sensory Perception (ESP). Let us begin with normal experience. In *Causality*, Kalupahana offers us one concrete example, and we should examine it. His one normal example is that of grabbing a live wire and receiving a vigorous shock.[26] We must not underestimate the rhetorical power of this illustration: the vivid picture that comes to one's mind of clasping one's hand around a bare wire and feeling the scrambling jolt of kilowatt power violently surging through every neuron in the body.

Though an effective illustration, when examined further it only reiterates that we judge moments of causality on the basis of constant conjunction. Imagine that this live wire is in inside a power shed out on a farm in the flatlands of Kansas. A tornado wiped out a rural county's power, but long after the power returns to the county, one of the prairie farms still has no electricity. The farm calls Bodhi, an electrician, because its power shed directly encountered the tornado's path.

However, Bodhi has a significant hangover from the night before and forgot his gloves for this call. He does not like gloves anyway. They make it hard for him to pull up his pants as they have a tendency to slip down his bulging midsection. Out of shame he doesn't tell his customer that he forgot his gloves, enters the feeble twisted shack and sees loose wires everywhere. He begins feeling all the loose power cables to see which one has the juice. He finds himself climbing all throughout this tall power shed, but he finds nothing. By now the prairie sun cooks him in the shed and his tight-ribbed tank top drips with sweat. He wipes his brow looking up. There, next to a power box, he sees a loose cable with promise. Getting a ladder, he climbs up into the recesses of the shed. But to reach the wire he finds himself almost leaning against a power box. He grabs the wire. Zzzzaaap! He awakes at the bottom of the shed now confident about what to do.

After two days of cable hunting and blueprint reading he finds where this wire should connect. He connects them and voila!

26. Ibid., 104.

Nothing happens. It turns out that a short in the power box caused the shock. Sweaty Bodhi had leaned against it while grabbing the loose cable.

In this counter-example, Bodhi has a justifed belief that the big cable at the top of the shed was the loose wire he sought. He was wrong. But the phenomenon of grasping the loose wire and receiving the significant shock from the power box felt the same. (Someone may want to dispute this. If they want, they can set up a laboratory situation, with experimental and control groups, and publish what nuances of violent shock quality each research subject suffered in each case.) It seems that even the wire illustration shows that the recognition of particular causal relations is still an inductive inference, a judgment.

Concrete examples also show something we see in common experience and something that any employer will look for in the employees he hires—the precious need for the development of wisdom in "seeing" causal relationships with a level of confidence.

Kalupahana's second example addresses the relationship of cause and effect where the cause and effect are separated in time. He tells us that in such a case we may allegedly sense the connection by ESP. We have already dealt with ESP to a degree. But my tactic will be somewhat different here.

Kalupahana reiterates the Buddha's empirical claim that he could perceive things beyond the five common senses by the use of the mind, which was believed to be a sixth sense:

> By means of the knowledge of the past existence and the knowledge of the decease and survival of beings, the Buddha was able to verify the problem of rebirth. In Buddhism, the propositions about the phenomenon of rebirth are inductive inferences based on the data of direct experience. . . . With knowledge of the destruction of defiling impulses, and also through the foregoing four forms of knowledge, one is able to verify the Four Noble Truths and the origin and cessation of defiling impulses. Thus having experienced particular instances of causation through sensory as well as extrasensory perception the Buddha arrived at a general theory of 'causality' or 'causal uniformity,' which he considered to be a universally valid principle[.][27]

27. Ibid., 106–7.

Now for the sake of argument, let us take the Buddha at his word and assume that by ESP one can directly perceive causal relationships. How would such a perception occur? Keeping in mind our discussion of the six senses, let's return back to chapter 5, which discussed the Buddha's epistemology. In the section entitled "Sense Experience," we opened our analysis with an exegesis of the Buddha's theory of perception. We quoted this section:

> *Depending on the visual organ and the visual object, O monks, arises visual consciousness; the meeting together of these three is contact; conditioned by contact arises feeling. What one feels, one perceives*; what one perceives, one reflects about; one is obsessed with. What one is obsessed with due to that, concepts characterized by such obsessed with, due to that, concepts characterized by such obsessed perceptions assail him in regard to visible objects cognizable by the visual organ, belonging to the past, future, and the present.[28]

Kalupahana then reminds us that what connects our nonsubstantial mental faculties with the nonsubstantial external world is dependence (*paṭiccasamuppāda*):

> The principle according to which sense experience begins to take place is "dependence" (*paṭiccasamuppāda*). The conception of a "self" (*ātman*) that functions as the agent is thereby eliminated.[29]

What allows us to perceive that alleged "causal relation" object out there is the fact that there is a causal relationship between that relation and our senses. Then when the two meet, that causes something else . . . contact! Contact *causes* perception. All of these causal relationships are necessary parts of perceiving one causal relation "out there." If these relationships are not the case, then the alleged "causal relation" does no one any good.

Causality (*paṭiccasamuppāda*) accounts for all inter-relation, including those that make perception possible. So the Buddha's view of causality must first be accurate for his epistemology to work, but the epistemology is what justifies any claim, including that

28. *Majjhima-nikaya* 1.111–112 quoted in Kalupahana, *History of Buddhist Philosophy*, 32; emphasis mine.

29. Kalupahana, *History of Buddhist Philosophy*, 32.

of causality. Here's the rub. Even if we have an objective, causal object out there to "observe," we must still use the Buddha's radical empiricist positivism, which requires a causal relationship between the empirical observer and the object out there in the nonsubstantial world. So we find ourselves in a circular argument. If there is no causal relationship between the perceived object and our own perception of it, then the causal law (*paṭiccasamuppāda*) can never be proven. So the Buddha seems to assume what he tries to prove, even though he tells us not to do that.

Some may think we are just taking an isolated text and building a case. In the Buddha's account of the twelve factors we see the same analysis of causality and perception:

> [D]ependent consciousness arises the psycho-physical personality; dependent upon the psycho-physical personality arise the six senses; *dependent upon the six senses arises contact; dependent upon contact arises feeling. . . .*[30]

Once again, we see the psycho-physical personality causally relates to the six senses, which causally relate to the "causal relation object" (CRO) that causes contact. Once again, we see the internal/external universality of causality which must first be assumed before a CRO can begin to serve us. And once again, causality must be assumed to be proved, something not allowable within the Buddha's epistemology.

There is a way to beat my accusation of circularity within the Buddha's epistemology and causal theory. All the Buddha would need to do is empirically verify each causal relation during the act of directly perceiving a causal relation.

ESP involves the sense of the mind (*mano*) causally relating to things not normally sensed through the other senses. To illustrate what would be involved in examining this process, let us only examine the CRO between the senses and the original CRO. We will call the CRO that evidences causality directly CRO1. The relation between CRO1 and the mind we will call CRO2.

To have a noncircular account of causal relations, we must empirically account for all causal relations within that act, so the mind must empirically verify the causal relationship between CRO2

30. *Saṃyutta-nikāya* 2.16–17 quoted in Ibid., 58; emphasis mine.

and the mind. That causal relationship also must be verified, for if it is assumed then the causal law once again is the support for the empirical verification and not vice-versa. So the mind must also verify the causal relationship between the mind and CRO2. If we verify that causal relationship empirically, then that relation becomes CRO3.

For a noncircular account of the empirical causal relation between the sixth sense of the mind and CRO3, we must also verify the relationship between CRO3 and the mind. The causal relationship between the senses and CRO3 may be termed CRO4.

The astute reader can see where this is going. To defend a solely empirical account of causality, we must be able to account for each element of the epistemological causal chain, without smuggling an act of faith into the proof. Such a labor is not possible since each act of verification creates another causal relation which requires further verification.[31] Plato's theory of forms ran into the same problem. Plato had the integrity to expose it as the "Third Man Argument" in the dialog *Parmenides*.

It would seem that any attempt at a process of empirically proving causal regularity will have to assume causal law somewhere in the process of empirical demonstration. The very act of empirically verifying it is fraught with causal relations. These "internal" causal relations cannot be verified as causal relationships without creating more causal relationships to verify, which further replicates the problem. Somewhere, one must assume causal law to prove causal law. At some point, then, the empirically-minded man must assume causal relationships even during the act of trying to verify *one*. So *paṭiccasamuppāda* is a metaphysical claim.

CONCLUSION TO THE CAUSALITY PROBLEM

In this chapter, we have examined Kalupahana's justification of causal law. We have found it wanting for four reasons:

1. It sets up a false either/or distinction between irreducible staccato moments and fluid causal relations.
2. The proof of causality in the live wire illustration proved to be

31. One may wish to argue that someone else could verify the other causal relations that may not be accessible to the fellow who is directly seeing a causal relation. The comments I make in chapter 14, "The Buddhist Problem of Other Minds," may be applied here.

an inductive (and conductive) judgment.

3. His ESP example combined with radical empiricism led to an infinite regress.
4. We concluded Kalupahana must still assume causality before being able to prove a causal moment.

TRANSCENDENTAL RECURSIVE CAUSAL PROOFS

The arguments presented so far suggest that to prove causality one must assume causal regularity. This makes causality something that must be proven transcendentally. Chapters 2 and 11 introduced transcendental arguments, a kind of logical argumentation that attempts to establish a transcendental proof. A *transcendental proof* seeks to prove something on the basis that it is a necessary precondition to intelligible human experience. A *transcendental argument*, then, aims to establish a conclusion on the basis that if such a conclusion were not the case, then the world would not be intelligible. Thus, transcendental arguments must have a recursive element to them.

If someone were to give a transcendental proof that provided the basis for, say, logic and reason, then that proof must also necessarily account for itself. For example, Plato posits the existence of the forms in books 6 and 7 of the *Republic*:

> We say there are many beautiful things and many good things, and so on for each kind, and in this way we distinguish them in words.
>
> We do.
>
> And beauty itself and good itself and all the things that we thereby set down as many, reversing ourselves, we set down according to a single form of each, believing that there is but one, and calling it "the being" of each.
>
> That's true.
>
> And we say that the many beautiful things and the rest are visible but not intelligible, while the forms are intelligible but not visible. (507b)[32]

In this passage, Plato summarizes the point he has been arguing, giving his account of intelligible things. Plato argues that immaterial forms in a special realm of forms make experiences of particular ob-

32. *Republic*, 180.

jects and characteristics intelligible. However, notice that if Plato's perspective is correct, then the reader's ability to make sense of the *Republic* dialog is also due to the immaterial forms. Plato's problematic thesis argues that it alone makes experiences intelligible.

Though people have been making transcendental arguments for millennia, Kant gave them trendy nomenclature. Kant argued that the mind shapes "phenomenal reality."[33] We have already summarized that Kant believed phenomena resulted from the interaction of the noumenal mind (the mind as it really is) and the noumenal world (the world as it really is). He tries to prove this by arguing that mathematics is both *a priori* and synthetic. He thought mathematics was certainly *a priori* since it deals with relating numbers in the mind and not experiences. But since he thought that mathematical mental operations move from relating quantities to concluding a sum, he believed that the mind adds something to the mix. Science had used math to study the external world. Science gave real, objective knowledge. However, if mathematics resulted from mental operations, it seemed that somehow the mind generated some of the objectivity of the surrounding world. This seemed, at least to Kant, to suggest that one's mind somehow shapes one's perceived reality. In arguing this way, he sought to provide an account of knowledge and phenomena. He also noticed that, if correct, his account would also have to justify his own ability to account for the mind's activities. Finally, transcendental proofs received a name.

Transcendental Argumentation in the Bible

Plato reasoned transcendentally long before Kant. However, this form of argument even precedes Plato. The author of the biblical Book of Isaiah uses this type of argument, but for a different purpose. (Some biblical scholars dispute whether the author or an author of this book is the prophet Isaiah. For ease of readability, I will use the name 'Isaiah' to identify the author.) In the middle of the Book of Isaiah—Isaiah's great exposition of the attributes of God to the Gentile nations (chapters 40–48)—the book stops to critique the idol worshiper and describes the idolater's resourcefulness.

33. This paragraph summarizes Kant's analysis of his own perspective in Kant, *Prolegomena to Any Future Metaphysics*. I have here emphasized his discussion in the Preamble and Part One.

Then, with some sharp satire, the book criticizes the idol worshiper's worldview:

> Surely he cuts cedars for himself, and takes a cypress or an oak, and he raises it for himself, among the trees of the forest. He plants a fir, and the rain makes it grow. Then it becomes something for a man to burn, so he takes one of them and warms himself; he also makes a fire to bake bread. He also makes a god and worships it; he makes it a graven image, and falls down before it. Half of it he burns in the fire; over this half he eats meat as he roasts a roast, and is satisfied. He also warms himself and says, "Aha! I am warm, I have seen the fire." But the rest of it he makes into a god, his graven image. He falls down before it and worships; he also prays to it and says, "Deliver me for thou art my god." They do not know, nor do they understand, for He has smeared over their eyes so that they cannot see and their hearts so they cannot comprehend. And no one recalls, nor is there is there knowledge or understanding to say, "I have burned half of it the fire, and also have baked bread over its coals. I roast meat and eat it. Then I make the rest into an abomination, I fall down before a block of wood!" He feeds on the ashes; a deceived heart has turned him aside. And he cannot deliver himself, nor say, "Is there not a lie in my right hand?" (Isaiah 44:14–20)

In verses 14–17, Isaiah points out the folly of hoping in a god that one manufactures. Isaiah narrates the worldview of the idolater by climbing inside his phenomenology of perception and the external culture that comes to exist by one's interaction with the physical world.[34] Notice his critique shows the worldview of the idolater. He burned half the thing he hopes will save him. If he can craft tools to build it, how much more can another tear it down and him with it? Not only does the worldview of this idolater not comport; more importantly, his *method* does not comport with his own worldview.

The Book of Isaiah goes on to link the idolator's idolatry to an inability to understand the internal contradiction and absurd praxis that one's method and system produces. In this passage, the cost of idolatry is not the pain of harsh fortune but the loss of one's

34. For more on phenomenology of perception and the way in which external physical culture creates a hermeneutical circle journey from the cultural object back to the participant in the culture, see Merleau-Ponty, *Phenomenology of Perception*. See also Ricoeur, *From Text to Action*.

discernment. Verse 20 begins "He feeds on ashes." The Hebrew literally reads "He herds ashes." On modern ears, this phrase loses much of its punch. The herd gave one milk and food. Often animals were capital for bartering. The herd provided skins for many household items. So people gave great attention to their flocks. The Book of Proverbs instructs the wise man to watch his flocks, for if the herd suffers loss by negligent hands, then the consequences will be felt by those of the family whose well-being depends on the herd's condition. When it says that the idolater herds ashes, the writer of Book of Isaiah is making his words count. The idolater invests his energies into caring for and hoping in something that can never produce anything for him. Yet in the act of herding, he brings to bear his considerable cognitive and physical resources and consumes them in serving the vision of his own created fiction. Isaiah tells us that his idolatry consumes him and offers him nothing but futility.

The passage goes on to show that he can no longer deliver himself because he does not recognize the lie. The right hand in Hebrew literature refers to one's power, skill, and strength. This passage harks back to the first chapter of Proverbs, which claims that forsaking God has necessary epistemic consequences. The one who forsakes wisdom loses the mental clarity to deliver himself in times of trouble (Prov. 1:20–33).

Thus, Isaiah produces a kind of informal, negative transcendental argument. With a *reductio ad absurdum*, he points to the inconsistency—no, too weak—the complete folly of the idolater's method. Instead of building his own prudence on the actual God who set up the world, the idolater must cleverly cast a fiction in that God's place. The resulting item becomes the means for this person to evaluate all of his own life. But in order to make the world intelligible, in order to account for the world around him, the idolater must also think in accord with the intention that made the natural seams, grooves, and joints of the world—the intention of the One who is the necessary precondition for the intelligible world. When the idolater does not, he will pay with the integrity of his mind. Thus, he must set aside some of the integrity of his mind in order to function. The author of Isaiah addresses this *reductio* not only to idol worshipers among his own people but also to those who had never even heard of Moses. He is addressing all idol worshipers.

Two Helpful Points

The Book of Isaiah makes two helpful points that we may now apply directly to the Buddha. First, the Buddha's method seems absurd. He offers an epistemology to prove *paṭiccasamuppāda*, but the causal law of *paṭiccasamuppāda* must first be assumed before his epistemology can work. He then demands that nothing can be proven recursively in a transcendental method. The Buddha then tells us not to have faith,[35] but his circle of epistemology and causality still require their adherent to "believe in order to understand." Absurdly, it is also the case that if one accepts the Buddha's epistemology, then he must *never* accept the Buddha's epistemology. But the Buddha, himself a brilliant rhetorician, presents his view in stages so that one can accept either his epistemology or theory of causality without realizing that he has also accepted the other. I am not saying the Buddha surreptitiously intended to deceive. I believe it was rather a well-intentioned mistake.

Second, when the idolater blinds his mind by choosing to put trust in his system, he makes it impossible to see his way out. One could prove causality by arguing from the impossibility of the contrary. After all, even a conclusion that causal regularity is not the case would still follow as the final step in a series of mental acts. Yet if such proofs are allowed, then one must also be able to transcendentally justify the adoption of that method of proof. In no time one finds oneself in need of an entire cohesive worldview that accounts for epistemology, metaphysics, value theory, and the mundane issues of life.

Buried within the Buddha's system is the deep, desperate need for a transcendental proof. Yet he chose to bar himself from even attempting one. His pragmatic decision to make the end of suffering his all-consuming goal conditioned him to reject any type of transcendental proofs when he denied the validity of anything but sense experience. The Buddha cannot say, "Is there not a lie in my right hand?"[36]

35. Recall that the Buddha distinguishes between faith in views and faith in an experienced teacher of enlightenment. Here I am obviously referring to the former.

36. Isaiah 44:20.

16

To End All Suffering

He shall wipe away every tear from their eyes; and there shall no longer be any death; there shall no longer be any *mourning, or crying, or pain; for the former things have passed away. . . .*

Revelation 21:4

BUDDHISM AS A SOFA BED

IMAGINE A NEIGHBOR GAVE you a big sofa bed. A really big sofa bed. He talked you into taking it. At the time you were sleeping on the floor (maybe this was when you were in college). He boasted of its utility. You decided to give it a try.

It turns out that, like all sofa beds, this one is lumpy, stiff, and uncomfortable. That bar in the middle of your back does not help either. You come back to your neighbor who gave you the bed. He tells you that the problem not with the sofa bed. It is in you! Though the bed feels uncomfortable, he says that your problem is your own desire for comfort. You continue to give it a try. But your stiff back and daily tired eyes finally persuade you to get rid of that sofa bed.

However, sofa beds are big and clunky, especially when unfolded and all sprawled out in the middle of your studio apartment. You recognize that getting it out of your apartment will be a considerable chore, an impossible feat if the unwieldy sofa bed remains open.

If we compare Buddhist philosophy to a sofa bed, the previous six chapters have been folding it up. In this chapter, we will brace ourselves so that in the next chapter we can try to move the sofa bed out the apartment door with one good heave.

The Buddha provided an account of logic, epistemology, and causality that present considerable problems. The Buddhist view of causality (*paṭiccasamuppāda*) leaves no way to account for the value of validity structures and their permanence over time. If the Buddha's view accurately describes the world, then we have no reason to think that validity is possible or persistent. It also seems that the Buddha's epistemology is a little too successful at its goal of undermining metaphysical claims since it turns even the claim that individuals exist beyond one's self into a metaphysical claim. The previous chapter argued that causality could not be proven without first assuming causality, and since it could not be proven from direct experience, it would seem to also fit into the category of metaphysical claim. Finally, we concluded that the Buddha's epistemology assumes the doctrine of *paṭiccasamuppāda* at the same time, but to know *paṭiccasamuppāda* one must first apply the aforementioned epistemology. So the Buddha's epistemology must reject itself.

Some may object that the method used here found problems within Buddhist philosophy because we are approaching Buddhism like Western absolutists. The chapter on Nāgārjuna concluded with observing that the Buddha and later thinkers like Nāgārjuna thought of philosophy as useful insofar as it is used as a tool to end suffering. The value of propositions is their usefulness. According to Nāgārjuna, logic and any other metalanguage must be thought of as tools, as "useful fictions," which help us to achieve our goals. In the *Alagaddūpama Sutta*, the Buddha thought of his teaching as a raft to get one across the river of suffering.[1] Once across, one throws away the raft. Likewise, the argument goes, you should do the same with Buddhism. Recall that Nāgārjuna did this with the sixty-third view, which was his own view.

1. *Majjhima-nikāya* 1.134–135. See Nanamoli and Bodhi, *Middle Length Discourses*, 228-229.

BUDDHIST PHILOSOPHY AND PRAGMATISM

Consider this short outline of a conversation between a Buddhist and a Christian:

> Buddhist: God is irrelevant. The Christian God can never be known.
>
> Christian: Why is that the case?
>
> Buddhist: Because God's existence is not an empirical claim.
>
> Christian: Then what do empirical claims tell us?
>
> Buddhist: That everything is caused.
>
> Christian: Including suffering?
>
> Buddhist: Yes!
>
> Christian: Why is ending suffering your greatest concern?
>
> Buddhist: Because I do want to end it.
>
> Christian: How do you know that the end of suffering should be your pursuit?
>
> Buddhist: Well, if you do not care to end your suffering then Buddhism is not for you.

I have had this conversation with a number of Buddhists. It has always seemed strange to me that the Buddhist usually begins with strong, definite claims about what can and cannot be known, but ends by telling me that Buddhism makes no claims—it is just a method I can choose if I want to end my suffering.

On what basis does a Buddhist blast away at the Christian worldview? How does a philosophy that begins with the strongest of statements about the inadequacy of revelation claims (in the Pali texts) end with the most subjective of appeals? Buddhism is definitely bold enough to declare what can and cannot be known. Yet it does not seem capable to declare whether or not its doctrines are true or whether its method should be chosen. It is just up to you and me to decide whether we want to choose it. What? In the face of Buddhism's bold declarations, it seems only right to ask the Buddha to give some explanation for his apparent doublespeak.

The explanation for this odd phenomenon takes us back to themes we have already covered in great detail. Buddhism begins with the goal of ending suffering. However, to begin one's journey on the Buddha's path, one must have 'right view' and 'right conception.'

This means accepting a way of looking at the world that involves the Buddha's radical empiricism and *paṭiccasamuppāda*. Only then does one have the right epistemology and 'ontology' to begin ending one's suffering. The Buddha organized his doctrine around soteriological goals.[2] All his analysis aims at insight into the human being and the world in order to end suffering. Supposedly, to search for more to this universe beyond what is basically given in one's experience will only lead to *dukkha*, the Buddha tells us. Should we believe him?

The Buddha's pragmatic focus defines his entire philosophy. This cannot be stressed enough. "Appeasement of the dispositions enabled [the Buddha] to look at conception itself as possessing pragmatic value rather than absolutist implication."[3] Even the forming of concepts in the human mind has what pragmatist philosopher William James called a "cash value." It accomplishes a function for us. Like James, the Buddha sees no need for absolute answers. As a radical empiricist, he only needs deal with what perceptions themselves directly presented. Recall in chapter 5 we learned that nonsubstantial items of empirical perception become the basis for the Buddha's system of logic. A pragmatic criterion establishes the difference between contrary and contradictory statements.[4] Neither a coherence nor correspondence theory of truth will do since the third line of the Buddha's four-cornered system calls into question both methods. Truth, then, is seen in terms of what has "become." "The best epistemological criterion for distinguishing what had come to be and what has not come to be is simply usefulness or utility."[5] Kalupahana goes on to say that:

> Equating the "not become" with "confusion" would then explain

2. Both Gethin and Williams make this point in numerous places in *Foundations of Buddhism* and *Buddhist Thought*. However, there seems to be a contradiction in *Buddhist Thought*, page 144, which begins a discussion of Tantric Buddhism, a tributary of Buddhist thought that is more interested in pursuing human sexuality as a tool to gain enlightenment. The text on this page disparages finding "original Buddhism" and viewing Buddhism as primarily soteriological. One can see how Tantric Buddhism seems to be breaking with the teachings in the *Nikāyas/Āgamas* that certainly seem to disparage sexual desire and encourage monks to turn away from it. It may be that this text was inserted by one of Williams' co-authors.

3. Kalupahana, *History of Buddhist Philosophy*, 27.

4. Ibid., 50.

5. Ibid., 51.

> a significant *epistemological fact*, namely, *the function of human interest or perspective as a determinant of the worldview* that continues to change in different directions. In this sense, the system of logic utilized by the Buddha allows for change and creativity without falling into the abyss of absolutism.[6]

Notice that the Buddha takes "human interest or perspective as a determinant of the worldview that continues to change[,]" and this is built even into the Buddha's approach to logic. The importance of Buddhist pragmatism must not be underestimated.[7]

These philosophical doctrines provide context to the Buddha's soteriological doctrines. However, the Buddha chose them because of what he wanted more than anything else: the end of suffering. "In his search for the truth about human existence motivated by a desire for release from the suffering inherent in it, Siddhārtha Gautama is said to have visited teacher after teacher. . . ."[8] The Buddha rejected Vedic and Upaniṣadic speculations they taught because they did not provide an end to *dukkha*. He adopted a method for the ending of ignorance, which leads to suffering. This end of ignorance requires an understanding of *paṭiccasamuppāda* through a radical empiricism that does not accept any metaphysical claims. The Four Noble Truths bring this understanding. But "noble" in this case does not mean regal, reverent, spiffy, or pompous. Instead, "noble truths" (*ariya-saccāni*) mean that these truths are fruitful (*atthasaṃhita*).[9] These truths are not mere rational statements. They bear fruit in one's life. "The Four Noble Truths are therefore more appropriately explained as factual truths with moral relevance."[10] In the *Discourse to Kaccāyana*, Kaccāyana receives the Buddha's counsel to abandon the notion of *ātman*, the conceivin- of a permanent self. Instead, he is supposed to take a view from nowhere. By abandoning the concept

6. Ibid., 52; emphasis mine.

7. The modern school of philosophy that defines truth in terms of utility bears the name "Pragmatism" or "Instrumentalism." William James, John Dewey, F. C. S. Schiller, G. H. Mead, and Richard Rorty are only a few of those associated with this school of thought. Kalupahana has written a book on Buddhist psychology interacting with the philosophy of William James. See Kalupahana, *Principles of Buddhist Psychology*.

8. Kalupahana, *Buddhist Philosophy*, 16.

9. Kalupahana, *History of Buddhist Philosophy*, 85.

10. Ibid.

of self, he becomes free to see life from the human perspective. "The pragmatic conception of truth presented by the Buddha is therefore not only epistemologically relevant but also ethically significant."[11] And ethics are not absolute but goal-oriented, soteriological through and through. Allegedly, Buddhism's claims are useful. For that reason they are "true." The Buddha's anti-absolutist stand makes accepting a utility truth criterion much easier. It is even the criterion for recognizing logical consistency. When a certain pattern of thinking does not help, then we can be "creative" to serve the interests of particular goals as we can see from the long quotation above.

Up to this point in *To End All Suffering*, I have been sorting the Buddha's doctrines to make them accessible. This had to be done to separate the philosophical arguments early Buddhism makes to show how they define what the Buddha offers as a cure to suffering. There is simply no way to look at the goal of Buddhism from a different worldview without looking very carefully and fairly at the philosophical apparatus that interprets that goal, which is what we have been doing in *To End All Suffering* until this chapter.

Since Buddhism begins and ends with the question of how to end *dukkha*, it is now necessary to examine the problem of *dukkha* within a completely different context, that of the Christian worldview. The Bible has much to say about the nature of human suffering and how suffering can be ended. Since this book is not about suffering *per se*, this chapter must be briefer than I would prefer. Once we understand the place of *dukkha* in the Bible, we will be able to watch the two perspectives address one another.

THE PROBLEM OF EVIL

Shann Ray Ferch, one of my colleagues at Gonzaga University, has written a powerful book: *Forgiveness and Power in the Age of Atrocity*.[12] In it he grapples with the deep challenges communities face in forgiving those who commit atrocities against them and their members. Ferch documents his own experience growing up on a Cheyenne reservation as a white American, and from that portion of his life he attempts to explain the perspective of the Cheyenne

11. Ibid.

12. Ferch, *Forgiveness and Power*.

concerning American atrocities committed against them, particularly the Sand Creek Massacre in which U.S. Cavalry Troops brutally murdered Cheyenne women and children, then mutilated their bodies. What gives *Forgiveness and Power in the Age of Atrocity* its own power is that Ferch does not write if from a detached, academic, third-person point of view. At several points he moves into the first person, absorbing the questions he asks and answers he provides in the book through his own personal narrative. The path to forgiveness takes personal risks and a willingness to be vulnerable. There is no other way to make such a case than to model what that vulnerability looks like. Shann told me that he had approached many publishers with the manuscript, but they either wanted him to make the book an impersonal academic treatise or a personal memoir. He finally found a publisher who was willing to take a chance. Suffering, like forgiveness, cannot be understood without a willingness to participate.

No biblical inquiry into the nature of suffering can sidestep the Problem of Evil, a problem with which all human beings have experiential contact. In this chapter, because of the way I am framing the Problem of Evil, a theodicy *per se* (a defense for God's existence by offering a justification for why God allows evil in the world) is not necessary, and Rupert Gethin is correct to point out that Buddhism need not pursue a strategy of theodicy.[13] Evil and suffering are more complex than the philosophical formulations of the Problem of Evil would suggest. This problem has three forms: (1) the Logical Problem of Evil, (2) the Evidential Problem of Evil, and (3) the Existential Problem of Evil.

The Logical Problem of Evil aims to fault the claim that God exists by finding a logical contradiction between the existence of evil and the existence of an all-good, all-powerful, all-knowing God. If the attribution is correct, Epicurus penned one of the most trenchant statements of this problem:

> Is God willing to prevent evil, but is not able? Then he is not omnipotent.
>
> Is he able, but not willing? Then he is malevolent.
>
> Is he both able and willing? Then whence cometh evil?

13. Gethin, *Foundations of Buddhism*, 68f.

> Is he neither able nor willing? Then why call Him God?[14]

This framing of the problem of evil questions God's concurrent power and goodness. If God is willing to prevent evil but he just cannot stop it, then he clearly cannot be all-powerful. If God is able to but not willing, then he must hate humans. If God is both willing and able, then it would seem the existence of evil is impossible, so where did it come from? Thus, if evil exists, God cannot, which is how Epicurus concludes his statement of the problem.

Christian philosopher Alvin Plantinga answered this logical formulation of the problem with a careful presentation of the free will defense, that God permits evil, but only for a time, because God is also guarding the good of human free will.[15] His presentation of this argument was so effective that for the last two decades the Logical Problem of Evil has become passé in professional discussions in academic philosophy. The debate has moved on to the so-called Evidential Problem of Evil, which I will discuss shortly. However, one other counter-argument should be used against the Logical Problem of Evil that will bear on the rest of this discussion.

What is evil? Is it suffering? If it is, then is any amount of suffering evil? The literature on the problem of evil usually defines evil as "gratuitous suffering." This definition of evil begs the question of what is the point at which suffering becomes *gratuitous suffering*. One answer is: when it gets to that point, we all just know it is too much. Notice that this is an appeal to the people. "They all just know!"

Another tactic is to ridicule the person who even raises this line of questioning. Perhaps one could list a series of deeply horrific events (we all know such things happen), and then respond, "Only a fool would question whether there is evil in this world!" However, even if we all agree that evil exists, it is very important we answer the epistemic question, how we know there is evil in this world. On what basis do we make the claim that evil really exists and that such-and-such a thing actually is in fact evil? What standard determines whether something is evil?

14. Barnes, *Understanding Science and Religion*, 92.

15. *God, Freedom, and Evil.*

Within the domain of Christian theology, this question is very important. If the so-called Problem of Evil is to be used against the God of the Bible, then whatever standard is used to measure evil must be powerful enough to establish an evil that is strong enough to overturn the existence of God. Personally, I despise cats. If I am in company with a cat for ten minutes my windpipe shrinks to the width of a rice grain. But I cannot say that because cats exist, God does not.

What standard is powerful enough to define evil so as to make the Problem of Evil work? There are many possible answers to this question. One possible answer is that evil is culturally relative. We get a group of people together and ask them what they do not like. The group labels that thing "bad." Then we ask them what they *really* do not like. Those things then become "evil." So the standard for evil is a strong opinion maintained by an influential group of people. It is clear an arbitrary standard is woefully inadequate to establish a kind of evil that can be applied to the Problem of Evil. If humans can simply get together and define evil arbitrarily, why not just arbitrarily define "God" as a being that does not exist? Cut out the middleman. Furthermore, different cultures have different standards for what constitutes evil as demonstrated by various totalitarian regimes in the last century.

Another possible option is John Stuart Mill's utilitarianism.[16] Here, the good is defined as that which causes the greatest pleasure for the greatest number of people. Evil is the opposite. However, utilitarianism is not useful to define evil if those who are suffering are in the minority. If the majority can make the claim that their good is the greater, then it is very hard for the oppressed minority to define their suffering as an evil, so long as utilitarianism is the *only* standard. Yet, once again, this standard is arbitrary. Why does J. S. Mill get to be God?

Another standard for measuring evil could be virtue ethics. Certainly, there is much to commend Aristotle's account, but, while virtue ethics is helpful in identifying noble and ignoble traits in a person, it lacks law-like force to define a thing as evil; Aristotle is honest and forthright about its imprecision at the beginning of

16. Mill, *Utilitarianism.*

Nichomachean Ethics. Once again, simply stipulating virtue ethics is arbitrary.

One possible response to the arbitrariness of human definitions of evil is "There are many ways to define evil. Just pick one. We can use just about any ethical theory." If we can arbitrarily use any theory, then what warrant do the definitions based on these theories have? And on what is that warrant based? Any standard that is simply posited by a person or a group runs into the same problem. What ultimately stands behind that definition is human choice. While this type of standard may be helpful for a person personally as she or he pursues her or his own moral development, it lacks a warrant for application to a community or a nation without some mechanism by which it can claim that warrant. Civic law gives this sort of mechanism such that the moral standard held by a collection of individuals can distanciate from each community member and become law in the community, by social contract, by precedent, etc. However, evil is evil whether law sanctions it or not. The Holocaust of the Jews may have been legal in Germany, but it was not moral. It was most certainly evil. But why? Not because of arbitrary human opinions. If it was evil because of arbitrary human opinions, then when the opinions change direction, as perhaps they will in the future, then today's evil will no longer be evil tomorrow.

For the Problem of Evil to work, there must be a way to define evil such that evil exists apart from human judgment. Where could we find a source for a standard powerful enough that it could measure evil? The Bible provides a clear answer to this question. According to the Bible, the standard for goodness is God. That which contradicts his moral character, which is reflected in his moral law, is evil. The biblical account of moral law as being rooted in God's moral character is sharply different from so-called *divine command theory*, which teaches that the moral law of God is morally binding simply because God commands it. The law of God is not arbitrary because he is the Creator of human beings—beings who, according to the Bible, were created to reflect God's personal moral nature, as God's moral law reflects his own moral character; as Jesus taught, "Be perfect. . . as my heavenly father is perfect" (Matt. 5:48). Thus, God could never command men to torture and rape because those actions do not reflect his own character. Thus, the Bible goes between the horns of Plato's dilemma in the *Eythyphro.* It is not the case that God makes good into good merely by his divine will. Nor is it that God is attracted to good things because the standard of good is outside himself. Rather, there is one God who is the measure for all good.

Thus, the Bible presents a worldview in which evil is the sort of thing which can actually be used in an argument so that there can even be the Problem of Evil. Rather than evil being based on a human judgment or human preference, the Bible explains that there is real evil in this world. It also explains what defines it and why that definition is not subject to human opinion. However, what makes possible the objective identity of evil is God himself. This creates a deep problem for the Problem of Evil, for if God must be the inherently good, creator/compass of the universe in order to even define evil so there can even be such a thing as real good, real evil, and a Problem of Evil, it becomes impossible to use evil to disavow his goodness or his power. Thus, the Logical Problem of Evil is a total non-starter in the Christian worldview.

Some may call this move unfair because evil is a topic discussed in value theory. Yet I am attacking the Logical Problem of Evil on the basis of its epistemology, and that is often considered a big no-no. It is some how unfair or unprofessional to challenge the one who wishes to use the Problem of Evil against the God of the Bible to come up with a standard to measure evil that is not based on human opinion because for some magical reason philosophers cannot skip over sub disciplines. If one is working in value theory, one has to stay in value theory. If one is working in epistemology, one cannot discuss value theory and vice-versa.[17] However, the history of philosophy should remind us that value theory and epistemology are not so divergent or disconnected. Plato's *Republic*, Hume's *Treatise*, and Nietzsche's *Twilight of the Idols* are only three of a *vast* sea of precedent works penned throughout the history of philosophy that display a studied philosophical tradition interlinking value theory and epistemology. Without having a definition of evil independent from the fiat of

17. Richard McClelland, my friend and colleague at Gonzaga University, raised this objection to me in email correspondence, dated May 8, 2012, after our debate at the Gonzaga Socratic Club on May 4, 2012.

human opinion, a person cannot use the objective existence of evil to disprove the existence of the Christian God.

The second version of the Problem of Evil is the Evidential Problem of Evil.[18] This one is framed not in terms of a deductive case but rather an inductive case. For this reason, Plantinga's free will defense has a limited effect upon it. The Evidential Problem asks people to consider whether there is enough evil in the world to cast doubt on whether a good God exists. Is there not too much evil? Too much suffering? Or is the amount of suffering consistent with what we would expect if in fact God were all-good and all-powerful? This argument is particularly compelling because it requires a person to be self-critical of her or his standards. How much is too much? Certainly all of us would want as little evil as possible. And there are so many examples of evil in this world. It seems reasonable that some evil must be gratuitous. Perhaps much of it we could call gratuitous.

Nonetheless, notice that even here the critical question is begged. What defines evil? Who gets to decide what is actually evil? And how much is gratuitous? By whose standard is a given example of evil gratuitous? The rhetorical strength of the Evidential Problem is the way that it makes a person think in terms of specific examples, which is exactly the kind of thinking that motivates us as human beings to want to do something about the evil we see around us in the world. Nevertheless, that same rhetorical force also makes us forget that the definition of evil is once again being assumed. The Bible presents many examples, which could be used as premises to support the evidential problem of evil, but on what basis can we define those things as evil? A moment's reflection should quickly return us to the question of the definition of evil.

Finally, we come to the Existential Problem of Evil. This is the immediate experience of feeling evil done and the direct questions that arise from it. When we experience injustice at the hands of others or experience great natural disasters, we are provoked to ask why. "Why, God, did you let this happen?" From the Great Lisbon Earthquake that struck that city on All Saint's Day, November 1, 1755, or the 9/11 Twin Tower attacks in 2001 or the the Boxing Day Tsunami in 2004 or the Earthquake and Tsunami that struck Japan

18. Martin, "Is Evil Evidence Against the Existence of God?"

in 2012 causing the meltdown at the Fukushima nuclear power plant, each event provokes deep questions because they are hard to explain. Why would God allow these things to happen? We also face the Existential Problem when we are denied a work promotion unjustly and our colleagues do not rise to our defense. The wife of a pastor I know in Seattle was injured in a horse riding accident, that was no one's fault, in which her brain was severed from her spinal cord inside her skull. She was in a near vegetative state for a long time. Gradually her awareness has returned, but her husband now takes care of her every need while pastoring his church. Why would God let that happen? What purpose did it serve to put this young family through so much suffering already, with so much suffering still to come?

The issues related to finding a warranted definition of evil render the Logical Problem and the Evidential Problem into non-starters. Nevertheless, the Existential Problem is not quickly solved; rather, it is foolish to even talk about it as the kind of "problem" one solves. We have left the realm of abstract questions. This problem asks not whether evil is in this world; instead, the question is "Why, God, are you letting *this* evil happen to *me*, or to this person?" The question of evil's definition is still relevant though. Consider the pain one might feel at the hands of a dentist. One goes to the dentist to have one's teeth fixed. What if at the end of the pain there was no fix? We discover the person we went to see actually only intended to give us pain. Notice how this realization changes the meaning of the pain felt during the procedure, transforming it from a thing endured for a greater wiser good into cruelty. Thus, the pain caused by a dentist who allows a patient to experience temporary pain in order to fix his or her teeth is quite different from the the dentist whose only intention is to cause pain. *Evil is in part defined by the position of pain within a narrative* and the outcome of that narrative. This means that the evil of suffering is not exactly in the experience but rather in the experience that is imbedded with meaning in a narrative, which is *a very important distinction*. We do not directly experience evil without it being situated in a narrative. Thus, evil is an interpretation, but it is not *just* an interpretation, any more than suffering in a dentist's chair is just a narrative.

Here, then, we come to common ground between Christianity and Buddhism on the topic of *dukkha*. The astute reader may recognize that we have been talking about evil, when evil and suffering are not the same things. A person can suffer pain in a dentist chair for a good reason without necessarily experiencing evil. Granted. However, bringing suffering to terms with both Buddhism and Christianity requires us to grapple with suffering while understanding that we are analyzing it within two differing narratives, the Christian and the Buddhist. Throughout the remainder of this book, we will be looking at the implications these narratives have for *dukkha* and what they say about how to end it.

TO END ALL SUFFERING

The Problem of Evil has a narrative thrust, a direction, an implied expectation. It obligates God to do something about evil. But could God end evil in an evil way? Could God act unjustly to bring about justice? Clearly, an evil course of action to end evil only adds more evil to the pile of wrongs. Injustice done to bring justice causes more injustice. Who will then right that wrong? A philosopher faces this problem when he tries his hand at fantasy writing by saying God could just stop evil by a postulated, ficticious, supposed, divine act X, Y, or Z.

The Bible teaches that God will finally judge the world at the end of history. There will be a day when all things are put right. The Old and New Testaments clearly teach that the Creator God of Israel is the judge of all the earth. However, this biblical fact alone sometimes may bring the sufferer little comfort. Suffering is present. Evil stares us in the face. Evil smashes us in the teeth because we are in the way on its road to power. Evil steals our hard-earned life savings in order to cover financial derivatives trades, and this without legal recourse. Every year evil continues to end the lives of millions of unborn babies around the world. Evil outsources torture to third world countries to keep its hands clean. Why should we pray to a distant God who abandons us to suffer in the midst of this evil world, yet has a plan to show up at the end and play "hero" at our expense?

What is God doing about suffering? How is he present in human history to end evil and suffering? N. T. Wright addresses this question directly in his book *Evil and the Justice of God,* which was helpful for developing and organizing the case that follows. The reader who is interested in exploring this matter further would be wise to read his book.

Instead of asking how God will end evil, Wright asks what has God decisively done to bring about evil's end. He opens his book with what he calls "The New Problem of Evil."[19] This problem has three parts. "First, we ignore evil when it doesn't hit us in the face. Second, we are surprised by evil when it does. Third, we react in immature and dangerous ways as a result."[20] John Lennon's request to "imagine" a world with no evil is a challenging chore since selfishness and self-centeredness motivate so much of what we do.[21] It is not so simple. Wright calls us to think about what makes for a wise ending of evil, and in that context he argues that God has already taken the decisive step to end evil and suffering in this world: God became man and lived among us, taking the decisive step to defeat evil through the life, unjust death, and resurrection of Jesus the Messiah. God vindicated Jesus in human history and time to make him the one who now holds all authority and power in heaven and on earth (Matt. 28:18–20).

It has always surprised me how some biblical scholars will speak of what various New Testament communities thought and did while ignoring obvious, glaring data in biblical texts. Only a few decades ago, many New Testaments scholars focused intently on the sayings of Jesus, asking which sayings Jesus did and did not say. The Jesus Seminar is perhaps the most famous of these efforts. But what is apparent from all of the canonical Gospels, even the Gospel of John, is that each Gospel argues from Israel's scriptures that the life and work of Jesus of Nazareth fulfills Israel's hopes and purposes.[22]

If Israel's history were a movie, the event that starts the plot, its "inciting incident," appears to be God's call of Abram out of Ur of

19. Wright, *Evil and the Justice of God*, 19.

20. Ibid., 23–24.

21. Lennon, "Imagine" on *Imagine*.

22. Wright, *Jesus and Victory of God*.

the Chaldeans (Gen. 12). God calls Abram because "in you all the nations of the earth shall be blessed" (Gen. 12:3). While God calls Abram and promises to bless him, ultimately the blessing will not be for him—or more accurately, not only for him. Why is God calling Abram?

The answer seems to be found in the first eleven chapters of Genesis in which three great evils occur: (1) man's rebellion against God followed by being cast out of the Garden (Gen. 3), (2) human wickedness and violence followed by the natural disaster of the Great Flood (Gen. 6–9), and finally, (3) human arrogance followed by the rupturing of language which divides humanity (Gen. 11).[23] Certainly the fall seems to lead to the Great Flood and the Tower of Babel, but all three events provide the context to Abram's call. God is creating a people through whom he will fix humanity's problem, yet we discover that they are still part of the problem.[24] They struggle with the same base nature, which they demonstrate by rebellion against God in the wilderness and the Promised Land. The same wickedness and arrogance lives in them, too.

Evil and suffering are major themes in the Old Testament. So much could be said (and has been said) about what each of the books of the Old Testament teaches about evil and suffering. Because of the limits of space, we will focus on three books in particular, namely, Isaiah, Daniel, and Job, which address the question of what God is doing and what God will do about evil and suffering.

We should bear in mind that while the Bible reveals that the nation of Israel and the Israelites are the chosen people, they are not chosen for themselves but for God and for the nations. They are chosen unto a purpose. They have a specific role to play in the world. By the light of wise living and the pursuit of righteousness and justice, they are to shine the light of God's wisdom and righteousness to the surrounding nations (Deut. 4:5–8). Yet they fail because they share the same character as the rest of humanity. They partake in the same faults that reflect the world of Genesis 3–11. Repeatedly, God's people aspire to the calling to which they have been called only to fall short of that calling, be it the nation as a whole in the time of the

23. Wright, *Evil and Justice of God*, 46.

24. Ibid.

Exodus generation (Exodus and Numbers), or the repeated cycle of idolatry in the Book of Judges (Judg. 3), or the northern kingdom of Israel (1 Kings. 12–2 Kings. 17), or the southern kingdom before the exile into Babylon (2 Kings. 21–25 and Jeremiah), or the complacent generation which returned from the exile but was complacent in rebuilding the Temple (Hag. and Zech.). What is most important here is that their failure is individual, corporate, and human. They are part of the problem.

However, they are also part of the solution. Throughout Israel's history we see great examples of faithfulness—examples of people individually and corporately overturning rebellion, wickedness, and arrogance: Moses, Joshua and the nation during Joshua's period of leadership, the Judges, Samuel, David, many in the northern and southern kingdoms who remained faithful, Daniel and his friends, those who returned to Israel and settled in the city of Jerusalem after the walls were rebuilt by Nehemiah, those who led and participated in the faithful revolt against Antiochus Epiphanes, the mother in 2 Maccabees 7 who counsels her sons through torture, and many more examples (Heb. 11). All of these people sought to overturn evil and were faithful to God's calling to be a people who shine the light of God's mercy on a world poisoned with the evils of Genesis 3–11. Admittedly, not all those listed above are the best examples. They are a motley crew to be sure, all too human.

The problem of a compromised Israel, a human Israel, is what the Book of Isaiah confronts head on as it engages with the question of what the nation's future will be. It recounts the failures of the people of the southern kingdom of Judah as a whole and of individuals as well, especially King Ahaz (Isa. 7), and even King Hezekiah (Isa. 39) who is presented heroically in the book, for the most part. But it also describes the fates of nations that surround Israel (Isa. 7–35). The second half of the book, sometimes called Second Isaiah by many scholars, speaks of a future comfort coming to the nation (Isa. 40:1–2). In this section, a new character comes to the forefront: the Servant, who is prominent in chapters 42–61. This Servant appears to be a king figure who will end evil and stop the suffering of the oppressed and hurting of *the nations* (Isa. 42:1–9). The spirit of God has anointed him—literally "messiahed" him—and made him a king to the brokenhearted, the oppressed, and to those in chains to deliver them (Isa. 61:1–2). Interestingly, this section also describes this "Servant" as "Israel" (Isa. 44:1). Isaiah 53 tells how the Servant will bring deliverance from suffering and evil by enduring suffering and evil himself. And he will endure until death, without doing any evil in return. Given the context of this portion of Isaiah, this Servant must be the messianic king figure, yet the Servant is also Israel. It follows that the calling of the nation of Israel is to suffer for the nations to end their evil and suffering, but the Book of Isaiah and the entire Old Testament affirm that the nation of Israel is not living up to this calling of being faithful, even to the point of death, in order to bring redemption to the world. So the question remains in the text: Who will fulfill the role of the Servant?

Daniel also presents a figure like the Servant of Isaiah, the "Son of Man." Like the Book of Isaiah, the Book of Daniel focuses on the nations, but more in terms of imperial power and the evils surrounding it. In the middle of the story stands Daniel, who, more than once, brings rescue and restoration on behalf of the God of the Hebrews to those who neither know God nor serve him. Like the character of Daniel in the book, the Son of Man also stands in Daniel 7 within the company of strong powers, or "beasts." Yet God exalts the Son of Man over these empires and gives him a kingdom that will not be destroyed (Dan. 7:14). As Wright observes:

> Daniel 7 is basically a court scene: God takes his seat, and judgment is given for the human against the beasts. This is what God's justice over the unjust world will look like. God's restoration of creation must come about through his proper overthrow of the forces of evil and his vindication of his faithful people. The questions we are left with at the end of Daniel are: Who are God's faithful people? How will it all work out? Who is the Son of Man?[25]

The Book of Job presents a very different view of the Servant. As I mentioned in chapter 2, Satan challenges God, not through a wager but by a false accusation. Satan tells God that humans do not choose righteousness because it is good; rather, they choose righteousness because God will bless them for it. God asks Satan to consider Job. Clearly Job is not that kind of man. He is righteous because he loves

25. Ibid., 67–68.

God and desires what is right. So God sets out to vindicate Job by letting Satan test Job. Job never accuses God. He curses everything else, but from God he just asks "*Why?*" Job is living in the Existential Problem of Evil. By the end of the book Job is vindicated and God sets things right in this world. More important, notice that Job defeats Satan's accusation regarding the possibility of human righteousness in this life because he is willing to suffer faithfully. God vindicates Job through suffering. Job is blessed afterwards, but the narrative context of that blessing in the book shows that God gives such things not as though he is a Skinner box, where one pushes the lever and out comes the sugar. Instead, God is governing the world toward righteous ends and one of them is defeating evil in heaven through righteousness and faithfulness on earth. Our life stories are ours, *but they are not about us.* If Job had made his highest goal to end suffering, then something very great would have been lost.

The sufferings of Christ share this same quality with Job's suffering. Jesus does not hide from evil and suffering. He faced it, head on, at a time in history in which the arrogant height of political power trampled justice and rampantly crucified in the interest of maintaining power and control. Jesus faced suffering at a time when the leadership of his own nation was fully corrupt, ripe for its own Great Flood. He faced evil at a time when, as we sometimes see in organizational development, certain practices and habits lead the organization to do unspeakable things. For fear, for envy, or indignation they "stone" people unjustly. Jesus faced evil and suffering alone, like Job, with no comforter.

It was common in the 1800s for theologians in Britain and America to aim their retelling of the Gospel story as a kind of sales pitch highlighting the benefits of becoming a Christian. A focus on conversion to the exclusion of works of mercy for the suffering and oppressed—or cultural advancements in the arts and scholarship—has led American Christains to almost completely abandon cultural and civic participation for a religion of mere personal devotion. Yet when seen in his historical context, Christ is not coming to be a sacrifice "just for me." He is come to reverse Genesis 3–11. Jesus participates in works of mercy and culture building, not as ends in themselves, but as performative metaphors that incarnate and explain the Gospel to human beings. Jesus takes responsibility to lead in all the details of his life and the lives of his followers. He is making all things new as the Messiah-Servant-King of the Book of Isaiah and The King over all empires. The gospels are the story of how Jesus becomes the lawful King, the one who has the authority and power *to end all suffering.*[26]

The coming of Jesus Christ into the world is also God acting to end suffering and evil because Jesus is the presence of YHWH, the Creator God.[27] Acting under all the moral requirements against which humans do evil, Jesus heals those who are suffering, especially those suffering from ailments that would make them ritually unclean and unworthy to enter the presence of God according to the Law of Moses. He also, in the end, fully identifies himself with the revolutionaries who had failed to bring the deliverance of Israel from oppression through their own revolutionary actions.[28] Jesus has table fellowship with sinners, those who do evil. God in Christ is meeting humanity in the midst of his own evil and suffering in order to rescue him from it. God the Son of Man humbles himself in order to bring those who do evil together to be changed by fellowship with God. Christ the man is reversing the arrogance of humanity at the Tower of Babel.

Jesus is also showing Israel what it means to be Israel. He shoulders the calling of Israel as the Servant of the Book of Isaiah. He bears all the reproach, suffering, shame, judgment; he takes everything that the Servant was to take onto himself in order to bring healing and redemption to the nations. Christ does this by taking on himself all the sin and failure and suffering of Israel. Since the role of Israel was to serve the nations by ministering to them the mercy and grace of God—something Israel could not do—Christ fulfilled the work that they could not do, which no other human could do. Thus, in Christ is the end of suffering for all men, in the here and now. Because Jesus Christ represented Israel to fulfill its calling, to enter the New Covenant with God's people is to be "in" Christ. This is something in which all nations can take part, to minister this powerful mercy and grace to our fellow human beings.

26. Wright, *How God Became King.*

27. Wright, *Jesus and Victory of God*, 477–662; Wright, *Evil and Justice of God.*

28. Wright, *Evil and Justice of God*, 84.

In Christ, we can be his body, his hands working to overturn evil and end suffering on this side of eternity. Jesus was judged falsely by the evil powers of this world, and was put to death because those in power either envied him or wanted to save themselves from being ground by the gears of secular power. In order to justify the sentence, Jesus was falsely accused of being a false prophet and a blasphemer (Deuteronomy 12–13) and was executed (as that passage instructs) for being a false prophet. This judicial pronouncement came from the lips of the high priest and the counsel of the Sanhedrin, specific governing bodies organized according to the Mosaic Law found in the Bible. In this situation, they both rendered a false judgment against Jesus who was who he claimed to be.[29]

Yet God the Father overturned this unjust, evil sentence and raised Jesus from the dead, giving him the kingdom of Israel, and because of his faithfulness in all things made him the King of *everything*. As the King of everything, he calls all his subjects to do what he did—to bring about the end of evil and suffering—but to do it his way, which will involve suffering on our part. God knows that this way of ending evil and suffering is best because our story is not just about us. God understands the causes of evil and suffering; therefore, in Christ he is ending suffering in the best way, one that involves our participation. This is why the New Testament does not end with the resurrection of Christ but goes on to recount the story of the New Testament Church. It tells the beginning of the end of suffering.

Jesus Christ did not come to end some suffering or some evil; he came to end it all. However, the way that Christ is ending suffering also involves human, willing participation in God's work in history. Some Christians may read me here and miss my point. I am not attempting to describe the mechanics of justification here or who is saved or how righteousness is applied. Others have written excellent books on those topics. I am addressing how God is ending suffering and evil in this world. The Book of Acts and the Epistles clearly teach that those who are living Christ's way are actually Christ's body to the world. We are his healing hands and feet in this world. Like Jesus, we throw ourselves into the breach to end

29. Wright, *Resurrection of Son of God*, 719–38.

injustice and suffering, or at least we should. Jesus Christ became King of everything so all humans who are his subjects would have the authority and the resources to be faithful to Israel's calling, which is the Christian Church's calling today—to minister the mercy and grace of God to all nations. This does not mean that the Church rules over God's grace. The Church is not the King. Jesus is.

King Jesus is working to bring the end of all suffering and evil, and the Bible promises he will be successful. "For he must reign until he has put all His enemies under His feet. The last enemy that will be abolished is death" (1 Cor. 15:25–26). As the Book of Revelation explains, "He shall wipe away every tear from their eyes; and there shall no longer be *any* death; there shall no longer be *any* mourning, or crying, or pain; for the former things have passed away" (Rev. 21:4; italics in the translation). God promises that King Jesus will succeed in stopping suffering and evil—all of it. Jesus Christ is ending, and will end, all *dukkha*.

In our present interreligious dialogue between the teachings of the Buddha and the teachings of Christ, we have to ask a very important question. If (a) Jesus Christ is ending all *dukkha* and (b) the Buddha's teaching contradicts the work of Christ in ending *dukkha* and (c) Jesus is the only one who can ultimately and finally end *dukkha*, would it then not be counter-productive to the goals of Buddhism to follow the Buddha's teachings?

Certainly Buddhist discipline increases awareness of habits, patterns of thinking, and cravings, and has other positive benefits. (I have benefited from breathing exercises and meditation.) Nevertheless, if one's goal is to really end *dukkha*, should not the teachings of the Buddha be abandoned for the teachings of Christ? Nāgārjuna abandoned the sixty-third view for 'nothing'. Maybe it is wiser to abandon the sixty-third view for *someone*.

BUT. . . . BUT. . . . BUT. . . .

Someone who just read the last section is saying, "No. I do not believe the Bible. What you just gave is not an argument. I want to see you prove the Bible first. Give me evidence. Logically prove that God exists. Logically prove that the miracles of the Old Testament happened. Prove to me that Jesus rose from the dead. Where is the empirical evidence? The Buddha did not trust revelation. The best faith can be mistaken. Prove it! Prove it! Prove it!"

I accept the burden of proof. But notice that for me to accept the burden of proof, there must be such a thing as "proof." The Bible presents a worldview in which proof—logical inference, evidence, causal regularity, scientific proof, personal identity, and the like—is not only possible but useful in discerning wisdom about the world and knowledge of God and his revelation in the Bible. Recall in chapter 2 (on methodology) that I compared God's composition of his written Scriptures (within Israel, within history) to a man who crosses a room using his memory to guide him to remind him of where things are and were. Likewise, the Bible is the public memory of a people who have experienced God's interaction with them over thousands of years. I explained that faith and evidence work together in a creative and critical hermeneutical circle, over a long period of time, through multiple epochs, culminating with the coming of his Son in history. This is what permits each biblical text to intertextually discourse with the others. Through this discourse, God demonstrates his trustworthiness over and over and over and over again, with future events reestablishing the faithfulness of previous revelation. God offers this testimony of himself in history to confirm and account for all the things necessary to confirm and account for any true, good, and right thing.

I accept the burden of proof. If I am to accept it, there must be logic, evidence, and a world in which such things make sense. This is why it was so important to painstakingly work through the Buddha's teaching on logic, personal identity, empirical evidence, and causality to establish that the Buddhist worldview does not account for the ability to prove worldview claims at all, especially its own. It is not able to even begin to ask for proof of the Christian worldview. The Buddha stands on no ground to reject the Christian revelation claim.

I accept the burden of proof because the Buddha cannot.

17

A Christian Critique of Buddhist Pragmatism

Therefore, Mālunkyaputta, remember what I have left undeclared as undeclared. And what have I left undeclared? 'The world is eternal'—I have left undeclared. 'The world is not eternal'–I have left undeclared. 'The world is finite'—I have left undeclared. 'The soul is the same as the body'—I have left undeclared. 'The soul is one thing and the body another'—I have left undeclared. After death a Tathāgata [enlightened one] exists'—I have left undeclared. 'After death a Tathāgata does not exist'—I have left undeclared. 'After death a Tathāgata both exists and does not exist'—I have left undeclared. 'After death a Tathāgata neither exists nor does not exist'—I have left undeclared.

Majjhima-nikāya, Cūḷamālunkya Sutta 1.431

For whoever wishes to save his life shall lose it; but whoever loses his life for My sake shall find it.

Matthew 16:25

AN ODD TABLE TALK

Suppose that a friend you met recently invites you to her house. When you arrive, your friend meets you at the door and walks you to a spacious dining room. In the center, a dozen people sit around a table, which is cleared of both food and even a tablecloth.

Instead, sitting in the center of the table beneath a suspended, dust-caked chandelier is a cage holding a cat.

Your friend introduces you to the gathering, but you find it hard to remember names because of the oddness of this scene and the question of why the cat is here.

Gradually, they return to their conversation. "If we cut down the back, it will just slide off the sides," one comments.

Another replies, "Yes, but the skin will get caught on the paws and the head. I think we should make an incision along the bottom from below the chin all the way to the tail. Then we can also make incisions along the inside of each leg and a circular cut around the wrists of each paw." That recommendation gets a number of "Hmmms" and head nods.

"But that will make a mess," replies a guest on the other side of the table. More "Hmmms" and nods follow.

You wonder if these are veterinarians. Maybe they are. Hopefully they are. You keep listening.

One of them near you paces, impatiently pounding a pack of cigarettes into his palm. "Look. We just sit here debating this. Let's just start cutting!" He flicks a cigarette between his lips, nervously lights, and draws a long pull on it that curls and twists the glowing leaves, igniting them into ash as the fire climbs through them.

Slowly, the unthinkable condenses in your mind. They really are debating how best to skin the cat on the table. You look at the cat, which moves nervously about its cage. It can sense something is wrong. Somehow it knows it is in danger. The table guest who spoke first turns to you and calls you by name. In this context, you find the sound of your name startling. The person asks what you think should be done.

You ask, "Why are you skinning this cat?" They all look at each other blankly. After a moment, they look at your friend who invited you. You expect her to answer their gaze. But she catches your eyes and wryly grins, gently biting the nail on the middle finger of her elegant right hand.

The man replies, "We're pragmatists. We are trying to find the best way to skin this cat."

"But why?" you ask.

Your friend takes her fingernail out from between her teeth but keeps her smile. She replies, "Because we want to."

THE PROBLEM OF PRAGMATISM

The pragmatic criterion of truth is "Truth is what works." However, one must ask the follow up question: "Works for what?" This question pragmatism cannot answer within itself. It must rely on something else, specifically, a *goal* to answer that question. A human must have already selected a goal, in order to ascertain whether a certain idea leads to a productive result related to that goal or not. A pragmatist can defend the "truth" of scientific concepts because scientific concepts produce technological advancements and lead to the discovery of more knowledge. Of course, this new knowledge must also be defined in terms of whether it "works." However, without the human goal of creating technology or making future discoveries or the like, pragmatism cannot say that knowledge is true whether that knowledge is scientific or any other kind.

The problem with a pragmatic theory of truth is its inability to answer the question of why one goal is chosen over another. Which is "truest" knowledge regarding cats in the example provided above? Is it the knowledge that permits one to skin the cat in the most efficient way? Or the way that causes the smallest mess? Or the way that causes the most pleasure for those seated around the table? It all depends on how the gathering around the cat defines their goal. That goal is what defines the utility of their knowledge.

No item can have utility without a purpose. A Swiss army knife may have great utility, meeting a number of different purposes. However, if we melt it down into a little puddle of molten ooze, the utility goes away. Once it cools and hardens, one potential utility returns: paperweight (if one has paper one needs to hold down). Utility is goal-directed. Put in terms of pragmatism, one must have a goal to achieve.

Pragmatism brings with it a great ambiguity. As early as 1908, Arthur O. Lovejoy had isolated thirteen different pragmatisms involving theories of meaning, the nature of truth, differing justifications of knowledge, and ontology.[1] People have different

1. Lovejoy, "Thirteen Pragmatisms," 39.

goals even in their theories of pragmatism. The Buddha clarifies this problem since he has the goal of ending *dukkha*. But the Buddha provides no criterion for evaluating whether we should have this goal. Nor can he really. If one wants to end *dukkha*, then one may adopt the Buddha's method. If one does not want to end *dukkha*, one need not consider the Buddha's method.

Kalupahana expounds that the Buddha held neither a correspondence theory nor a coherence theory of truth.[2] Instead he embraced a pragmatic criterion of truth. In chapter 13, we concluded this was the one option available for explaining the nature of logical norms. Based on Nāgārjuna's method of rejecting all metalanguage analysis, the Buddhist may choose not to think about these problems because such considerations supposedly get us away from experience, and, therefore, away from the knowledge that will end suffering. The Buddha will only allow knowledge to be justified by the epistemology criticized in chapters 10–14. Also one may choose not to think through the serious problems with the Buddhist theory of causality (chapter 15), but believe that carefully considering them will facilitate too many philosophical speculations about reality that do not lead to the ending of suffering. When I consider my own conversations with Buddhists, our points of discussion always seem to hinge on the pragmatic value of the Buddha's teaching (*dharma*) to end suffering. In our context here, we must ask, "Why make ending *dukkha* our highest goal?"

SPIRITUAL HOSPICE CARE OR SPIRITUAL CURE: THE "MEDICAL ETHICS" OF REDEMPTION

I teach a graduate course in medical ethics for Gonzaga University's graduate program for Advanced Practice Registered Nurses. Because of the aging of the "Baby Boomers" in the United States, I have my students write a philosophical paper on end-of-life care. A number of my students write papers on hospice care and palliative sedation. Hospice care is care generally given to relieve suffering in people who are either terminally ill or who are so advanced in years

2. "The Buddha is thus left with only a pragmatic criterion of truth, and this is what we come across in the Discourse to Prince Abhaya (*Abhayaraja-kumara-sutta*)," In *Continuities and Discontinuities*, 50–51.

that death is near. Palliative sedation, on the other hand, is sedation given to a patient, usually a terminally ill patient, to relieve pain and suffering, but which does not heal one of illness. In the 1990s, the practice used to be called "terminal sedation" because once sedated, the patient remained sedated till death. However, this practice became controversial as some empirical evidence suggested that palliative sedation may hasten or cause death. But other empirical findings seem to contradict those findings and show palliative sedation does not hasten death. This matter is hotly debated in the literature.[3] However, the reason why it is debated is that medical providers know that if a doctor can cure someone, the doctor should. If a person is suffering and is terminally ill, hospice care can make the person more comfortable. Palliative sedation can remove one's pain by giving one a sleep from which one shall never wake. Nevertheless, it is unethical to give a person who is not near death either type of care.[4] They should not even be called "treatments" since they do not heal anything. They only make a person more comfortable. Basically, *they numb*. It can be argued that palliative sedation is the most powerful kind of numbing one can receive. Its purposes do not result in physical health. It has only one goal: *to end suffering*.

We recognize that it is unethical for a doctor to give hospice care or palliative sedation to a person who could be cured. Why? Because health is more than the end of suffering. The goal of ending suffering is not weighty enough. In fact, if a doctor or medical team knows only how to numb pain but not how to heal, they lack the knowledge of medicine necessary to fulfill the Hippocratic Oath.

"The image often used in Buddhist texts is not of the Buddha as philosopher, but the Buddha as a doctor, 'the great physician'."[5] However, this metaphor can be misleading, as I will now demonstrate. Consider the only spiritual care that Buddhism claims to offer. In chapter 9, we reviewed what the the Buddha teaches about nirvāṇa (Pali: *nibbāna*). He taught that putting an ending to ignorance leads

3. Claessens, Shotsmans, and Broeckaert, "Palliative Sedation."

4. As I have defined these. Some one could be temporarily sedated to help that person with extreme pain, to promote rest leading to recovery. But I am not discussing that type of sedation.

5. Williams, *Buddhist Thought*, 25.

to a reversal of the chain of causality, based on the doctrine of *paṭiccasamuppāda* (dependent arising), bringing an end to birth and death. In the *Cūḷamālunkya Sutta,* this leads to a number of difficult philosophical problems, including the question What happens to the Buddha after death?

> Therefore, Mālunkyaputta, remember what I have left undeclared as undeclared. And what have I left undeclared? 'The world is eternal' —I have left undeclared. 'The world is not eternal' —I have left undeclared. 'The world is finite' —I have left undeclared. 'The soul is the same as the body' —I have left undeclared. 'The soul is one thing and the body another' —I have left undeclared. After death a Tathāgata [enlightened one] exists' —I have left undeclared. 'After death a Tathāgata does not exist' —I have left undeclared. 'After death a Tathāgata both exists and does not exist' —I have left undeclared. 'After death a Tathāgata neither exists nor does not exist' —I have left undeclared.[6]

In the *Cūḷamālunkya Sutta*, the Buddha's central thesis is he does not speak on these matters "Because it is unbeneficial, it does not belong to the fundamentals of the holy life, it does not lead to disenchantment, to dispassion, to cessation, to peace, to direct knowledge, to enlightenment, to nibbāna."[7] This admission is startling because it shows how the Buddha has built his entire worldview around the goal of ending suffering, an integral part of which is stepping off the wheel of *saṃsāra,* the endless cycle of reincarnation. To do this, the Buddha must help a person to stop reincarnating. However, the Buddha does not answer the question of whether one exists after accomplishing this feat, and there is a reason for this. Logically, if one reverses the causes of becoming and, thus, birth, it would seem that one stops what we know as life. Some Buddhist traditions teach that *nibbāna* experienced by an *arahant,* an enlightened one, after death is a kind of Buddhist heaven. But this is really a story for the masses that is inconsistent with the implications of the Buddha's teaching in the Pali texts. If one follows the implications of the enthymeme of the Buddha's teaching, it would seem that ending the causes of

6. *Majjhima-nikāya, Cūḷamālunkya Sutta* 1.431, quoted from Nanamoli and Bodhi, *Middle Length Discourses.*

7. *Majjhima-nikāya, Cūḷamālunkya Sutta* 1.431 quoted from Ibid.

suffering means ending of the causes of life. The Buddha does not care to address this question though. He is a one-issue philosopher. Anything that gets in the way of the cessation of suffering should be cast from one's mind.

To underscore this point, the Buddha tells several short parables in the *Cūḷamālunkya Sutta* comparing the man seeking enlightenment to a man who is wounded.[8] He asks Mālunkyāputta if he were wounded with a poison arrow, would he wait to be treated until he found out what caste the doctor was from? Or would he care about the doctor's race? Or from what tree the arrow was made? After sharing these parables, the Buddha then asks what good it would do to answer these questions when one is dying of the poison. But we must be very careful that we think through his metaphor of the wound that leads to death. Ignorance, dispositions, craving, and the rest of the causal chain lead to suffering. So in the parable, death is the counterpart to the condition of suffering. This means that health is also a metaphor, which is why it is not important whether the Buddha's teachings do actually lead to final, ultimate death, a complete cesstion of existence. The question the Buddha cares about is whether the person's suffering has been ended. The Buddha is more concerned with spiritual hospice care than spiritual cure and the restoration of a person to a full life as a person. Whatever that full life is, it must be a life without suffering. Richard Gombrich explains the Buddhist quest for liberation from suffering:

> To attain it is open to any human being, and it is ultimately the only thing worth attaining, for it is the ony happiness which is not transient. A person who has attained it will live on so long as his body keeps going, but thereafter not be reborn. Thus he will never have to suffer and die again. For Buddhists, religion is what is relevant to this quest and nothing else.[9]

8. *Majjhima-nikāya, Cūḷamālunkya Sutta* 1.429 quoted from Ibid.

9. Gombrich, *Theravāda Buddhism*, 24, quoted in Williams, *Buddhist Thought*, 3. The context of Gombrich's comment in his own book is very interesting, and relevant for our discussion here. He recognizes the totalizing claims Buddhism makes of what actually can free a person from suffering. However, he recognizes that for the Buddhist, the Hindu gods are merely more powerful beings, providing earthly benefits. This is true. However, he makes the mistake of mapping this conception of the place of the Hindu gods onto Christian faith. He attempts to show that there are beliefs held by Western Christians (British Christians to be

The Buddha's religion, his *dhamma*, only promises the end of suffering. The Buddha's spiritual hospice care does not aim at preserving life. That is beyond the scope of his "treatment."

How does this contrast with the teaching of Jesus Christ? Jesus taught to choose suffering if one must, and Jesus promises in this life there will be suffering for those who follow him. Jesus explains, "For whoever wishes to save his life shall lose it; but whoever looses his life for My sake shall find it" (Matt. 16:25). Jesus tells his disciples one should not try to save one's life, but rather prioritize his kingdom first (Matt. 6:33). What he is referring to here is a particular attitude toward life that trusts God is faithful to his promises. Jesus is asking his disciples to make a long-term investment based on the teaching of the Old Testament. If you entrust yourself to God's promises, the covenant God has made with his people, God will pay up. God will reward a person who puts their trust in God's promises to humanity, with what is actually best (Rom. 8:28). What Jesus is promising is not a regulative concept, a lie to encourage moral behavior. It is not a trick to get us to do something good. Jesus is teaching that we should be so focused on heeding his word that we do not seek to save our lives, *per se*. The Greek text of Matthew's Gospel is so emphatic on this point that instead of using the Greek word for biological life (*zoe*) it renders Christ's words into Greek using the word for soul (*psuche*).[10] So, in Greek the passage reads: "For whoever wishes to save his soul shall lose it; but whoever looses his soul for My sake

precise) which have nothing to do with Christian faith, for instance, beliefs about certain subatomic particles. Gombrich assumes that secular beliefs are neutral beliefs. However, beliefs do not exist without people to believe them. It is a kind of reism to think that beliefs exist without believers. If a Christian holds beliefs in such a way that that a belief has no relationship to Christ, then St. Paul teaches he is thinking disobediently (2 Cor. 10:5), since in Christ are hid all the treasures of wisdom and knowledge (Col. 2:2–3). If St. Paul's insights are applied to subatomic particles, particle physics is not a secular discipline, but rather the testimony of the awesome, kind, and creative power of God (Ps. 19:1-6) and a testimony to YHWH's great wisdom in the way he planned the universe before he made the first elementary particles (Prov. 8:26). Christ makes totalizing claims, not only about the end of suffering but also particle physics (John 1:3,: Col. 1:16–17).

10. Dr. Joost Nixon, Senior Pastor at Christ Church, Spokane, WA, pointed this out to me.

shall find it."[11] Paradoxically, but without contradiction, Jesus is asking his disciples to take up their crosses and die to themselves, along with accepting the possibility that they may be killed by Rome as revolutionaries. Jesus came so that we might have life and have it more abundantly (John 10:10). While the end of suffering is included in what Jesus came to give, it is not the final and ultimate goal of his work. He aims to transform us into his likeness. He calls his people to suffer with him for others so that they, too, can be transformed into his likeness, in order to love one's neighbor as one's self (Matt. 22:39), to love others the way that Jesus Christ loves (John 15:11). Our capacity to love others, to lay down our lives for them, even to suffer for them, is a greater good than the end of suffering because through love and humility God has promised that his humanity will inherit all things (Matt. 5:5). And better than any sort of material wealth is the selfless fellowship that humanity will share in Christ and with Christ, and with God, in this life and forever. As St. Paul writes:

> The Spirit of Himself bears witness with our spirit that we are children of God, and if children, heirs also, heirs of God and fellow heirs with Christ, *if indeed we suffer with him* in order that we may be glorified with Him. (Rom. 8:16–17; emphasis mine.)

God is a king who adopts his subjects to give them an inheritance with his son.

Contrast the Buddha, who offers spiritual hospice care. He makes no promises about abundant, flourishing life. His goal is not life because, from his worldview, abundant life *is the problem.* We have too much of it, over and over and over again. He wants to step off the merry-go-round. He wants to end the pain, to make it stop. It is important to see clearly what we read in the *Cūḷamālunkya Sutta* and other Buddhist texts, that the Buddha uses the goal of ending suffering as a rhetorical device to stop people from asking more

11. The word that is probably being used here is the Aramaic word for life, which is the cognate of the Hebrew word *nephesh,* which refers the full life of an organism, roughly equivalent to Aristotle's use of *psuche* in both *On the Soul* and *On the Parts of Animals.*

questions because the Buddha holds a pragmatic criterion of truth.[12] The pragmatic criterion cannot speak to the whether its own goal is best, but must evaluate everything in terms of whether it works to accomplish the goal. However, we also discovered in chapters 10–16 that the Buddha's teachings in the *Nikāyas*, on logic and reasoning, personal identity, empirical evidence and causality each mutually annihilate the others. Thus, Buddhist pragmatism puts Buddhism in a very interesting predicament.

THE QUESTION OF MOTIVE

The desire to end suffering becomes the basis for the Buddha's method. However, the Buddhist method cannot justify that people ought to choose its method over another. For some people, the goals of Buddhism may not fit. *So for some people, the Buddhist epistemology and causal theory may not be needed.* If *each and every* person did not need Buddhism, then *Buddhism would have no utility.* Therefore, it would be confused (*musā*) or in Western terms, false.[13] If the world is set up in such a way that Buddhism cannot really end *dukkha*, then Buddhism is false for every one on its own terms. Remember this point!

Now the Buddha very clearly said in the *Samyukta-āgama* that causal law:

> . . . is neither made by me or by another. Whether the Tathāgatas (enlightened ones) were to arise in this world or not, this pattern of things is eternally existent. Concerning this [pattern of things] the Tathāgata (enlightened one) has insight, is fully enlightened"[14]

Buddhism claims that the world we experience actually operates in the way the Buddha described. Buddhism also claims insight into the way that knowledge works. However, the epistemology that the Buddha used to justify his claim in the *Samyukta-āgama* must rest on his goal, the ending of suffering.

12. Please take seriously my exhortation in the first chapter to read the *Nikāyas* for yourself and read other Buddhist philosophers. I am not making a case from a few proof texts.

13. See chapter 5 for an extended discussion on Buddhist logic.

14. *Daizōkyō* 2.85 b–c (*Tsa a-han ching* 30.16) in Kalupahana, *Causality*, 92.

How does this pragmatic criterion of truth impact interreligious dialogue between Christianity and Buddhism? In chapter 2, I introduced the concept of the Point to Adjudicate, which is explained in the ancient Roman oratory text *Rhetorica ad Herennium. Ad Herennium* explains the Point to Adjudicate within the context of legal argumentation, though the concept can be applied in many other contexts. The Point to Adjudicate:

> . . . will be established from the meeting of the prosecutors Central Point and the defendant's Justifying Motive, as follows: When Orestes says that he killed his mother to avenge his father, was it right for Clytemnestra to be slain by her son without a trial? This then is the proper method for finding the Point to Adjudicate. Once the Point to Adjudicate is found, the complete economy of the entire speech ought to be directed to it.[15]

Here in *To End All Suffering*, I have followed *Ad Herennium's* advice and directed the complete economy of my discourse toward it. In chapter 2, it was too early to identify the Point to Adjudicate. But that time has come.

The Point to Adjudicate is where the central point of one side meets the justifying motive of the other. In this case, because the Buddha defined his entire pragmatic philosophy around the goal to end suffering, the Point to Adjudicate is the question of the motive that leads one to choose this goal since there is nothing else behind the goal except one's desire to chose it.

One might object that defining the Point to Adjudicate as I have above is unfair because *there is more to Buddhism than just choosing this goal.* Agreed. That is why it was so important to work through the complex interlocking organic whole of early Buddhist philosophy, first to explain Buddhist doctrine, and then to show how these various doctrines unravel when they are applied to each other.

Some also might object that pragmatism also can be used to justify religious claims. William James, one of the fathers of modern psychology, attempts to defend pragmatism's value for supporting religious claims:

> [Pragmatism] widens the field of search for God. . . . She will count mystical experiences if they have practical consequences.

15. [Cicero], *Rhetorica Ad Herennium*, 53.

> She will take a God who lives in the very dirt of private fact—if that should seem a likely place to find him. Her only test of probable truth is what works best in the way of leading us, what fits every part of life best and combines with the collectivity of experience's demands, nothing being omitted. If theological ideas should prove to do it, how could pragmatism possibly deny God's existence? She could see no meaning treating as "not true" a notion that was pragmatically so successful. What other kind of truth could there be, for her, than all this agreement with concrete reality?[16]

James argues that pragmatism cannot "possibly deny God's existence." Nor can it affirm the God of the Bible who claims the right to write the truth—the kind of truth that our vacillating goals can never touch, the kind of truth that defines our being.

Pragmatism, the philosophy that "truth" is only a synonym for usefulness, flies in the teeth of Jesus teaching. Jesus claimed to be the way, the *truth*, and the life (John 14:6). God reveals that his word is truth (John 17:17). Christ requires that all thoughts be taken captive to him and not to a surreptitious philosophy (2 Cor. 10:4–5). But pragmatism defines truth outside of God's being and will, which is a straight denial of Christ's teachings as they would have been understood during this period of history, within the worldview of his discourse community: Second Temple Judaism. James' emasculated "truth" can hold no concord with the Christian gospel.[17] This ancient faith is useful, but it is so because it is true and not vice-versa, as Paul writes, "if Christ has not been raised, your faith is worthless;

16. Aristotle, "Posterior Analytics," 18.

17. Though I have argued that Jamesian pragmatism is disobedient, I am not saying that truth has no component of usefulness. Concepts that bear truth should also be helpful to us as tools.

Some might argue that pragmatism is correct as an ultimate test for truth because truth can be defined as the most useful thing. Such a definition of truth cannot be challenged. But this defines truth in terms of only one of its aspects. Humans are upright ambler bipeds, but they are more. Those who stop here demonstrate foolishness since usefulness must be understood in terms of a goal. If the goal of a man is contrary to the Christian gospel, his "truth" will never agree with God. If there is to be a Christian pragmatism, it must be defined not in terms of the utility of Christian doctrines but in terms of God's goal.

Yet such talk creates the epistemological problem of verifying our knowledge of God's goal. This means that a "Christian pragmatism" is revelation-dependent, and therefore Christian pragmatism is epistemologically incomplete in itself.

you are still in your sins. Then those who have fallen asleep in Christ have perished. If we have hoped in Christ in this life only, we are of all men most to be pitied" (1 Cor. 15:17–19).

So the Point to Adjudicate stands, and we return to the justifying motive behind the choice to make the ending of suffering the ultimate worldview-defining goal.

What justifies it? Well, if the Buddha's teaching is justified by the goal of ending suffering, then, the answer is: nothing.

It is just a choice. But if we reflect further, there may be one more justification, which the will that chooses Buddhism can give. An additional reason why a person would make the ending of suffering, not just a- important goal to accomplish in the light of a higher goal, but *the highest goal.*

"Because I want to."

"Because I want to." Think about each of these words in light of the exposition of Buddhism given in chapters 3–9, and the careful study of the collapse of the Buddha's teaching in chapters 10–15. Each of these words fall apart when viewed in the light of the Buddha's teaching, especially the words "*I want.*" It is ironic that a Buddhism driven by a pragmatic criterion of truth, which is what the Pali *Nikāyas* teach, is driven by desire, by craving. Some have compared philosophy to a cheap sweater. If you pull one thread from the Buddha's philosophy, you will find that thread, which winds through radical empiricism, *paṭiccasamuppāda,* and all the other doctrines, eventually is tied to the thing that says "I want." Many terms could be used to describe it. Which one should we choose? The psychophysical personality? The seat of the mind/emotions? The willing person? To keep things simple, let us call it *the heart.*

"Because I want to." The Buddha's method works in the will that wishes to end its suffering. The method requires a certain epistemological outlook defined by that goal. However, the Bible identifies a broader context for comprehending the causes of *dukkha.* God requires us to obey with a perspective that sees even *dukkha* in relation to him. The pragmatism of the Buddha's all-consuming method isolates *dukkha* from the one who has decisively brought about the beginning of the end of suffering through his promise and through his work in the world. Therefore, the Buddha's method can neither explain the nature of *dukkha's* causes nor the effectual end

of them. God has recognized and explained why, how, and that *the Buddha's method is not ultimately useful.*

This may be psychologically uncomfortable for a Buddhist to consider because the interconnected web of doctrines seems to be fixed on reasonable empirical grounds. This is why the previous chapters were necessary—to show how these doctrines actually vivisect human knowledge and dismember the unity of the human person. They also explain how the whole web of the Buddha's teaching is suspended from this one point, the will that says, *"Because I want to."*

Yet it must be seen clearly that if what Jesus Christ has said is true; if what he did on the cross in human history two thousand years ago worked, if he continues to work through human history through his Spirit and through his people to end suffering in humanity, then the Buddha's teachings—well-meaning though they might be—actually prolong suffering, even eternally, based on *profoundly* selfish "Because I want to" thinking. So profound, in fact, that it has generated the massive, intricate architecture of Buddhist doctrine.

If Buddhism is built on this heart's desire—"Because I want to"—then what does the Gospel say? "*Let it go*" (Matt. 5:29–30). If this is keeping a person from embracing the promises of God in Christ that lead to the end of suffering, *let it go*. Nāgārjuna cast away the sixty-third view. This is just one more.

Buddhist teaching is often compared to an onion. If one keeps peeling away the onion layers (the doctrines, philosophy, all the dialogues, exercises of mental discipline), one will only find more layers, until, at some point, one gets to the center—and finds nothing. Just a tabletop covered with torn onion layers. Yet the last seven chapters have uncovered something different. The teachings of the Buddha have critical weaknesses that *To End All Suffering* has explored. As a kindness to Buddhists, it must be made clear that the center of onion petals is not emptiness; rather, it is the will of the practitioner, naked, shivering, squinting at the light, thrashing to pull the onion layers back over him to cover himself. But if a Christian loves his or her Buddhist friend, and if it can be done in a way that communicates love and kindness, the Christian should point out what is actually at the center of the onion, what is really holding the onion together—a human will that has chosen to make ending *dukkha* life's ultimate goal, despite what anyone says to the contrary. Where Buddhist friends may strive for spiritual hospice care, a Christian friend should be willing to suffer long with them that they might have life. As the Buddhist tries to pull the onion petals back over his or her head, the Christian friend should hold the onion petals down, preventing Buddhist will from grasping them, and then graciously but firmly say, "No. Look. Here is where you stand."

"Because I want to."

Let it go.

WHAT ABOUT OTHER RELIGIONS?

At the last, the Buddhist may want to turn to another worldview or religion beyond Buddhism to show that Christianity is not the only worldview that can account for functional logic, epistemology, and causal theory.[18] Such a move needs to be respected, and giving it a complete reply would require a book like *To End All Suffering*, which itself would be an interreligious dialogue between that religion or philosophy and the Chrisitian faith. Applying the method I have employed here to other religions requires that one step into other worldviews, each in the same way we have for Buddhism. Even so, once the Buddhist steps out of Buddhism to answer these questions, our debate is over.

THE POWER OF A FRIENDSHIP THAT WILL NOT AGREE TO DISAGREE

The next few hundred years may be the wealthiest period of abun-

18. Some slippery philosophers have claimed that one can use an opponent's system without making worldview commitments. Once you can show contradictions in that system, then the opponent will be motivated to leave his system of thinking and embrace Buddhism. The problem with this type of thinking is that if the arguments have no proof value beyond merely getting a person to accept them, then they are rhetorical tricks. Such tricks cannot be used to substantiate any of the Buddha's claims regarding causality, epistemology, and logic since they do not *prove* anything. They merely motivate. But in such a method, where moving an opponent from this position to another is the only goal, the proof can be seen in no other terms other than "that which motivates." The fellow using this type of argument commits a sly bait and switch where the logical structures are used to motivate his opponent to embrace a claim, which can be no truer than the fact that the former opponent now embraces it. See chapter 13 on Nāgārjuna.

dance in human history. Emerging technologies promise to solve problems that have contributed to human suffering for millennia. Though it is possible that we may use up more resources here on earth, already companies are working on practical means to mine the solar system and find new resources. The Internet is linking the globe together in remarkable ways that promote the sharing of ideas, and increased learning. Soon impoverished countries will have access to the Internet and will be able to gain knowledge, which will enable them to solve problems, produce useful goods and services, and create wealth that could help to mitigate much physical suffering in this world. These resources can be used to heal or to kill. These new technologies also will present new ethical challenges requiring dialogue and debate.

Perhaps the most remarkable of all current developments is the work being done on developing universal translator technologies that will permit people of different language groups to speak to one another as freely as they speak to people of their own language. When this development is considered in light of the story of the Tower of Babel and of the Pentecost of Acts 2, the development is one of the most exciting things that has happened in the last several millenia of human history. Human beings will be able to share ideas and increase the division of labor and thus increase prosperity in ways we cannot even imagine now. The future is indeed bright.

In this emerging global linguistic community, Buddhists and Christians across the world will have the opportunity to interact productively in daily life and on the job as they work together in various ways throughout the world's productive economy. My hope is that both of these traditions pursue the examples of their founders in their willingness to interact and debate ideas with charity. These two traditions have the opportunity to reason with one another with a graciousness, clarity, fervor, winsomeness and peace that could leave the world thunderstruck by their example. This book is my feeble attempt to play a part in bringing about such a world. Rather than glossing over differences, we could see a world where Buddhists and Christians continue their respectful discourse—where interreligious dialogue is combined with diligent service and care for our fellow human beings. For *this* is true religion (James 1:27).

Biblical and Apocryphal Abbreviations

Acts	Acts
Col.	Colossians
2 Cor.	2 Corinthians
Dan.	Daniel
Deut.	Deuteronomy
Eccles.	Ecclesiastes
Exod.	Exodus
Gen.	Genesis
Hag.	Haggai
Heb.	Hebrews
Hosea	Hosea
Isa.	Isaiah
James	James
Jer.	Jeremiah
Job	Job
John	John
Judg.	Judges
1 Kings	1 Kings
2 Kings	2 Kings
Lev.	Leviticus
Luke	Luke
2 Macc.	2 Maccabees
Mark	Mark
Matt.	Matthew
Num.	Numbers
Prov.	Proverbs
Ps. (pl. Pss.)	Psalms
Rev.	Revelation
Rom.	Romans
1 Sam.	1 Samuel
2 Sam.	2 Samuel
Zech.	Zechariah

Bibliography of Works Cited

Adler, Mortimer J. *The Synopticon: An Index to the Great Ideas*. Edited by Mortimer J. Adler. 60 vols. Vol. 1, Great Books of the Western World. Chicago: Encyclopedia Britannica, 1993.

Alter, Robert. *The Art of Biblical Narrative*. New York: Basic Books, 1983.

Aristotle. *Categories and De Interpretatione* (Categories and On Interpretation). Translated by J. L. Ackrill. Clarendon Aristotle Series, edited by J. L. Ackrill and Lindsay Judson. Oxford: Oxford University Press, 1975.

———. *Categories; On Interpretation; Prior Analytics*. Translated by H. P. Cooke and Hugh Tredennick. Edited by T. E. Page. Vol. 325, The Loeb Classical Library. 1938. Reprint, Cambridge: Harvard University Press, 1949.

———. "Posterior Analytics." In *Great Books of the Western World*, edited by Mortimer J. Adler. Chicago: Encyclopedia Britannica, [1952] 1993.

———. "Prior Analytics." In *Great Books of the Western World*, edited by Mortimer J. Adler. Chicago: Encyclopedia Britannica, [1952] 1993.

———. *Rhetorica*. Translated by W. Rhys Roberts. Edited by W. D. Ross. Vol. 11, The Works of Aristotle. Oxford: Oxford University, 1924.

Augustine. *Confessions*. Translated by Maria Boulding. Hyde Park: New City Press, 2001.

———. *Exposition on the Book of Psalms*. Translated by A. Cleceland Coxe. Edited by Philip Schaff. Vol. 8, Nicene and Post-Nicene Fathers: First Series, 2nd ed. Peabody, MA: Hendrickson Publishers, 1995.

———. *On Christian Teaching*. Oxford: Oxford University Press, 2008.

Bacon, Francis. *The New Organon and Related Writings*. New York: The Liberal Arts Press, 1960.

Barnes, Jonathan. *Posterior Analytics*. 2nd ed. Clarendon Aristotle Series, edited by J. L. Ackrill and Lindsay Judson. Oxford: Oxford University Press, 1994. Reprint, 2002.

Barnes, Michael Horace. *Understanding Science and Religion: Introducing the Debate*. London: Continuum International Publishing Group, 2010.

Budziszewski, J. *What We Can't Not Know: A Guide*. 2nd ed. San Francisco: Ignatius Press, 2011.

Calvin, John. *Institutes of the Christian Religion*. Translated by Ford Lewis Battles. Edited by John T. McNeill. The Library of Christian Classics. Philadelphia: The Westminster Press, 1960.

Cassuto, Umberto. *The Documentary Hypothesis*. Jerusalem: Shalem Press, 2006.

Chesterton, G. K. *Heretics/Orthodoxy*. Nelson's Royal Classics. Nashville: Thomas Nelson Publishers, 2000.

[Cicero]. *Rhetorica Ad Herennium*. Edited by G. P. Goold. The Loeb Classic Library. Cambridge, MA: Harvard University Press, 1989.

Claessens, Patricia, et al. "Palliative Sedation: A Review of the Research Literature." *Journal of Pain and Symptom Management* 36, no. 3 (September 2008): 310–33.

Clark, Andy. *Being There: Putting, Brain, Body, and World Together Again*. Cambridge: MIT Press, 1997.

Collender, Michael. "Complexity and Hermeneutic Phenomenology." PhD diss., University of Stellenbosch, 2008.

Collender, Michael, and Matt Deller. "Scoping Complex Systems for the Joint Task Force Commander." *Campaigning: The Journal of the Department of Operational Art and Campaigning (DOD)* no. Fall 2008: 35–79.

Cook, Johann. *The Septuagint of Proverbs: Jewish and/or Hellenistic Proverbs?: Concerning the Hellenistic Colouring of Lxx Proverbs*. Leiden: Brill Academic, 1997.

Corless, Roger. *The Vision of Buddhism*. New York: Paragon House, 1989.

———. "The Mutual Fulfillment of Buddhism and Christianity in Co-Inherent Superconsciousness." In *Buddhist-Christian Dialogue: Mutual Renewal and Tranformation*, edited by Paul O. Ingram and Frederick J. Streng. Honolulu: University of Hawai'i Press, 1986.

Daye, Douglas D. "Major Schools of the Mahāyāna: Mādhyamika" In *Buddhism: A Modern Perspective*, edited by Charles S. Prebish, 76-96. University Park: The Pennsylvania State University Press, 1989.

Descartes, Rene. *Descartes: Meditations on First Philosophy: With Selections from the Objections and Replies*. Edited by John Cottingham. Cambridge Texts in the History of Philosophy, edited by Karl Ameriks and Desmond M. Clarke. Cambridge: Cambridge University Press, 1996.

Ferch, Shann Ray. *Forgiveness and Power in the Age of Atrocity: Servant Leadership as a Way of Life*. New York: Lexington Books, 2011.

Frame, John. *Cornelius Van Til: An Analysis of His Thought*. Phillipsburg, NJ: P & R Publishing, 1995.

———. *The Doctrine of the Knowledge of God*. Phillipsburg, NJ: P & R Publishing Company, 1987.

Friedman, Thomas. *The World Is Flat 3.0: A Brief History of the Twenty-first Century*. New York: Picador, 2007.

Garfield, Jay. *The Fundamental Wisdom of the Middle Way: Nāgārjuna's Mulamadhyamicakārikā*. Oxford: Oxford University Press, 1995.

Goodall, Dominic, ed. *Hindu Scriptures*. Berkeley: University of California Press, 1996.

Grene, Marjorie. *The Knower and the Known*. Berkeley: University of California Press, 1974.

Hirakawa, Akira. *A History of Indian Buddhism: From Sakyamuni to Early Mahāyāna*. Translated and edited by Paul Groner. Honolulu: University of Hawai'i Press, 1990.

Hiriyanna, M. *Outlines of Indian Philosophy*. Oxford: George Allen & Unwin, 1970.

Hume, David. *A Treatise of Human Nature*. Edited by L. A. Selby-Bigge. Oxford: The Clarendon Press, 1888.

Husserl, Edmund. *The Crisis of European Sciences and Transcendental Pheno-*

menology: An Introduction to Phenomonological Philosophy.* Translated by David Carr. Edited by John Wild. Northwestern University Studies in Phenomenology and Existential Philosophy. Evanston, IL: Northwestern University Press, 1970.

Ichmura, Shobei. "Sunyata and Religious Pluralism." In *Buddhist-Christian Dialogue: Mutual Renewal and Transformation,* edited by Paul O. Ingram and Fredrick J. Streng, 95–114. Honolulu: University of Hawai'i Press, 1986.

Ingram, Paul O. "Interfaith Dialogue as a Source of Buddhist-Chrisitan Creative Transformation." In *Buddhist-Christian Dialogue: Mutual Renewal and Transformation,* edited by Paul O. Ingram and Fredrick J. Streng, 77–94. Honolulu: University of Hawai'i Press, 1986.

Ingram, Paul O., and Frederick Streng, eds. *Buddhist-Christian Dialogue: Mutual Renewal and Tranformation.* Honolulu: University of Hawai'i Press, 1986.

Jayatilleke, K. N. *Early Buddhist Theory of Knowledge.* Delhi: Motilal Banarsidass, 1980.

Robinson, Richard H., and Willard L. Johnson. *The Buddhist Religion: A Historical Introduction.* 3rd ed. The Religious Life of Man Series, edited by Frederick J. Streng. Belmont, CA: Wadsworth, 1988.

Kalupahana, David. *Buddhist Philosophy: A Historical Analysis.* Honolulu: University of Hawai'i Press, 1976.

———. *Causality: The Central Philosophy of Buddhism.* Honolulu: University of Hawai'i Press, 1986.

———. *Ethics in Early Buddhism.* Honolulu: University of Hawai'i Press, 1995.

———. *A History of Buddhist Philosophy: Continuities and Discontinuities.* Honolulu: University of Hawai'i Press, 1992.

———. *The Principles of Buddhist Psychology.* Edited by Kenneth K. Inada, Suny Series in Buddhist Studies. Albany: State University of New York Press, 1987.

Kant, Immanuel. *Critique of Pure Reason.* Translated and edited by Paul Guyer and Allen W. Wood. The Cambridge Edition of the Works of Immanuel Kant. Cambridge: Cambridge University Press, 1999.

———. *The One Possible Basis for a Demonstration of the Existence of God.* Translated by Gordon Treash. New York: Abaris Books, Inc., 1979.

———. Immanuel Kant: *Prolegomena to Any Future Metaphysics: That Will Be Able to Come Forward as Science: With Selections from the Critique of Pure Reason.* Edited and translated by Gary Hatfield. 2nd ed. Cambridge Texts in the History of Philosophy, edited by Karl Ameriks and Desmond M. Clarke. Cambridge: Cambridge University Press, 2004.

Khun, Thomas. *The Structure of Scientific Revolutions.* 2nd ed. Chicago: University of Chicago Press, 1990.

Lakoff, George, and Mark Johnson. *Philosophy in the Flesh: The Embodied Mind and Its Challenge to Western Thought.* New York: Basic Books, 1999.

Lamotte, Etienne. *History of Indian Buddhism: From the Origins to the Saka Era.* Translated by Sara Webb-Boin. Louvain-la-Neuve, Belgium: Peeters Press, 1988.

Lehrer, Keith. *Theory of Knowledge.* Boulder, CO: Westview Press, 1990.

Lennon, John. "Imagine." *Imagine.* 1971, Apple Records R-11531.

Liu, Quanhua. "Presuppositionalism is Not the Way to Go." The Gonzaga Socratic Club. http://guweb2.gonzaga.edu/faculty/calhoun/socratic/Liu_resp_to_

Collender.pdf (accessed Decem-ber 12, 2012).
Martin, Michael. "Is Evil Evidence Against the Existence of God?" *Mind* 87, no. July (1978): 429–32.
Martin, Robert M. *The Meaning of Language*. Cambridge: MIT Press, 1995.
McGrath, Alister. *The Intellectual Origins of the European Reformation*. Oxford: Basil Blackwell Ltd., 1987.
Merleau-Ponty, Maurice. *Phenomenology of Perception*. Translated by Colin Smith. 2nd ed. Routledge Classics. London: Routledge, 2002.
Mill, John Stuart. *Utilitarianism*. Edited by Mortimer J. Adler. 60 vols. Vol. 40, Great Books of the Western World. Chicago: Encyclopedia Britannica, 1993.
Mizuno, Kogen. *Buddhist Sutras: Origin, Development, Transmission*. Tokyo: Kosei Publishing Company, 1989.
Nanamoli, Bhikkhu, and Bhikkhu Bodhi, trans. *The Middle Length Discourses of the Buddha: A Translation of the Majjhima-Nikāya*. Boston: Wisdom Publications, 1995.
Nietzsche, Friedrich. *Twilight of the Idols*. Translated by Duncan Large, Oxford World Classics. Oxford: Oxford University Press, 1998.
North, Gary. *Autonomy and Stagnation: An Economic Commentary on Ecclesiastes*. Dallas: Five Point Press, 2012.
———. *Predictability and Dominion: An Economic Commentary on Job*. Dallas: Five Point Press, 2012.
Osinga, Frans P. B. *Science, Strategy and War: The Strategic Theory of John Boyd*. Strategy and History, edited by Colin Gray and Williamson Murray. London: Routledge, 2007.
Packer, J. I. *Concise Theology: A Guide to Historic Christian Beliefs*. Wheaton, IL: Tyndale House Publishers, 1993.
Plantinga, Alvin. *God, Freedom, and Evil*. Grand Rapids, MI: William B. Eerdmans Publishing, 1977.
Plato. *Republic*. Translated by G. M. A. Grube. Revised by C. D. C. Reeve. 2nd ed. Indianapolis: Hacket Publishing Company, 1992.
Quine, W. V. *From a Logical Point of View*, Logico-Philosophical Essays. New York: Harper and Row Publishers, 1953.
———. *Philosophy of Logic*. Edited by Elizabeth and Monroe Beardsley. Foundations of Philsophy. Englewood Cliffs, NJ: Prentice Hall, 1970.
Reagan, Charles E. *Paul Ricoeur: His Life and His Work*. Chicago: University of Chicago Press, 1998.
Ricoeur, Paul. *The Conflict of Interpretations: Essays in Heremeneutics*. Evanston, IL: Northwestern University Press, 1974.
———. *Freud and Philosophy: An Essay on Interpretation*. Translated by Denis Savage. New Haven: Yale University Press, 1970.
———. *From Text to Action: Essays in Hermeneutics, II*. Translated by Kathleen Blamey and John B. Thompson. Evanston, IL: Northwestern University Press, 1991.
———. *Interpretation Theory: Discourse and the Surplus of Meaning*. Fort Worth: Texas Christian University Press, 1976.
———. *The Just*. Translated by David Pellauer. Chicago: University of Chicago Press, 2003.
———. *Oneself as Another*. Translated by Kathleen Blamey. Chicago: University of

Chigago Press, 1992.

———. *The Rule of Metaphor: Multi-disciplinary Studies in the Creation of Meaning in Language*. Translated by Robert Czerny with Kathleen McLaughlin and John Costello, S. J. Toronto: University of Toronto Press, 1979.

———. *The Symbolism of Evil*. Translated by Emerson Buchanan. Boston: Beacon Press, 1967.

———. *Time and Narrative: Volume I*. Translated by Kathleen McLaughlin and David Pellauer. Chicago: University of Chicago Press, 1990.

Rubin, Danny, and Harold Ramis. "Groundhog Day." DVD. Directed by Harold Ramis. USA: Columbia Pictures, 1993.

Russell, Bertrand. *Our Knowledge of the External World*. London: Open Court Publishing, 1914.

———. *The Problems of Philosophy*. London: Williams and Norgate, 1912.

Thomas, Edward J. "Buddhism in Modern Times." *University of Ceylon Review (Colombo)* 9, (1951).

———. *The Life of the Buddha as Legend and History*. New York: Barnes and Noble, 1956.

Tuck, Andrew P. *Comparative Philosophy and the Philosophy of Scholarship: On Western Interpretation of Nāgārjuna*. New York: Oxford University Press, 1990.

Van Til, Henry R. *The Calvinistic Concept of Culture*. Grand Rapids, MI: Baker Academic, 2001.

Walshe, Maurice, trans. *The Long Discourses of the Buddha: A Translation of the Dīgha-Nikāya*. 2nd ed. Boston: Wisdom Publications, 1995.

Warder, A. K. *Outline of Indian Philosophy*. Delhi: Motilal Banarsidass, 1971.

Wittgenstein, Ludwig. *Philosophical Investigations*. Translated by G. E. M. Ascombe. Oxford: Basil Blackwell & Mott, 1958.

———. *Tractatus Logico-Philosophicus*. London: Kegan Paul, Trench, Trubner & Co., 1933.

Wright, N. T. *Evil and the Justice of God*. Downers Grove, IL: IVP Books, 2006.

———. *How God Became King: The Forgotten Story of the Gospels*. New York: HarperOne, 2012.

———. *Jesus and the Victory of God*. Christian Origins and the Question of God. Minneapolis: Fortress Press, 1996.

———. *The New Testament and the People of God*. Christian Origins and the Question of God. Minneapolis: Fortress Press, 1992.

———. *The Resurrection of the Son of God*. Christian Origins and the Question of God. Minneapolis: Fortress Press, 2003.

Yandell, Keith, and Harold Netland. *Buddhism: A Christian Exploration and Appraisal*. Downers Grove, IL: InterVarsity Press, 2009.

Subject/Name Index

C

D

G

H

I

J

K

L

M

N

Q

R

S

V

W

Y

Z

Index of World Religious Texts

Qur'an Passages

Biblical and Apocryphal Passages